THE UNIVER~
OF BIRMING~

APPROACHING RETIREMENT

Social divisions, welfare and exclusion

Kirk Mann

Dedication
For Isiah and Rochelle

First published in Great Britain in November 2001 by
The Policy Press
34 Tyndall's Park Road
Bristol BS8 1PY
UK

Tel +44 (0)117 954 6800
Fax +44 (0)117 973 7308
e-mail tpp@bristol.ac.uk
www.policypress.org.uk

© The Policy Press 2001

British Library Cataloguing in Publication Data

A catalogue record for this book is available from the British Library

ISBN 1 86134 282 9 paperback 2158463

A hardcover version of this book is also available

Kirk Mann is Senior Lecturer in Social Policy and Sociology at the University of Leeds.

Cover design by Qube Design Associates, Bristol.

Front cover: photograph supplied by kind permission of John Cleare, and is of Mike Banks, a former commando, climbing the Old Man of Hoy at the age of 71.

Contents

List of figures and tables

Figures

Tables

Acknowledgements

First and foremost I would like to thank Linda for putting up with me while I have been working on this book. Surprisingly she has never suggested that I ought to consider retiring from the project. My 'respondents' must also be acknowledged because I have sought their opinions whatever the social situation and despite their protests. Thus my random and snowballing samples of family and friends, my 'focus groups' of dog walkers, mates in Mojo's, fellow allotment diggers, my Mum's bowls club, Jodie, Marie, Debbie and Carolyn, my neighbours and the succession of students taking my course at Leeds, have all been regularly canvassed and queried as I have struggled to clarify my ideas. In the UK, Moira Doolan, Pete Dwyer, Carol Smart, Fiona Williams, Malcolm Harrison, Alan Deacon, The Policy Press referees and (especially) John Hamill, have all provided useful feedback, comments and suggestions on draft chapters. Zygmunt Bauman has been an inspiration to me since I was an undergraduate and more recently he demonstrates that some 'retirees' can be highly productive. Jay Ginn helped with my maths, some perceptive comments, and with Sara Arber, has provided a stream of scholarship and research that I have drawn on. Thanks also to Arthur Gould and Einer Overbye who responded in the best academic tradition to my queries about Sweden.

I am grateful to colleagues at Leeds University in the Department of Sociology and Social Policy for a vital period of study leave, and to the Department of Social Policy, Social Work and Sociology at Sydney University for making me so welcome during it. The Menzies Foundation provided much needed assistance with airfares and expenses. In Australia the seminars I attended at the Social Policy Research Centre at the University of New South Wales were a crucial source of information and debate. Merrin Thompson, Annette Falahey, Stuart Rees, Diana Olsberg, Robert van Krieken, and Peter Saunders, all helped me to appreciate key aspects of Australian scholarship, social policy and society. Helen Meekosha, Stephanie Short and the outstanding Fines (Michael and Ina) provided mateship, encouragement for my ideas, some lively debates, and some invaluable sources of stimulation.

Dawn Rushen and Rowena Mayhew at The Policy Press have gently guided me in the production process and final stages of this book. Their copy-editing and layout suggestions have made this a more accessible text and, in contrast to publishers who shall remain nameless, they have been remarkably prompt and supportive at every stage.

Finally I would like to thank Mike Banks, who features on the front cover, climbing the rock 'The Old Man of Hoy' at 71 years of age, and John Cleare who took the photograph. It has reminded me of what people are capable of, and why my task was a relatively simple achievement. For me this image has captured the ambiguity, difficulty and risk that confronts anyone approaching retirement (that is, everyone). It is, simultaneously, inspiring, gendered (masculine), disciplined, dynamic and frightening. Not unlike the way many people feel as they approach retirement.

However, if the above are to get any credit, I would also like to blame them for the shortcomings and mistakes. Unfortunately, that would be grossly unfair and these remain my responsibility.

Acronyms and glossary of terms

ABI	Association of British Insurers
ACTU	Australian Council of Trade Unions
Actuarial principles	assumptions used to consider risks, costs and contributions. Data on life expectancy, length of time in a scheme, increases in earnings, and so on, are used to ensure the fund is able to meet its future commitments
Actuaries	people who make calculations based on actuarial principles
Annuities	usually an annual income, paid monthly, that an insurance company, bank or other provider, guarantees for the remaining life of the purchaser
AVCs (Additional Voluntary Contributions)	payments made by an individual into a private scheme that are designed to complement an existing occupational scheme. These allow the contributor to buy extra years in their occupational scheme thereby enabling the individual to retire earlier or to 'catch up' with lost years
AWE	average weekly earnings
DB (Defined Benefit)	retirement income is usually calculated as a ratio or percentage of former earnings. For example, the employer promises to provide a pension based on 40 years' service that will give an annual income after retirement of 60% of final year's salary, plus a lump sum equal to three times final year salary. Pro rata reductions will apply for less time in scheme or early retirement

DC (Defined Contributions)	retirement income is based on contributions made (individual plus any employer contributions). Contributions will usually be invested to produce a 'fund' that is then either paid as a pension, or used to buy an annuity
DSS	Department of Social Security
EU	European Union
Fiscal welfare	tax incentives, loopholes and privileges that subsidise or promote welfare provisions; for example, pension contributions may be tax free
Friendly Societies	non-profit-making membership associations providing a range of welfare benefits, including sickness, unemployment and pensions. They grew rapidly in late 19th century Britain and are also often referred to as mutual societies
FSA	1986 Financial Services Act
FSAVCs (Free Standing Additional Voluntary Contributions)	like AVCs, private pensions purchased separate from, but additional to, any employer schemes. They differ from AVCs because they are 'free standing', that is, they are not tied to an existing scheme
Fund managers	companies are usually appointed by trustees to be the 'fund manager'. These will employ people who are fund and investment managers
Funded scheme	payments into a fund are set aside for the future payment of a pension. Usually separate from the employer's business with additional assets accumulated by being invested in the finance markets
GDP	Gross Domestic Product

GPP (Group Personal Plans)	private personal pensions that a life insurance or mutual society operates but usually organised by the employer. Can offer lower administrative charges or, by grouping specific types of employee, can spread actuarial risk for members (quite common in the US)
IMF	International Monetary Fund
Lump sum payments	a one-off payment on retirement based on the number of years of service and final salary in DB schemes. For example, 40 years' service may guarantee a lump sum equal to 150% of final salary or three times annual value of pension. Pro rata reductions apply, usually tax free up to £150,000
MIG (Minimum Income Guarantee)	a 'new' means-tested benefit introduced by the Labour government
NAPF (National Association of Pension Funds)	the fund managers' association. Their journal *Pensions World* is an accessible and surprisingly forthright source of information
NI (National Insurance)	contributions pay the basic public pension on a 'pay as you go' basis (see below)
Occupational welfare	often called 'fringe benefits', non-wage welfare and perks. Can include employer nurseries, discounted mortgages (common for bank employees), work clothes/uniforms, company cars but, most importantly, a company funded pension
Pay as you go	pensions are paid from contributions currently being paid and no fund exists for future liabilities/claims. Current workers pay current pensioners
PIA (Personal Investment Authority)	one of the regulators

PIU (Performance and Innovation Unit)	reporting to the British Cabinet Office. (See Cabinet Office, 2000.)
Portability	the ability to take the pension, contributions and any accrued 'earnings' an individual may have generated and transfer to a different employer, or private scheme. The idea is that the pension goes with the person and not the provider
SDW	social division of welfare – see Figure 1 for a summary
SERPS	State Earnings Related Pension Scheme
SGC (Superannuation Guarantee Charge, 1992)	Australian compulsory occupational pension scheme introduced in 1992
SIB (Securities Investment Board)	the chief regulator of financial services with responsibility for the supervision and proper conduct of investment bodies, including pension funds
SIP (Statement of Investment Principles)	trustees must agree a SIP that addresses any ethical considerations they feel the fund membership would support. This has to be compatible with their legal duties to maximise investments in the interests of the members and beneficiaries
SRI (Socially Responsible Investments)	usually a commitment by the trustees of the fund to avoid certain types of investment that are deemed 'unethical' but can mean identifying desirable investments. Can also extend into using voting rights as shareholders to promote responsible investments

Stakeholder pension   introduced in 2001 by the Labour government, these are aimed at low earners and operate much like any personal pension. Lower administration charges and tax privileges apply, various providers are approved, including the TUC, mutual societies, banks and insurance companies

Trustees   nominees who oversee the pension funds according to trust law. In the UK they are often lay trustees, meaning they are not necessarily experts, but some will be

TUC   Trades Union Congress

Unfunded scheme   usually a 'pay as you go' (see above) arrangement, without any 'fund' to meet future liabilities

Introduction

This book focuses on the meaning of retirement and how individuals and societies may approach it in the future. Crucial issues are raised about the balance between work, leisure and care, which involves reconciling people's expectations and desires with the costs involved. At the start of the 20th century only the privileged few could expect to retire and have an income that would enable them to enjoy their retirement (Macnicol, 1998). An age-related income was guaranteed in all OECD (Organisation for Economic Cooperation and Development) nations during the 20th century and the idea that older workers should have the right to retire was firmly established in the popular consciousness. By the start of the 21st century the average age at which people exited the paid labour force – not quite the same as retirement, as we shall see later – was closer to 60 than 65 (OECD, 1998a). Some 'retirees' are undoubtedly forced to retire early due to illness, disability, pressure from employers or their spouse, or because they resign themselves to the reality of age discrimination in the labour market. For others retirement and the idea of time to do as they please is eagerly anticipated. Although the prospects for retirees in the 21st century might seem to be healthy there are some ominous and disturbing signs. In future it may only be those who have saved, or who have contributed enough to a reliable fund, who can expect to retire.

Anthony Giddens, one of Britain's best known and most widely quoted sociologists, has argued that the concept of retirement needs to be reconsidered, that the retirement age should be abolished and that pensioners are the clearest example of welfare dependency that can be found (1998, pp 119-20). He is not alone, however, in wanting to radically rethink the concepts of 'retirement' and 'pensioner'. The OECD (1998a, 1998b; Visco, 2001) has advocated major reforms that would, in effect, scrap the statutory age of retirement around the world. The US and Sweden are among a number of countries that have already introduced a graduated age of retirement, which means that younger people can expect to retire later than their predecessors. The British government is also considering whether "The very concept of 'retirement' needs to be challenged" (PIU, 2000, p 47).

It is against this backdrop, one in which any idea of a right to retire is being undermined and the welfare 'dependency' of retirees is to the fore, that this book was written. One of the book's principal aims is to ensure that any rethinking about retirement is explicitly informed by broader conceptual approaches which focus on the interplay between welfare, in its various guises, social divisions and exclusion. Social policies are never free of theory, but often the theoretical assumptions underpinning policy are implicit. Here explicit links are made between some social theories and a major policy arena.

Interestingly, calls for retirement to be reconceptualised are part of a wider debate over the future of social policy, and society more generally (Giddens, 1994; Hillyard and Watson, 1996; Lister, 1997; Jordan, 1998). As Lewis et al (2000) notes: "The process of 'rethinking', of course, implies a challenge to existing ways of thinking" (p 20). However, rethinking the meaning of retirement, without remembering the contribution of previous thinkers, may be innovative but it may also unwittingly reproduce some traditional, and mistaken, ideas. A second aim, therefore, is to set out some of the approaches that inform current thinking about society and social policy, and to explore their respective strengths and weaknesses in relation to retirement and pensions policies. Each chapter uses a different approach and provides a different lens through which we may study and understand retirement and pensions policies. Although they are, in many respects, competing approaches, a third aim will be to show how they can be reconciled within the flexible framework of the social division of welfare (Titmuss, 1958; Mann, 1992). However, before setting out the case for a more theoretically informed debate over retirement and pensions policy, it might be helpful to explain who this text is intended for, and why retirement and pensions policy should be taken seriously.

Expectations, desires and costs

Although this book hopes to engage with a broad constituency, it was written with an undergraduate student readership in mind. It is meant to be an accessible and provocative introduction to some of the contemporary debates surrounding social policy in general, and retirement and pensions policy in particular. As the typical reader I had in mind was one of my students, so I shall begin this text with some similar introductory questions that I have asked them over the years. These questions should illustrate the importance of retirement and pensions policy and the answers usually raise some further fundamental questions about how to approach these issues theoretically.

• *When do you expect to retire?*

Although some 'mature' students said that they expected to retire at the age of 65, the majority hoped to do so before they were 60, and about a third of the students I teach each year expect to retire before the age of 55. My annual survey is hardly representative, but I would suggest that it does indicate a widely held desire to retire at a relatively young age. This is a desire, however, that may be frustrated by government policy, economic demands, social restraints, or personal circumstance.

• *How much are you currently saving toward your retirement pension?*

Although some students have previously paid some National Insurance (NI) pension contributions, only one student (out of about 100) said that they were currently paying into a private pension scheme. Again this is not very surprising, as very few students have an income that would enable them to set aside anything towards a meaningful pension. But without contributing to a private or occupational pension fund in the near future, any desire to retire before the age of 65 is unlikely to be fulfilled.

• *Once you are in full-time paid work what proportion of your income do you expect to contribute towards your retirement pension?*

Answers ranged between 10-25%, but the majority favoured a figure close to 15%, which is at the lower end of what private pension providers would consider to be viable; this would not fulfil the expectations of most of my sample of students. (Dismay has often followed when it is pointed out that mortgage, student debt repayments, holidays and a host of other expenditures will also have to be met.)

• *What do you expect to do when you have retired?*

Travel featured strongly, and there was a general expectation among my unrepresentative sample of having sufficient resources to 'enjoy' their retirement.

The point of asking these questions is two-fold: first, to relate retirement and pensions policy to the desires and expectations of a (mainly) young group of people. Second, to emphasise the disparity between their desires and their readiness to consider how these might be fulfilled or indeed, frustrated. Many graduates will be able to retire early and, provided that they are able to make adequate contributions, may only have to make minor revisions to their retirement expectations. If they are able to access a 'good' occupational pension scheme and/or pay sufficient contributions into a private scheme they should be able to look forward to their retirement years. If, however, their employment record is regularly interrupted by unemployment, illness or caring responsibilities, then these expectations may have to be revised. For some (albeit a small minority of graduates), the experience of retirement will not be one they can enjoy by travelling, for example. Instead, it will be a period of exclusion from the labour market and the consumption patterns enjoyed by much of society. There are widening social divisions between the different 'types' of retiree and there is little prospect of that trend being halted (Walker, 1999; Walker with Howard, 2000).

Income inequalities will not be the only divisions within the pensioner population in the future. The age at which people exit the paid labour force, and the degree of choice they have over when they do so, will also be significant. The phrase 'time for retirement' is useful in this context to illustrate the way that time itself is a resource that is unevenly, and unfairly, distributed in society.

> For example, a graduate teacher could consider retiring at the age of 55 with an income close to the national average. It is assumed here that they pay Additional Voluntary Contributions (AVCs) to 'top up' their public sector occupational pension scheme. This would mean that their paid working life lasted for approximately 30 years. A cleaner working at the same school will probably have at best a pension worth 60% of her (for it is more likely that the cleaner will be a woman) formerly low wages after 40 years. This will not be an adequate income and she is therefore likely to have to work until the age of 65, a potential working life of nearly 50 years! Moreover, even then, her income will probably be considerably lower than that of the graduate teacher. If the cleaner has 'time out' to care for children or relatives, or if she is unemployed for any length of time, the contrast becomes even starker. She may end up working for twice as long as the graduate but with only half the income and, because life expectancy varies with social class, the cleaner could well receive her pension for half the time that the graduate teacher is able to claim theirs (based on data in Ginn and Arber, 1992a, 1993; Vincent, 1995; Walker with Howard, 2000).

The point is not that pensioners are 'victims' to be pitied (this further diminishes the status of the poorest), but that there is the very real prospect of deep social divisions developing between different 'types' of pensioner.

In order to explain the persistence of social divisions in retirement I will take an approach that draws on the concept of the social division of welfare (henceforth, SDW). Such an approach takes a firm standpoint, but not simply in the interests of the retired population, for there are profound implications for society as a whole in simply accepting current trends. Put most simply, a divided and divisive society will be less comfortable, more fractious and less secure for everyone (Bauman, 1998). Addressing the blatant social divisions that affect the pensioner population will also affect taxpayers, current and future generations of workers, and may impinge on some cherished social norms. Perhaps the most important feature of an approach based on the SDW is not that some pensioners are very poor, while others are quite well off, or that some pensioners are welfare dependants, but that we are all interdependent. Everyone, rich and poor alike, will be dependent on some form of welfare in retirement. The main difference is which feature of the SDW we have to rely on and how to acknowledge the different ways this impacts on *us* and how *we* then view *others* and their welfare. I will elaborate on the above points in the next chapter. Before exploring the SDW in more depth, however, I will clarify the key components of the concept. This is followed by an outline of the book that indicates how each chapter poses a challenge to an approach based on the SDW, challenges that will, hopefully, be resolved in the course of the book.

The social division of welfare

Titmuss (1958) used the idea of a SDW in the 1950s to illustrate the way that critics of 'the welfare state' failed to appreciate what it was they were discussing. Welfare was, and still too often is, defined simply in terms of the benefits that the poorest receive, but this neglects the host of benefits available to the middle classes. Titmuss pointed out that even when certain state policies were intended to address similar needs, they were often defined in a way that highlighted the benefits the poorest received but neglected the benefits available to the better-off. Why, for example, does the NI-based pension count as welfare, but tax relief on private pension contributions does not?

Likewise, the advantages of being in an occupational pension scheme are well known, but are rarely seen as part of 'the' welfare state, despite the crucial role of the state in facilitating, and in respect of many public employees, providing them (Hannah, 1986).

Figure 1 provides a summary of the SDW and some of the different types of retirement pension provision that currently exist in the UK. This is neither a detailed nor comprehensive model, but it should provide a rough guide to the account set out below.

Titmuss (1958) suggested that there were, in fact, three systems of welfare, which he identified as: social welfare, occupational welfare and fiscal welfare. However, I have added a fourth division: informal welfare. The differences between these divisions of welfare are largely related to the mechanisms of delivery. Thus social/public welfare has been the most visible (a point that will be emphasised in a number of chapters) with direct transfers from the state to claimants; age-related NI pensions and social security transfers being the most obvious examples in the UK. Too often commentators assume that public welfare is the only form of welfare. Following Adrian Sinfield (1978), the term 'public' welfare, rather than 'social', is used to emphasise both the visibility of this type of welfare and the way it is often assumed by the public at large to be the definitive part of 'the' welfare state (Mann, 1992).

Second, there is occupational welfare provided by employers or their nominated intermediaries, for example, company pensions that are related to length of service and rely on employee and employer contributions. Occupational pensions are funded – meaning that unlike the UK public welfare scheme of NI, huge resources are set aside to pay pensions in the future. These funds are then invested in the finance markets to generate additional resources. The Australian system of 'super' (superannuation) provides a good example of how the state can make occupational pensions compulsory and of welfare being provided through a different route to that often assumed, in the UK, to be *the* way to provide welfare. Australian examples feature in a number of chapters to illustrate the different ways that similar welfare needs can be addressed, or frustrated (Mann, 1993; Olsberg, 1997; Castles, 1997). A recurring theme in this book will also be the power and significance of the occupational pension funds, how they are managed and to whom they 'belong'. In effect the crucial question is: if occupational pensions are part of the wage/labour contract – paid to attract or retain labour – are they deferred wages and should there be greater control over the investment decisions they make?

Third, fiscal welfare consists of tax concessions that promote or underpin particular policies; for example, private insurance pensions in the UK and US that are tax privileged. It should be remembered, however, that

Figure 1: A simplified model of the social division of welfare and retirement income in the UK

	Public welfare	Occupational welfare	Private/fiscal welfare	Informal welfare
Types	Income Support, NI, social security, SERPS	Occupational schemes – private company and public sector DB	Personal pensions, via insurance company, bank, Mutual Society FSAVCs, AVCs (top ups), Stakeholder, Annuities, Savings	Income derived from or shared with partner or spouse Unpaid care provided on basis of need
Funded by	state: general taxation, employer and own contributions	Employer: plus own contributions (with tax privileges) and usually relies on investment in the finance markets	Market: usually just own contributions but employers increasingly offer DC schemes instead of company pensions. Tax privileges are vital	Spouse's pension rights, if any
Recipients	70% of women pensioners have to claim means-tested support	Roughly 70% of recipients are men but more women are accessing them	16% of people in scheme 65% of recipients are men, but more women appear to be accessing these	Less than 10% of men rely on their spouse's pension or savings. Care prior to retirement (especially childcare) mainly provided by women
Reliability	NI and SERPS have seen numerous changes to entitlements	Generally very reliable but Maxwell scandal highlighted dangers. Market failures could pose problems	Misselling scandal highlighted flaws and funds rely heavily on finance market performance	As reliable as any marriage or household arrangement
Value	Basic NI = 15% AWE, SERPS = maximum of 20% of former earnings	Maximum = 66% of former earnings. Average = 40% AWE but median = 5% AWE due to small value to many. Lump sums are also paid	Varies enormously. The more that is paid in the more that is paid back – minus administration costs	Depends on distribution within household and varies greatly with spouse's pension rights, if any
Flexibility	Inflexible in terms of household but flexible in relation to paid employment, unaffected by job changes	Fairly inflexible 'golden chains' for some	Very flexible Can change employer and retain rights. Can vary contributions	As flexible as any informal household arrangements

occupational schemes can also be favoured by fiscal policies. In the US fiscal policy has been vitally important in promoting private pensions and this may have influenced Conservative governments in Britain in the late 1980s. Certainly the additional tax privileges that were introduced for private pensions and for various occupational pension 'top-up' schemes, such as AVCs, promoted a 'personal pensions stampede' that was poorly regulated (Disney and Whitehouse, 1992; Dilnot et al, 1994; Dobbin and Boychuk, 1996). Despite this experience it will be suggested in subsequent chapters that the providers of personal pensions have been more flexible in their response to the needs of specific social groups than either the occupational or public welfare providers. Again, it is the different ways that similar needs can be addressed that has to be borne in mind. Thus fiscal welfare plays a crucial role in the overall pattern of the SDW (Kvist and Sinfield, 1996).

The fourth division of welfare, albeit not identified by Titmuss, is the system of informal welfare (Rose, 1981). This consists of those benefits, services, income and resource transfers that are not arranged or provided by the state. Informal welfare is usually established according to household arrangements between spouses/partners, family or, less common, friends. Informal welfare is by no means sloppy or unstructured but it does exist outside of the formal state mechanisms; but it, too, may be promoted in one form rather than another by state policies. Childcare and elder care, along with privately negotiated, but socially structured, domestic arrangements over resources would all be examples of informal welfare (Mann, 1992, p 26). For many women who provide informal welfare the effect is to make them dependent on their spouse's pension. They will derive their retirement income, at one stage removed, from the same source as their spouse. Of course this assumes that the provider of informal welfare both has a spouse and that he (for it is usually men who rely on women to provide informal welfare and women who rely on their spouse's pension rights) has a good occupational or private pension. Divorce, illness, unemployment and disability can all disrupt this informal arrangement. Furthermore, there are a great many women who provide informal welfare for relatives or children who do not have a spouse to rely on (Arber and Ginn, 1995a).

For Titmuss, critics who focused on the cost of public welfare not only ignored the cost of occupational and fiscal welfare, they also promoted a more sectional and socially divisive society. Indeed, Titmuss claimed that only public welfare served to promote social unity and to reduce social divisions generated by the increasingly specialised division of labour

(Titmuss, 1958). Titmuss therefore favoured universal public welfare measures that were capable of embracing every section of society and which would enhance social solidarity. He regarded occupational pensions as a new law of settlement, in which employees were tied to their employer, and hence their place of residence. Employers were blamed for trying to "buy good industrial relations" (p 53) by offering occupational welfare to retain labour while skilled core workers, managers and professional groups were implicitly at fault for pursuing sectional self-interests. Private insurance pensions he condemned as various forms of "special indulgences according to a privileged group" (p 72). He roundly criticised Beveridge for not promoting a properly funded scheme of NI that would have been attractive to all and, in the 1950s, suggested that pension provisions were increasing social divisions, undermining social unity and promoting social injustice (Titmuss, 1958).

As a polemical essay the SDW has much to commend it. In contrast to Titmuss's carefully argued and presented case, critics of 'the' welfare state can seem crude and naive for treating welfare as a unitary and coherent whole. Their blinkered approach conveniently allows them to ignore the benefits that accrue to other, often more privileged sections of society (Mann, 1992, 1998). For the supporters of public welfare the essay represented a call for an extension of the state's public welfare activities along more equitable lines. Indeed, Titmuss's work in general, but arguably the essay on the SDW most of all, was a central plank in the defence of welfare for most of the second half of the 20th century (Walker, 1984; Goodin and Le Grand, 1987; Deacon, 1993). Unfortunately, as Sinfield suggests, the SDW has largely been treated as a descriptive tool, despite its theoretical potential (1978, p 131). By outlining other theoretical approaches to retirement and pensions policies, and drawing on aspects of these, it is hoped that the reader will be persuaded of the SDW's full potential.

Limitations and (some) other approaches

Before setting out the structure of this book I would like to identify the book's limitations and also some other approaches that might have featured, but do not. For example, a comprehensive historical account that relied on E.P. Thompson's (1968; Kaye and McClelland, 1990) work would have placed much more weight on 'the making' of the SDW (Mann, 1992). A view of social policy from below, that is made in response to the social and political pressures exerted by subordinate social actors, albeit in constrained and contested circumstances, has, nevertheless, informed much of this text. Intra-class divisions, contests over the labour process and access to the paid labour market, the consequences of informal care, forms of social closure, cultural expectations relating to home and work, and how all of these have impacted on the SDW feature in various chapters. However, a detailed historically informed approach does not, but fortunately there are some very good accounts already available (Hannah, 1986; Sass, 1997; Macnicol, 1998).

On the other hand, very little attention has been paid to the policy makers or to a 'top-down' view. Thus the social engineering tradition within social policy might have featured as a separate approach (Mann, 1998). From Bentham to Beveridge there has been a desire to construct the 'good society' at the top and to impose it on welfare subjects (Lee and Raban, 1988). Managing and engineering populations, notably the retired population, could be seen as one of the central objectives of social policy and sociology (Katz, 1996; Hillyard and Watson, 1996). According to this approach, pragmatic solutions to social problems have emerged in response to the empirical evidence. The data showed reformers what they needed to do, with welfare evolving accordingly (Fraser, 1984). Change was orchestrated by a small elite who, having considered the problems, set about providing solutions. The relatively benign versions of this approach are described by Williams (1989) as welfare collectivism and Fabian socialism. The poorest were frequently portrayed as victims to be pitied and helped. Images of frailty and a vocabulary of assistance were used to enlist sympathy but, like children, the poor were to be seen and not heard (Hockey and James, 1993). The poorest had no voice of their own, and it was implicitly thought that their views could safely be articulated by pressure and lobby groups *for* but not *of* them (Beresford et al, 1999). It is an approach that, with the explosion of social movements after the 1960s, is now largely discredited. Whether the use by politicians and policy makers (and some researchers) of focus groups, selected service users, and consumer groups is much more than a token gesture is debatable. Managing critical voices could also be seen as the most recent effort at 'civilising' populations and social movements. Indeed, another approach to retirement and social policy not covered here is to see welfare developments in terms of a 'civilising process' (Elias, 1982; de Swaan, 1988). Viewed in this light the construction of retirement becomes part of the management of society and the self. That is, individuals learn to behave in ways that are socially prescribed. Age-related expectations about what is appropriate behaviour are deeply embedded in society.

Retirement serves as a marker, reminding those of us who wish to grow old disgracefully to 'act our age'. Meaning, of course, comply with the cultural and social norms or suffer the ridicule that will certainly follow. As Vincent (1999) argues, these age-related stereotypes about what is appropriate behaviour can insidiously serve to govern the self (Rose, 1996). Chapters Three and Five touch on this approach, but a powerful case could be made for a more sustained account. However, and while offering profuse apologies to these (and any other) approaches not mentioned, there are always limits to what can be covered.

From advocates of the approaches provided here there may also be objections. Squeezing accounts into their respective chapters may perhaps have bruised some scholars, but hopefully the injury is not permanent. The intention has been to show how each approach provides both a challenge to the SDW alongside some crucial insights into features of retirement and pensions policy. In effect, each approach poses key questions that anyone committed to welfare and social justice should consider.

Furthermore, it is vital to recall that the weaknesses attributed to the approaches in this book would probably be contested by their advocates. They are presented here to promote and extend debate, not to foreclose it. One of the assumptions underpinning this exercise is that debate, in and of itself, is worthwhile. If retirement is to be reconceptualised, and if the process of rethinking social policy is not to be the exclusive preserve of senior politicians, think-tanks and established academics, the various approaches need to be set out and accessible to a broad constituency. An assumption underpinning this book is that there are things to be learnt from listening to others, and that by debating the respective merits of different approaches a clearer picture will emerge. Selling this rather liberal, optimistic and humanistic approach is not easy in a climate of cynical self-interest and uncertainty, but it is preferable to pessimism or fundamentalism.

Structure of the book

Chapter One explores the SDW in more depth and a case is made for applying this mid-range theory more generally. Four key challenges can be identified and need to be addressed if the SDW is to be applied to pensions and retirement policy:

- the structural restraints that confront individuals; in particular, the political economy of capitalism, gendered relations of care and power; and recurring patterns of discrimination and disadvantage;
- the influence of 'choice' and patterns of consumption on policy makers;
- the power and 'science' of the pensions experts;
- the breaking up of traditional social and political constituencies that previously underpinned the sort of welfare settlement advocated by Titmuss.

Each of these challenges provides some distinctive insights into specific features of pensions and retirement policy. Although it is claimed here that these challenges can be reconciled with the SDW, it is important to repeat that they are different and distinctive approaches. Chapters Two to Five make the case for approaching retirement and pensions policy from the perspective of one of these challenges. The intention is to both introduce the reader to a number of different approaches and to show how each of these has an important contribution to make to any analysis. The main strengths and weaknesses of each approach are set out in summary form, as bullet points, at the end of each chapter. The aim is to show how, within the framework of the SDW, the strengths of each approach can be retained without having to take on board the weaknesses.

Chapter Two approaches pensions and retirement policy from the perspective of political economy, which comes in two forms, orthodox and radical versions. Whereas orthodox versions stress the benefits of market forces and suggest that competition, rather than regulation, will enable the needs of older people to be met (Green, 1996; Simpson, 1996), radical versions believe capitalist markets are inherently flawed (Deaton, 1989). Both versions of political economy identify the state as crucially important. In the 1970s these opposing versions developed their respective critiques of 'the welfare state', and by the 1980s pensions and retirement were being identified, albeit from different standpoints, with welfare crisis (Friedman and Friedman, 1980; Walker, 1981; Phillipson and Walker, 1986). However, some critics query the continuing relevance of ideas that focus primarily on industrial capitalism. For example, the fact that the majority of the poorest pensioners are women is difficult to explain by simply looking at market forces and class interests (Rose, 1981; Groves, 1987; Williams, 1989).

Chapter Three uses an approach derived from consumption theorists (Dunleavy, 1986; Harrison, 1986) and Laslett's (1989) notion of the 'third age', to explore how pensions and retirement are both a key to, and a product of, particular consumption sectors. Treating retirees as discerning consumers with desires and aspirations, rather than as victims or as a 'burden', promotes more positive images, and this may be empowering for those who can identify with these images (Featherstone and Hepworth, 1995; Aldridge, 1997). Similarly, an approach that views retirees as consumers may encourage them to seek redress from pension providers. It may also enable more diverse lifestyles, household forms and relationships to be viable. Gay and lesbian partners, for example, may find that the market is better able to address their retirement needs than universal public welfare provisions (Berkery and Diggins, 1998). For some observers, however, a more consumerist model of welfare is developing that threatens traditional citizenship rights (Dwyer, 1998; Walker, 1999). Thus approaching retirement from the perspective of consumption has the potential to illuminate diverse needs, but also how these reflect existing patterns of power, privilege and disadvantage.

Attention is turned to some of the most powerful, but least visible, players in the arena of retirement and pensions in Chapter Four. Here the focus is on the professionals and power brokers involved in providing, calculating and managing retirement pensions. Actuaries, pension analysts, fund managers and other pension experts operate in a world that is very different to that of the average prospective pensioner. A failure to discuss these welfare experts would be like discussing health without mentioning the medical profession or a discussion of education that neglected teachers. Chapter Four is informed by the work of Foucault (1976, 1977) and scholars who have drawn on his approach (Poster, 1984; Rose, 1994; Ewald, 1991; Defert, 1991; Katz, 1996). In short, Foucault questions the claims of experts and the manner in which their expertise is established. Pension experts use a language and science that is peculiar to them, and yet a computer program that tracks the finance markets will often provide as good a return as any fund manager (Blake, 1992a, 1992b; Myners, 2001). Despite this, many people regard pensions as complicated technical features of a world that is largely alien to them. The need is for good expert advice, professional independent knowledge that will make the mysterious world of pensions understandable. Chapter Four also uses the example of superannuation in Australia between 1987-92 to show that even committed social reformers may feel constrained by a fear of contradicting the experts.

Chapter Five approaches the world of retirement pensions with some trepidation. Like many younger people who say that they cannot imagine what the world will be like when they retire, this chapter stresses uncertainty. Traditional ideas about 'the male breadwinner/female carer' and the role of public welfare in sustaining these have few advocates today. Instead of the state doing so, individuals are called on to address the potential risks and needs they may confront (Beck, 1992). But there are also likely to be new challenges to social exclusion mounted by older people and this will, as Phillipson notes, "... present a fresh and radical agenda ... a new type of ageing has emerged, one that calls into question traditional social gerontological research" (1998, p 140). It is this uncertainty that observers of 'postmodernity' consider to be one of the features of contemporary social life. Chapter Five explores this sense of uncertainty and questions whether a 'right to retire' can be sustained in a world where this 'right' may depend on the success of the finance markets in developing countries. For some we need to go 'beyond Left and Right' and seek a 'third way' (Giddens, 1994, 1998) to find policy solutions that reflect changes in society and paid work. Others (Beck 1992, 2000) stress the way that risks have to be addressed and confronted by individuals and national governments in a context that is profoundly global. A key feature of the approach outlined in this chapter is the need to acknowledge the decline of tradition, without refusing to take an ethical standpoint in defence of some traditional social values, such as social justice.

Whereas the approaches set out in Chapters Two to Five provide challenges to the SDW, albeit ones that can be resolved, Chapter Six shows why these challenges are significant, and why an unreconstructed version of the SDW is inadequate. The chapter considers patterns of early retirement in a number of countries using the theoretical model provided by Esping-Andersen (1990), which is one of the more sophisticated attempts to compare social policy. Nevertheless, his neglect of informal welfare, that so many women provide and rely on, has provoked some criticism (Lewis, 1992, 1997). In the case of retirement this may conceal women's inability to 'exit' when they wish to (Arber and Ginn, 1995a). Furthermore, and like Titmuss, Esping-Andersen appears to privilege public welfare over other forms of welfare that may provide welcome opportunities for early retirement. The chapter compares early exit patterns in Australia, the UK, the US and Sweden, and considers whether this is a desirable 'choice' or the result of exclusion. This is seen as particularly significant because governments and the OECD (1998a, 1998b; Visco, 2001) are promoting a longer working life for economic reasons, irrespective of whether this is socially or politically desirable. Amid the vocabulary of labour market and economic needs, that speaks of retired people and older workers as a resource (like the minerals that industry needs to use), it is necessary to recall a language and ethic of care (Sevenhuijsen, 1998, 2000). Thus politics and ethics will be seen to matter, as Esping-Andersen rightly asserts, and global economic forces need not determine social policies. An approach based on the SDW enables us to observe the different ways and means by which welfare enables, and restrains, the possibilities.

The final chapter draws on and reviews all the foregoing accounts. In short it will be claimed that the SDW continues to provide a framework that can accommodate different approaches, and can make visible the injustices associated with retirement pensions. Because virtually everyone in the developed economies is, in effect, approaching retirement, the implications of rethinking what it means – as we are urged to – are very considerable. Retirement and pensions policy operate within a long time frame with changes often taking 30 or more years before they are fully appreciated. It is important, therefore, that different approaches and various voices (Williams, 2000) are heard, and carefully considered.

ONE

Social divisions, exclusion and retirement

Introduction

This chapter approaches retirement using the concept of a SDW. Thus we begin with an account developed within the 'orthodox' tradition of social policy (Lee and Raban, 1988). The basic features of the SDW were set out in the Introduction; the task here is to show how Titmuss's original essay, suitably revised, continues to provide an invaluable descriptive and analytic approach. The chapter initially sets out Titmuss's approach in a little more detail. However, Titmuss's account is not without its flaws and questions of economic, social and political power, that acknowledge the close correspondence with gender, class and 'race', have to be posed. Revisions to the original idea from Sinfield (1978) and Rose (1981) that have developed the conceptual features of the SDW are then explained in turn. The chapter provides some evidence of the different elements of the SDW and identifies informal welfare as a fourth element. Rights, security, choices, forms of dependency, and income are all related to the different elements of the SDW. Towards the end of the chapter the idea of welfare regimes is briefly introduced alongside questions about the different means by which welfare can be provided. It will hopefully be shown that the SDW continues to provide a useful framework for exploring the different forms of welfare that have developed for retirees.

Titmuss's approach

Richard Titmuss was the first Professor of Social Administration to be appointed in the UK, taking up his post at the influential London School of Economics and Political Science. He was formerly the government's official historian for social policy during the Second World War and he later worked closely with members of the Labour government. He trained a generation of scholars (Lee and Raban, 1988, pp 72-8) who themselves went on to distinguished academic careers, and there is little doubt that he has had an enormous influence on the study of social policy (Esping-Andersen, 1990; Deacon, 1993). The SDW was first set out by Titmuss in a lecture in 1955, and initially published in 1956, although it is most often cited from his collected *Essays on 'The welfare state'* (1958). Titmuss places 'the welfare state' within quotation marks to indicate reservations about the idea of a single, unitary system of welfare. The essay needs to be read as a response to critics on the political 'Right' within the Conservative Party who saw the post-war welfare reforms as expensive for the middle classes, unnecessary for many of the working classes and potentially debilitating for all social classes (Titmuss, 1958, pp 34-7). Titmuss claimed that these views were promoting a misleading stereotype of welfare services and was determined to show that the critics operated with a definition of welfare that conveniently ignored the benefits that went to the middle classes. The essay should be read, therefore, as a polemic and not as a developed theory although, as this chapter will demonstrate, it has the potential for development and synthesis.

Titmuss identified three welfare systems that were operating to meet similar needs, albeit through different mechanisms. He argued that:

> Considered as a whole, all collective interventions to meet certain needs of the individual and/or to serve the wider interests of society may now be broadly grouped into three major categories of welfare: social welfare, fiscal welfare, and occupational welfare. When we examine them in turn, it emerges that this division is not based on any fundamental difference in the functions of the three systems (if they may be so described) or their declared aims. It arises from an organizational division of method, which, in the main, is related to the division of labour in complex, individuated societies. (1958, p 42)

Alongside the social welfare system, such as social security and NI, Titmuss identified occupational welfare (paid by employers) and fiscal welfare (tax relief). Retirement pensions provided Titmuss with one of his best examples of how wrong the critics were to simply focus on social/public welfare. He pointed out that the cost of occupational pensions to the Exchequer, and this was in 1955, was £100 million in lost tax revenue due to the fact that contributions were tax free. Likewise private, life assurance schemes that paid a lump sum on retirement, benefited from £35 million of fiscal relief. These figures were "substantially in excess of the present Exchequer cost of national insurance pensions" (Titmuss, 1958, p 51). Subsequently he estimated that the various tax privileges associated with occupational and private pension provisions were worth two to three times the cost of the NI scheme (1958, p 69). Thus, by using his knowledge of the life assurance business and of actuarial principles, Titmuss was able to convincingly show how retirement pensions were highly regressive in their effects. That is, the more a person earned the more they were effectively subsidised by the tax system; the less a person earned the less they got from any type of income transfers. In effect, Titmuss argued that the critics of 'the' welfare state failed to understand the meaning of welfare and were therefore incapable of assessing the true costs of the different welfare mechanisms.

Titmuss feared that critics would undermine universal welfare principles by misrepresenting the costs and benefits associated with the different welfare systems. This in turn would encourage people to pursue their own sectional or self-interests and thereby widen social divisions. Only universally provided public welfare services could bind everyone together because all other forms of welfare excluded some sections of society. The long-term effect for society, if everyone pursued their welfare needs in a sectional fashion, would be an increase in the numbers of people who were 'unattached' from society; simultaneously aware of their dependency and their failure (1958, p 55). Whereas right-wing critics claimed public welfare undermined social well-being, for Titmuss, universal welfare services were the antidote to social divisions and fragmentation. Publicly provided universal welfare measures are the glue binding a disparate society together. Furthermore, since industrial societies create needs and dependencies then, according to Titmuss, these ought to be addressed equitably. Failure to do so would promote social divisions. In the case of pensions, the state creates dependency by setting a specific retirement age. However, the needs that flow from dependency in retirement are treated very differently according to which element of the SDW a person has to rely on. By and large Titmuss believed that the middle classes benefited most and the working classes least from the SDW. Consequently, for Titmuss, the critics were wrong on all counts. They failed to define welfare adequately, misrepresented the costs to the middle classes, ignored the benefits that the occupational and fiscal systems provided, misunderstood the part that welfare plays in holding society together and were themselves in danger of promoting the fragmentation of society of which they made so much.

The division of labour

At the heart of the SDW is a theory of how the growth of 'needs and dependencies' has occurred. Titmuss identifies certain 'natural' dependencies and cites child bearing and 'infirmity' in old age as examples. He distinguishes these from 'culturally determined dependencies' such as unemployment and compulsory retirement. Subsequently even this distinction has been queried with women's and disability movements, highlighting the way their respective needs are socially constructed (Rose, 1981; Townsend, 1981; Williams, 1989; Oliver, 1990; Morris, 1993). However, Titmuss was concerned to stress the way that industrialisation generates a range of socially specific needs. Among these social forces he points to "subtle cultural factors", labour market access and most significantly claimed that: "... the dominating operative factor has been the increasing division of labour in society and, simultaneously, a great increase in labour specificity" (1958, p 43). Titmuss viewed these concepts from a perspective heavily influenced by Durkheim's study, *The division of labour in society* (1933). Elsewhere Titmuss (1968, 1970) was prepared to draw on a range of ideas and writers (Deacon, 1993), but Durkheim clearly informs the essay on the SDW and Titmuss concludes by pointing the reader towards Durkheim's work (1958, p 55).

The division of labour was crucially significant for Titmuss because it individuates society. That is, as tasks become more detailed, more specialised and impersonal, so too does 'society'. Titmuss appears to accept Durkheim's view that, unless carefully held in check by their attachment to social norms and values, individuals will experience anomie and social estrangement. For Durkheim anomie generates individuation, moral relativism, nervous and psychological breakdown, and potentially a rise in the rates of suicide. Without state intervention this might ultimately produce higher levels of crime and social disorder. For Titmuss, overcoming the isolation (anomie) generated by the division of labour requires a welfare system that recognises and addresses "individual dependencies and their social origins and effects" (1958, p 44). Only publicly funded welfare measures can hope to tackle these. Fortunately, according to this view, interdependence also encourages a respect between individuals for the autonomy, and dignity of others, that is, moral individualism. The growth in the SDW is, therefore, a function of, and a response to, the dependencies created by the division of labour (Mann, 1992).

Occupationally related pensions provided one of Titmuss's clearest examples of how the division of labour promoted the SDW. He observed that occupational pensions arose from "the drive to buy good human relations in industry" (1958, p 53). In a period of very low unemployment and strong local and national trades unions there was a tendency for occupational pensions to be a central part of the wage/labour negotiations. In order to attract and retain employees, particularly skilled workers, employers were prepared to extend the membership of their pension schemes. Trades unions saw a chance to improve their members' benefits and increasingly pressed employers to follow suit. Therefore, the ability of workers to persuade their employer to provide access to an occupational pension, and the desire of employers to offer this, reflects the labour market and industrial relations conditions of the day (Fitzgerald, 1988; Mann, 1991,1992). Sectionalism and social divisions flowed from the fact that pressure was greatest from those professional and trades union groups with the most leverage. Employers sought to tie their most valuable workers to the organisation with pension schemes that were effectively "new laws of settlement" (Titmuss, 1958, p 73), but the least skilled and the weakest sections of the labour movement were excluded. The state, via the Exchequer, bore the costs, because most of these benefits were deductible against tax due, both in relation to the respective contributions by employers and employees, and in the reduced tax liabilities of the pension funds themselves (1958, p 50). Whereas Titmuss believed that the state had a duty to promote social cohesion via the provision of universal welfare measures, it was often doing the opposite. Instead of resolving market inequalities and social injustices in the way needs arose and dependency addressed, the state was enhancing such inequalities. The result would be a widening of social divisions and "two nations in old age" (1958, p 74).

Class, power and the state

Sinfield (1978) has made a strong case for developing Titmuss's original essay by considering the close correspondence between class, power and the SDW. He states:"The greater power of certain classes or organisations to influence the allocation of scarce resources is a central issue for any analysis of the social division of welfare" (1978, p 149). The ability of professional groups, civil servants and some trades unions to apply pressure for improved pension rights from their employer is a good example. Moreover, this ability requires some measure of power to be exercised in relation to the labour market and the labour process (that is, the detailed manner in which the work is undertaken). For example, access to the professions and the civil service has historically exhibited some significant and recurring recruitment patterns. Until very recently those recruited were overwhelmingly white, male and from middle-class backgrounds. Having the right credentials such as A levels, university degrees and professional qualifications, and an increasing insistence that recruits have these (credentialism), has underpinned exclusionary closure for much of the 20th century. This has, in turn, restricted entry, and minimised labour market competition, thereby enabling professional groups to exert pressure for benefits that were tailored to their needs and reflected their perceived commitment to their vocation (Parkin, 1979; Mann, 1992). In the UK access to an occupational pension has been a key component in the remuneration package of many professional groups (Green et al, 1984; Hannah, 1986). Social closure has also occurred within the labour market more generally. For manual workers access to the most attractive, and well-rewarded, trades and industries has often been restricted to relatives, friends or neighbours, whereas women and people from ethnic minority groups were frequently excluded. Again this was intended to reduce labour market competition, protect trade skills and ensure a high degree of homogeneity among the workforce, characteristics which help explain "why some classes are more successful than others" (Therborn, 1983). Consequently, it should be no surprise that among non-professional groups, those most likely to have an occupational pension have generally worked in large companies, in skilled trades, or in public sector industries and utilities, with well-organised trades unions (Green et al, 1984; Mann and Anstee, 1989). Although some unskilled and semi-skilled trades and industries (for instance, car factories and mining) relied on post-entry 'closed shop' agreements – with trades union membership being a condition of employment once the individual was offered a job – other trades used control of the labour process, particularly access to an apprenticeship, to press employers to improve their pension rights. The continuing significance of the labour process and how it impacts on the SDW is illustrated by the fall in membership in the declining industries of the 1980s and 1990s and, in contrast during the same period, the very generous pension packages offered to information technology (IT) staff (*Pensions World*, December 2000). However, it is important to recognise who has exerted pressure and who has historically managed to get an occupational pension, with white, male, full-time employees and professionals the most successful (Mann, 1992).

The previous effects of closure in the paid labour market on retirement incomes will be discussed shortly, but it should be stressed here that the patterns will not be fully apparent for some time yet. There is inevitably a time lag of 30 to 40 years for the full impact to be appreciated and there are often countervailing pressures to consider. For example, racial discrimination in Britain during the 1960s and 1970s has, among others, two important implications for retirement incomes. First, discrimination often excluded non-white workers from certain private sector industries, trades and professions (Daniel, 1968; Modood et al, 1997). Second, public sector employment, in the health service, public transport and local authorities for example, appears to be much higher for some people from non-white ethnic minority groups than for the population as a whole (Modood et al, 1997). On the one hand, this would suggest exclusion from a good company pension scheme, underpinned by the higher contributions and wages that are associated with private sector skilled and non-manual employment, will result in many people from non-white ethnic minority groups having very poor retirement pensions. On the other hand, public sector employment often provides a relatively generous occupational pension, compared with some private sector industries (for example, construction) provided employment is maintained for many years. Most people migrate when young, and thus any firm conclusions are difficult until the current Census data has been fully analysed, and possibly not until after the 2011 Census. Academic research also appears to have been limited to relatively small samples and with a focus on qualitative issues concerned with ageing more generally. This is despite calls from the researchers concerned for more extensive projects and widespread recognition for the work they have undertaken (Blakemore, 1985; Boneham, 1989; Blakemore and Boneham, 1994; Berthoud, 1998; Nesbitt and Neary, 2001).

In 1996 people from non-white ethnic minority groups were all less likely than their white counterparts to have an occupational pension. The contrasts are most apparent between the Pakistani/Bangladeshi and the 'white' community in respect of occupational pension scheme membership (14% to 58% respectively), whereas 'black'/African Caribbean retirees are more likely to have to rely on means-tested public welfare benefits (for example, Caribbean, 70% – white, 39%). Social exclusion and social closure, in conjunction with the decline in specific sectors of the economy (for example, textiles), means that similar patterns are likely to be observed for at least the next 20 to 30 years (Modood et al, 1997; Berthoud, 1998; Nesbitt and Neary, 2001; Hamill, 2002: forthcoming).

Discrimination, social networks and social closure have clearly enabled some sections of society to access better pension rights than others. The central point is that the power to influence the allocation of resources and the desire to 'buy' good industrial relations is not random or meritocratic. Social groups and classes organise to protect and extend their relative privileges and in so doing exclude others. Whereas Titmuss believed (correctly) that if this situation was not tackled by the state it would promote social divisions in retirement, he paid much less attention to the way that the political economy of capitalism promotes inequality (Kincaid, 1984). Thus the detailed division of labour is not an unfortunate and unnecessary accompaniment of industrialisation that the state can rectify, as Titmuss claimed. Rather, a capitalist labour market requires competition, leading to social closure and divisions. Thus the state, via the legislation it enacts, mirrors existing social divisions and makes them concrete in the SDW (Mann, 1992). As Sinfield made plain, the question of how power is mobilised by interest groups and subsequently recognised by the state is crucially important. In contrast to Titmuss's optimistic belief that the state could resolve social divisions and inequality, primarily through egalitarian welfare measures, it seems more realistic to expect those interests that are the most powerful to be the ones that have the most influence.

In his discussion of time and security Sinfield provides a further insight into the inegalitarian method of service delivery that the three divisions of welfare conceal. He draws on another of Titmuss's essays (*Income distribution and social change*, 1962) to show how the insecurity of living on public welfare is in contrast to the benefits paid through the fiscal and occupational systems of welfare. The tax system, for instance, makes long-term planning easier for the very wealthy. Occupational benefits such as pensions (assuming that they are in a 'good' scheme) similarly make it easier for recipients to plan many years ahead. For example, final salary pension Defined Benefit (DB) schemes, common in the public sector in the UK, entitle members to a lump sum on retirement that is often worth several thousands of pounds but can go as high as £150,000 before tax is due (IDS, 1999, p 91). Without long-term continuous and well-paid employment the amount will be low, but for a significant minority the lump sump can be used to pay off outstanding mortgage debt, to buy a new car, or it can go towards a holiday home abroad. In contrast, public welfare tends to generate insecurity because it is only possible to plan in the short term, often on a daily basis. Public welfare provides no tax free lump sums that might be used to clear debts, or be set aside to cover household repairs, home insurance and so on. Even the mechanism by which the pension is paid can often consume the one resource public pensioners appear to have – time. Getting a pension through an automated bank transfer is clearly preferable to queuing at the Post Office counter. However, a very significant proportion of pensioners in the UK do not have bank accounts. Their working lives were characterised by pay packets or, for many women, a proportion of cash from their husband's pay packet. Monthly salaries paid directly into bank accounts are fairly recent developments and more common for white-collar workers who are less likely to rely on public welfare (Pahl, 2000). Whether the Post Office will become a more efficient service in the future remains to be seen, but at present the queue of pensioners waiting to collect their benefits is an all-too common sight. Thus relying on the state pension not only consumes time but it makes the recipient more visible.

By stressing the visibility of public welfare, Sinfield anticipated points that have more recently been developed by scholars who draw on the work of Foucault (1976; Poster, 1984; Hillyard and Watson, 1996). First, the visibility of public welfare ensures the focus of welfare debates is primarily on public welfare. This is similar to the point, outlined earlier, that Titmuss made regarding the way stereotypes of 'the' welfare state are misleading. Particularly important in this context is the way the media and newer 'modes of information' (Poster, 1984) discuss welfare topics. For example, the supposed *burden* of an ageing society is frequently associated with public pensions (Warnes, 1993; Giddens, 1998; Mann, 1998). Similarly, public welfare dependency and 'welfare cheats' are viewed very differently to those who get fiscal welfare/tax handouts and 'tax cheats' in the press (Golding and Middleton, 1982; Cook, 1989). The effect is to scrutinise and regulate the public welfare recipient, in this case, pensioners.

Second, the visibility of the public welfare recipient has a longer history that it is as well to recall, and it is a history that stigmatises public welfare to this day. Public humiliation for beggars and vagrants in the 17th century consisted of putting them in the stocks so that they would be physically and publicly shamed. Later Bentham's plans for workhouses, designed as total institutions like his prisons, exposed the poor, many of whom were old and infirm, to the stigma of pauperism. Waiting for charity, typified in the line of the Christian hymn, 'The rich man in his castle, the poor man at his gate', reaffirms the visibility of the poorest. Today, it is the Post Office, the bus queue and the charity shop, rather than waiting at the rich man's gate, that serve to identify the poorest pensioners. Third, the greater visibility of public welfare also reinforces divisions and distinctions between dependent groups with similar needs. Rather than seeing different, but equally valid, welfare mechanisms addressing socially constructed needs, the various elements of the SDW are normatively valued. Thus occupational pensions are perceived as 'earned' and are, therefore, deserved, but public welfare is given, like charity, and therefore stigmatised. state-organised contributory pensions, such as the NI scheme in the UK, overcame this distinction for some, but as the value of the basic pension has declined, many pensioners have had to top it up with means-tested benefits. Moreover, the NI scheme is unfunded, which means pensions are paid from the contributions received. There are no investments and no pot of money that is specifically identified with the contributor. (This is often referred to as a 'pay as you go' system with current workers paying for current pensions.) Media headlines emphasise that the public welfare system is an unbearable burden for younger workers (Walker, 1996, p 2). Consequently, and despite the contributory principle, it can often seem that the recipient of public welfare is less deserving.

Fourth, and as a consequence of the previous factors, the greater visibility of the public welfare recipient can construct the subject as a victim, to be pitied and helped. Dependency on public welfare makes the recipients, like children, objects of concern, investigation and regulation (Hockey and James, 1993). This in turn can reinforce ideas that *we* (the non-poor, young and independent) have of ourselves and *our* caring society, thereby legitimating the status quo.

Fifth, Sinfield stresses the part that the different elements of the SDW may play in reconstructing the economy and society generally. Again, the way welfare is viewed and discussed can be crucial. There has been a shift away from treating retirement as a 'right' towards seeing it as a privilege that can have negative effects on the economy (OECD, 1998a; Visco, 2001; PIU, 2000). For those who have them, occupational and private pensions bestow rights that must be protected because these were earned, albeit with tax subsidies paid for by the population at large. The responsible, reflexive, saver is contrasted with the welfare dependency of people who passively expect the state to support them (Giddens, 1998, pp 115-21). The contrasts are between dependence and independence, passive recipient and active planner. In this scenario the visible image of public welfare dependency is set against the consumer citizen. This is not an authoritarian process of social transformation but an insidious drift from citizenship to consumerism that individuals warmly embrace. Needs and dependency are negative qualities but desires and independence are positively associated with the post–modern self (Bauman, 1998). In effect, identities themselves are reformed in relation to the vocabulary and perceptions that the different elements of the SDW generate.

Finally, the visibility of pubic welfare draws attention away from the hidden injuries and benefits associated with the other elements of the SDW. The focus is on the public pensioner and the problems they pose *us*, and this can all too neatly serve to classify a population of failures (Katz, 1996). Yet occupational and private pension funds, and the tremendous resources they hold – the bedrock of the major stock markets – supported by fiscal handouts and benign legislation, attract very little critical attention. Indeed, a major strength of the SDW is the fact that it expands our view of what welfare is and draws our attention to the less visible pension penalties, and privileges, that can be imposed by other forms of welfare (Ginn and Arber, 1993).

Gender, care and informal welfare

In 1981 Rose made a powerful case for drawing on the twin traditions of the 'Titmuss paradigm' and the (then) new social policy that stressed political economy. In particular she claimed:

> The Titmuss concept of the 'Social Division of Welfare' with its potential openness for the examination of the contradictions of race, age and sex as structured by social policy offers a tradition of empirical enquiry which refuses the automatic reduction of all oppressions to that of class. (1981, p 479)

Instead she expanded our understanding of the SDW by posing the simple question 'Who cooks the dinner?' (Rose,1981), although she might have added 'And who washes up, cleans the house, takes time off paid work to look after the children and who collects them from school?' In effect, Rose was asking the question of 'Who cares?', and at what cost to their general welfare? Focusing on the paid labour market, as Titmuss did, reveals the close correspondence between this and his three forms of welfare, but it neglects entirely the informal, unpaid forms of welfare that underpin relationships in many households (Rose, 1981; Lewis, 1997). The providers of care are effectively excluded from the more privileged features of the SDW, producing significant differences between men and women in terms of occupational, fiscal and public welfare benefits, particularly retirement pensions. By adding a fourth category – informal welfare – to Titmuss's account, the unpaid welfare activities that do not conform to these three 'systems' can be acknowledged and addressed. Following Rose the focus here is on the 'pension penalties' (Ginn and Arber, 1993) that are imposed on care providers, but this narrows the debate and requires a brief caveat before proceeding.

By identifying informal welfare as a fourth element to the SDW, Rose was engaging with an established debate that had been wrestling with women's complex relationship to welfare, work and care for some time (Oakley, 1974; Wilson, 1977; Lewis, 1986; Ungerson, 1987). The key themes in this debate returned to the top of the agenda in the 1990s (Lewis, 1992, 1997; Orloff, 1993, 1997; Ungerson, 1997; Sevenhuijsen, 1998, 2000; Shakespeare, 2000). Care is identified here as a fundamental aspect of welfare. Indeed, an ethic of care, that acknowledges the complex web of dependence, independence and interdependence, could be seen as the definitive feature of welfare. Since care is recognised as public welfare when a nurse cares for a sick child in hospital, it is clearly a form of welfare when a mother cares for a sick child at home. However, both the focus on care providers and the concept of 'informal welfare' could be misleading. Care is not always benign; it may be intrusive, unwelcome, patronising and controlling. For older people and disabled people, being cared *for* without any say over *how* it is provided, or if at all, is especially significant. The cared for can all too easily be equated with being a burden or passive victim, the carer a martyr sacrificing themselves for others (Warnes, 1993). Ensuring that every form of care and dependency has a 'voice' (Williams, 2000), including the voice of those who depend on informal care, is one of the major challenges for social policy, and society. At present some forms of welfare are privileged because they have a formal voice and formal rights (Sevenhuijsen, 1998, 2000; Shakespeare, 2000).

Likewise the concept of informal welfare requires a little clarification since it can imply an unstructured, even casual and ad hoc, set of arrangements (Mann, 1992, pp 25-6). But despite the apparent chaos in many households, and the recurring negotiations that take place, the pattern of caring responsibilities has demonstrated considerable continuity over time and between countries (Lewis, 1986; Morris, 1990). Responsibility for providing informal welfare, childcare in particular, is much more likely to fall to women. The focus discussed later is on the implications of these socially constructed patterns for women approaching retirement. Nevertheless, it is necessary to bear in mind these reservations regarding the vocabulary of care and the concept of informal welfare in the discussion that follows.

Rose's approach is important because it explores women's relationship to welfare explicitly using the SDW concept. Her essay demonstrates both the descriptive durability of the SDW and its conceptual flexibility. Rose focused on the provision of care, advocated a detailed (micro rather than macro) analysis of resource allocation and distribution systems – both formal and informal – and she locates these within their historical context. For example, the establishment in the 19th century of the male 'breadwinner' and female carer model had profound implications for subsequent public welfare provisions (Rose, 1981; Williams, 1989). Unfortunately Rose's attempt to link feminist scholarship, radical political economy and the 'Titmuss paradigm' has often been overlooked and only rarely explored or elaborated (Williams, 1989, p 129). An important exception, however, is the work of Sara Arber and Jay Ginn, which has provided a sustained account of the pension penalties imposed on many women by the SDW (Arber and Ginn, 1995b; Ginn and Arber, 1992a, 1992b, 1993, 1996, 1999, 2000). Their research informs much of the following discussion of the main influences on women's access to the SDW and experience of retirement. Of course, not all of the following will impact on all women, as will become apparent. However, for many women the key variables affecting their security in retirement will be:

- caring responsibilities
- the form that dependency takes
- actuarial assumptions
- state policies
- the experience of the paid labour market.

These will now be explored in turn.

Who cares?

The answer to Rose's rhetorical question is that men and women undertake quite different and distinct types of responsibilities within households. Women are traditionally 'the carers' and men 'the breadwinners'. A raft of social and labour market policies have underpinned these arrangements, but until the last quarter of the 20th century they were often taken for granted. Indeed, women's caring responsibilities were frequently portrayed as natural, such as child bearing.

The informal assumptions made about caring are significant because the long-term consequences are rarely fully appreciated for many years.

This point is emphasised by the fact that in 2002 even the youngest man above the state pension age will have been born before 1937, every woman before 1942. (Consider for a moment the phenomenal social changes and events since then.) Put another way, someone born in 1979 will not, even if the retirement age is not raised, be entitled to the state pension until 2044. Thus gender divisions in retirement in 2001 have their roots in the patterns of paid work, caring, family structure and opportunities from the 1950s and 1960s, or earlier in a great many cases, all before the resurgence of feminism in the 1970s it should be noted.

In a world where quick fixes, instant responses and immediate solutions tantalisingly suggest everything can be 'sorted', it is crucially important to recall the time frame over which pensions develop.

The point that stands out above all else is that caring for children and working part time restricts women's access to public, fiscal and occupational welfare.

For example, in 1999/2000 occupational pensions in the UK provided 59% of all pensioner households with some income. This was worth on average (the mean value) £102 per week, although the typical (median value) amount was £59. For single male pensioners the average value of an occupational pension was £55 per week but for a single female pensioner it was only £33 (Cousins et al, 2000).

However, building up a meaningful occupational pension depends on access to full-time, well paid, continuous employment. Childcare responsibilities severely restrain access to such paid work and, as Ginn and Arber noted, "The gender gap in occupational scheme membership becomes substantial in the reproductive life phase and persists until women's customary retirement age" (1993, p 63).

In the early 1990s childless women in the age group 20-29 were eight times more likely to belong to an occupational pension scheme than mothers in the same age group. Childless women aged 20-59 were five times more likely to belong to an occupational pension scheme than women who had children. In contrast, men with a child in the household are *more* likely to be members of a scheme than men without. Thus for women who do not have children, particularly women under 40 years of age, the pattern of occupational and private pension membership looks fairly similar to that of men's (Ginn and Arber, 1993, 1996, 1999, 2000; Ginn, 2001).

It seems reasonable to propose that the 'male breadwinner' myth, combined with women's socially prescribed responsibility for childcare, continue to be the major factors accounting for this pattern.

Dependency

The form that dependency takes is important because many women have few formal rights to a pension of their own. Public welfare in the UK has encouraged married women to be financially dependent on their husbands by a series of allowances (Rose, 1981). A combination of the Wives Allowance, (that is, the ability to opt out of the pensions' component of the NI scheme) and the safety net of Widows Benefit led many women to believe that they would be able to comfortably rely on benefits derived from their spouse. Thus relatively few women built up any worthwhile NI pension contributions. Among female retirees in the UK just over a third have a pension of their own, but as many as 25% of these have inadequate contribution records and will not be getting the full rate. A further four million women pensioners rely on either their spouse's pension or means-tested benefits (Davies and Ward, 1992; Walker with Howard, 2000, pp 247-8).

By providing informal welfare many women have found to their cost that their formal welfare rights are diminished. Citizenship rights, based on contributions and activity in the paid labour market, provide carers with responsibilities but few formal entitlements (Twine, 1992). As Lister (1997) has observed, it is a model of citizenship predicated on activities that are more typically associated with men. Occupational, fiscal and public welfare benefits are defined in law and claimants can assert their rights formally if they have to. Relying on someone else's pension rights bestows no formal entitlement and claims have to be pursued informally. How resources are distributed within households is likely to be as uneven following retirement as it is previously.

The lack of formal rights has been most apparent in the last 20 years as the divorce rate has risen. The implicit informal contract many women thought they had, in which they cared for children and often the 'breadwinner', and in return could anticipate sharing in their husband's retirement income, has often been fractured. The family home and other resources could be subject to court orders but until 2000 pension rights in the UK could not. For some women this has meant that having cared for their children and spouse for most of their adult lives, they had little or no pension rights in their own name, nor any claims that the state would recognise, to that of their former husband's. Despite legislation enabling 'earmarking' and pension 'splitting' associated with 'clean break' divorce settlements that take pension rights into account, there is considerable confusion among occupational pension fund managers as to how they are to deal with an ex-spouse's pension rights. Few funds wish to retain the ex-spouse as a member. Nor are private insurance companies currently fighting for this business and it may be some time yet before there is anything like a 'clean break' that would give divorcees formal pension rights (*Pensions World*, April 2001).

Moreover, without protecting and enhancing the rights of women who have spent their adult lives caring for others, there is the danger of reinforcing their isolation in the name of economic independence. Indeed the vocabulary and meaning of independence for younger women may not be embraced, or appropriate, for older women. For many women pensioners economic independence from their spouse is not a liberating experience but more often a time of mourning. Relatively few widows will welcome economic independence in these circumstances (Wilson, 1995). Among the retired population there are 50% more women than men and this imbalance increases in older age with three times as many women over the age of 85 as men. Thus, most men can approach retirement confidently, having a partner with whom they can share the experience, but most women will not (Arber and Ginn, 1995b). In this context male mortality rates are significant and these are as much a legacy of previous gender divisions as childcare responsibilities, and because of the way the post-war 'welfare settlement' was managed, the two are not unconnected.

Nor can gender divisions be considered without reference to other social divisions, the most obvious of which is 'race' in the US and social class in the UK.

For example, in the US an African American male aged 45 can expect, on average, a further 27 years of life, but a white American woman of the same age can expect to live for a further 40 to 45 years (Elo, 2001; US Census Bureau, 2001). Similarly, a comparison of 1998 data for the North East and South East of England reveals that the death rate per thousand for men in each cohort 55-64, 65-74 and 75-84 is approximately 15% higher in the North East. Men in the North East die at almost twice the rate per thousand of women in the South East in the 55-64, 65-74 age cohorts and at a rate 60% higher in the 75-84 cohort. Women in the North East die at a rate per thousand approximately 50% higher in each age cohort than in the South East (*Regional Trends*, 2001, Table 3.14:9). When this data is set alongside that provided for social class in both areas it is tempting to correlate the two. Thus in the South East there are proportionately more than twice as many people engaged in professional occupations, 50% more in managerial and technical occupations, but at the other end of the scale, roughly 30% less employed in unskilled and semi-skilled work (*Regional Trends*, 2001, Table 3.6).

(Correlation and causation, of course, should not be confused. Within these large areas there are considerable numbers from all social classes, although a more refined account would be likely to see these divisions widen).

The point is that both women's economic dependence, and male patterns of health and illness, reflect socially constructed ideas regarding gender and responsibilities. These ideas and patterns were commonplace 40-60 years ago, and it makes no sense to discriminate or penalise any form of dependency that has been promoted by successive government policies over several generations.

Actuarial assumptions

Actuarial assumptions based on the type of data above has been a further obstacle to women's economic security in retirement. Any contributory system that simply provides a return in line with the funds paid in, and the predicted amount of time that the claimant will draw their pension, is likely to disadvantage women. Apart from interrupted patterns of paid employment associated with caring for children and/or relatives, part-time work that bestows few contributory pension rights and a retirement age of 60 (to be equalised by 2020) that has curtailed the length of time women can build up pension rights, women live longer and when earning get paid less, than men. Without some form of redistribution actuarial principles will invariably replicate demographic and income inequalities.

The State Earnings Related Pension Scheme (SERPS) was intended to address some of these obstacles by calculating the pension rights over a shorter time frame. This second tier system was intended to replace up to 25% of former earnings but this was cut to 20% in 1986. By 2030 the Government Actuary estimates the value of the basic pension (NI) if uprated with prices, will be 10% of male and 14% female average weekly earnings (AWE), while the second tier SERPS will have fallen to the equivalent of 16% of AWE for both men and women. If the value of these schemes was linked to earnings rather than prices, the picture is slightly better, but even then the best the state can promise is a pension with a combined worth of 32% male and 35% female AWE (Government Actuary, 1999, p 20). In 1998 it was estimated that only 17% of the UK paid labour force were still contracted into SERPS but 65% were women. Of all those in the scheme (men and women), 70% earn less than half of the average full-time male earnings (Budd and Campbell, 1998, p 4). Consequently the value of SERPS for most members, mainly women, is particularly unattractive. Moreover, even for a member of SERPS earning above the 50% of average incomes, the likely benefits will only be marginally above the basic state pension. Appropriately the Commission of the European Community described the SERPS benefits as "derisory" (Ginn and Arber, 1992b, p 261).

However, rather than enhancing SERPS, the two major political parties in the UK have instead promoted personal/private and stakeholder pensions. Both have disadvantaged women and particularly working-class women.

State policies

The Conservatives saw private insurance-based pensions as the solution and encouraged these with generous fiscal measures. Private pensions appear to have been an attractive option for many women in the 1980s and early 1990s. Motivated by appallingly low public pensions, very few rights in respect of informal welfare and a SERPS scheme that was being undermined, private pensions promised many women independence. By 1993 roughly five million people were members of private pension schemes. These were underwritten by massive tax subsidies (£6 billion) and the pensions industry often targeted women, with clever advertising, aggressive sales techniques, and often in people's homes. Private pensions 'belong' to the individual and as such break with the idea of women deriving their welfare from their spouse. They also allow for a measure of flexibility and mobility in terms of changing jobs, career breaks, and caring responsibilities that occupational schemes do not. For younger women who anticipate above-average earnings and want a pension that does not tie them to a single employer, private pensions may offer a reasonable package, but many women were misled. By 1992 it was clear that some companies were misselling pension policies by encouraging people to move from occupational schemes to private/personal schemes. Equally important were the cases of people transferring from SERPS into private schemes and the low paid who have, in effect, taken out such minuscule provisions that they have purchased next to nothing. There was clearly a desire on the part of many women to try and ensure that they could approach retirement with a little more security. Unfortunately their aspirations were misplaced because their contributions were generally too low to generate a sizeable investment fund, particularly after the deduction of administration and commission charges by the insurance companies. Two thirds of women contributing to personal pensions were earning less than £200 per week and as such were ill-advised, to put it mildly, to have taken out private pensions (Davies and Ward, 1992; Ginn and Arber, 2000).

Since 1997 the Labour government pursued a similar route but, by negotiating with the pensions industry and careful targeting, designed a package that should avoid the worst features of the misselling scandal. Stakeholder pensions were designed to encourage people earning between £9,500 and £20,000 a year to take out a second tier pension. With a 1% ceiling on administration charges and also subsidised by tax relief (up to 40%), the possibility of having variable contributions, and even contribution breaks, they too initially appeared quite attractive for women and the lower-paid looking for a more flexible way of saving for their retirement. But there were concerns raised as soon as they were available in April 2001 when it was suggested that, because of the tax relief, stakeholder pensions would be particularly attractive to higher earners with a spouse who was either not in paid work, or working part time (*The Observer*, 1 April 2001). Younger people who expect to see their incomes rise later in their careers, but who are not able to commit a large slice of their income to pension saving initially, may also benefit from being able to make an early start. However, there are some disturbing indications that in many respects the stakeholder pensions will simply reinforce the SDW and impose responsibilities without enhancing the rights of the poorest. Stakeholder pensions are cheap (in terms of administration charges) Defined Contributions (DC) schemes that promote private, market-based, provisions, with all the risks that this can entail. They are flexible at the contribution stage but offer the individual little choice or control over 'their' fund once they retire. Only 25% of the accrued funds can be taken as a cash lump sum and the remaining 75% of the fund has to be used to buy an annuity, that is, a guaranteed income for the rest of someone's life. Annuities can be criticised for a number of reasons:

• they are an inflexible form of saving;
• they often provide a lower return than could be realised from, for example, putting the equivalent amount into a mortgage on a more expensive home;
• they lack even the minimal levels of control and transparency associated with occupational funds;
• and if the annuity purchaser dies the fund usually dies with them, to the benefit of the provider – usually an insurance company.

For women, annuities are generally an unattractive option because the fund actuaries adjust the income according to life expectancy. Because women in general live longer than men, their annual income from the same stakeholder contributions could be as much as £1,000 per annum less. However, equalising annuities would mean transferring resources from, in the main, low-paid working-class men, who die the youngest but who can hardly be blamed for this, to women in general. Some women would undoubtedly be the wives of middle-class men taking advantage of the tax breaks (up to 40%) offered by the stakeholder scheme. The well-respected pensions and financial journalist Maria Scott (*The Observer*, 1 April 2001) has made it quite clear that she feels many people on low incomes would be ill-advised to join a stakeholder scheme. In any event, working-class women will still get very small incomes from stakeholder pensions that in many cases will simply take them marginally above the level at which the new means-tested benefits (Minimum Income Guarantee: MIG) will be paid (Walker, 1999; IDS, 2000).

Paid work

The experience of the paid labour market for many women in the UK is different to that of most men. The close correspondence between paid labour market activity, full-time continuous employment, access to a good occupational pension and gender is also clearly apparent from the data.

Membership of occupational pension schemes reached a high point in 1967 with 12.2 million people and 52.6% of the total labour force (full- and part-time) being members of a scheme. However, during the 1950s and 1960s the proportion of women in the paid labour force (full- and part-time) who were members of an occupational pension scheme actually declined from 27% in 1956 to 21% by 1967, but for men it rose from 49% in 1956 to 63% by 1967 (Ginn and Arber, 1993, p 3). Among full-time paid employees membership of occupational pension schemes has declined a little, but in 1990 72% of men and 63% of women were members. Over 90% of men in the public sector but 59% in the private sector, and 88% of women in the public sector and 49% in the private sector (all full-time) were members of an occupational pension scheme (Goode, 1993, p 17).

Occupational pensions are also the major reason for rising incomes for retired people.

In 1999/2000 59% of pensioner households were getting an occupational pension (see Figure 2). Remarkably 52% of single pensioners had an occupational pension. Among pensioners who retired in the previous five years a slightly higher percentage (64%) were getting an occupational pension. These trends are likely to persist for the next 10

Figure 2: Proportion of pensioner units in receipt of occupational pension income (1999/2000) (%)

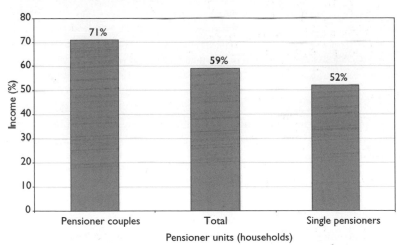

Source: Cousins et al (2000, p 51)

years or so, mirroring events in the (full-time) paid labour market up to the mid-1980s with a levelling off, and probably a decline, in the proportions benefiting thereafter.

However, the appearance of increasing pensioner incomes has to be heavily qualified, because it overlooks those excluded from schemes and the pitiful value of the pension to the poorest 20% of the retired population; typically £4 for a single person and £13 for a couple per week (Cousins et al, 2000, p 55). Again, women who worked part time or who were not engaged in the paid labour market will be the least likely to have any meaningful occupational pension rights. Even those that did fully engage in paid labour will, because their incomes have been lower than men's, have a smaller occupational pension.

Furthermore, part-time work, changing employers, periods out of the paid labour market and lower incomes – all features of labour market behaviour associated more strongly with women – will significantly affect pension entitlement.

> The Goode Report (1993, vol II) indicated that men were three times more likely to be drawing an occupational pension, and that in the crucial age cohorts of 35-44 and 45-55, men were, proportionately, nearly twice as likely to be members of an occupational pension scheme as women. Even when women work for an employer who provides an occupational pension they have in the past often been excluded from it if they work part time. In 1993 only 34% of part-time female workers whose employer had a scheme were members of it. With 33% of women of working age never having been a scheme member, compared to 18% of men, it is apparent that many more women than men will either have an inadequate occupational pension of their own, have to rely on their spouse's pension, or have none at all (Goode, 1993, vol II, pp 16-18).

The consequences of these assumptions, welfare measures and decisions, can be observed in the situation that confronts many women in retirement. In the UK the poorest pensioners are those who live alone, who rely on the state pension, and those who are over 75 years of age (that is, they were in their late teens and 20s when the Beveridge Report [1942] was published). Women predominate in each of these categories.

> Of the 3.9 million pensioners living alone in 1996, just over 3 million were women. Of these, roughly 1.5 million women were over the age of 75, and

approximately 1.2 million were relying on the basic state pension of 15% of AWE (based on data in Midwinter, 1997; Walker with Howard, 2000).

The overwhelming majority of these women will have had to apply for means-tested benefits. Thousands of others will have been deterred from claiming safety-net benefits by the stigma that is still associated with residual means tests in Britain.

State legislation has reinforced gender divisions in retirement in a host of ways that are overlooked if the focus is simply on paid labour. What is blatantly apparent is that every aspect of the SDW described by Titmuss is gendered. However, this does not adequately capture the disadvantages that women confront. In order to do that the informal pattern of provision and negotiation within households has to be fore-grounded. State legislation, trades union and labour market exclusion, actuarial principles, market misselling, discrimination, and informal welfare mechanisms all combine to weave a web around women's experience of retirement. This is not confined to women, however – many men will experience similar patterns of inequality and disadvantage in retirement. Exclusion, unemployment, illness or, in some cases caring, will see many men approaching retirement with trepidation. Moreover, as Rose (1981) made plain, discrimination and disadvantage are structured by class and 'race' as well as gender.

'Race'

A further note on 'race'/ethnicity is needed here to highlight one of the vital issues for social policy in the near future, difference and identity. Exclusion and closure in the paid labour market on the basis of 'race' and ethnicity were touched on earlier but there are also significant variations between, and within, minority ethnic groups. The data is still rather thin, and again we need to recall the time frame of migration and settlement for different ethnic groups; some tentative points can be made, however. It appears that 'black'/African Caribbean women are marginally more likely to be members of an occupational pension scheme than white women, but Pakistani and Bangladeshi women rarely have either an occupational or any private pension rights of their own. Although approximately 20% of Pakistani and Bangladeshi men are members of an occupational pension scheme, and 9% of private schemes, this is still less than half the rate for white, 'black' and Indian men (Berthoud, 1998).

The importance of access to paid labour, and the fact that unemployment rates are also more than double the national average for the Pakistani and Bangladeshi communities, has to be borne in mind. However, religious and cultural differences may also play a part and in any event need to be considered (Nesbitt and Neary, 2001). Historically, Papal edicts, religious belief and discrimination certainly combined to exclude Catholics and Irish migrants from the benefits of Friendly Society membership in the 19th century (Mann, 1992, pp 38-9). And if, for example, religious beliefs are offended by compelling membership of an occupational or private pension – because, for example, they depend on usury (profits from money lending) – some minority ethnic communities may well approach retirement rather differently to the ethnic majority. Thus, Nesbitt and Neary (2001) identified cultural values among Pakistani and Bangladeshi men in Oldham that emphasised traditional patterns of intergenerational support, rather than formal pension rights, as the mechanism to provide welfare for retirees. However, compulsory pension saving might undermine these traditional and informal commitments to welfare within specific communities.

On the other hand, formal pension rights might be perceived by some sections of the community, for example, younger women, as a welcome opportunity to break with traditions that commit them to providing informal welfare across generations. Of course, eradicating discrimination and exclusion would be prerequisites for meaningful choices by individuals and communities, but the history of social policy is littered with well intentioned, but misplaced, 'normalising' solutions (Rattansi, 1994). It may be that, asking questions about the significance of cultural identity will produce answers that emphasise similarity and shared values, irrespective of ethnicity. Failing to ask, however, can neglect the policy implications arising from difference and diversity. If, as Williams (2000) suggests, social policy has to recognise and listen to the dissident voices of marginalised and excluded groups, it cannot simply presume that one form of welfare 'fits all', or that the excluded speak with one voice.

Welfare regimes

Titmuss's essay on the SDW asserted the need for universal, non-means-tested, public welfare measures that would bind society together. Simultaneously he identified alternative forms of welfare to the public system that served to meet similar needs, albeit in ways that were likely to widen social divisions. In Esping-Andersen's (1990) approach, the SDW is combined with radical political economy, Korpi's (1978, 1983) work on class forces and Marshall's (1950) model of citizenship, in order to compare welfare provisions in the developed economies. His impact on comparative social policy has been considerable and his synthesis has influenced a generation of scholars. Esping-Andersen features at length in Chapter Six but merits a brief mention here because his revision of the SDW served as a timely reminder of the different means by which welfare could be provided. Moreover, Titmuss's neglect of power and class, his benign view of the state, his functionalist account of the division of labour and consequent misreading of how dependencies arise, are all implicitly addressed by Esping-Andersen. The glaring omission in his account, however, is informal welfare (Lewis, 1992, 1997). This in turn poses questions about the way he sees the representation and articulation of working-class interests.

Intra-class divisions and sectional scrambles for a relatively more privileged place in the SDW have been profoundly significant in many countries. In Britain the labour movement has historically played a key part in making the SDW by drawing a line between 'respectables and roughs', 'labour aristocrats and residuum', 'deserving and undeserving', and by excluding *others*. In the 19th century, Friendly Societies enabled millions to escape the Poor Law; in the first half of the 20th century the insurance principle maintained the deserving/undeserving distinction; and in the last 30-40 years the 'respectable' working class sought access to fiscal and occupational welfare (Mann, 1984, 1992). In the US trades unions were to the fore in pressing for retirement pensions from their employers, with a number of major industrial disputes during the 20th century (Stevens, 1996; Sass, 1997). Occupational welfare in general and retirement pensions in particular have developed in much the same way in the US as in most European Union (EU) countries. A two tier system of benefits has the social security system as the safety net and industrial/company and private insurance schemes providing an earnings-related (or contribution-related) additional tier. The main difference is that in the US, it was more effective to apply pressure to industries and companies than to coordinate pressure on the federal state (Rein, 1996; Sass, 1997). In Australia, 'The wage earners welfare state' (Castles, 1985) also largely reflected the interests of those who advocated it: full-time, male, wage earners. In contrast to the US, Australian labour had a centralised wage award system that made it relatively easy to press for social reform. However, compulsory saving and state insurance schemes were rejected as hidden taxes in favour of a relatively generous means-tested benefit (the Age Pension is 25% of AWE), high disposable incomes and a progressive system of direct taxation.

The point is that while the Swedish trades union movement and Social Democratic Party has traditionally pressed for the state to improve public welfare for all, in Britain, Australia and the US organised labour has often pursued welfare through different means and mechanisms. The legacy of the Poor Law in English-speaking countries has meant that public welfare has rarely been seen as desirable and the state has not been regarded as the most reliable provider. Moreover, and as industrial trades unionism has been marginalised in the UK and US toward the end of the 20th century, consumer interests and consumption cleavages have assumed a greater role in representing interests (see Chapter Three). The SDW is therefore becoming wider and broader with more sections of society able to access occupational and fiscal welfare, but creating a bigger gap with those who cannot. As Bauman (1998) has observed, the poorest, the non-consumers, are further removed from the most privileged forms of welfare. Simultaneously the social, political and economic forces driving the development of the SDW have seen occupational and fiscal welfare extended to the apparently contented majority. Retirement, and the way fiscal welfare is used to support it, is one of the clearest examples of this trend.

Fiscal welfare is most apparent in supporting the private market provision of insurance based pension schemes. Privately funded personal pension funds are generally operating in the wider life assurance and savings market, normally through insurance companies. They can also be arranged by businesses and employers or via a mutual savings society. In the UK the stakeholder schemes are a type of group plan with DCs. Many employers in the UK have also moved their recent recruits into DC group plans following the trend in the US to Group Personal Plans (GPPs). Without fiscal support the private pensions industry in many countries would, however, struggle to be attractive savings mechanisms. In effect private pensions are purchased like any other investment product, but in order to encourage take-up the state disregards all, or part, of the individual's (and/or the employer's) contributions when assessing their tax liabilities. In the US private plans had been tax privileged since at least 1913 but they became more attractive after 1926 and were further enhanced in the 1930s. Sass (1997) provides some useful insights into how sectional interests, particularly those of higher earners, were served by a tax system that effectively promoted pensions as a system of avoidance. In many countries both the contributions and the income from the investment funds attract a privileged tax status. By providing retirement 'perks' individual employers and companies have often pursued their wider labour market strategies, for example, trying to attract skilled labour or reward executives, alongside some generous schemes for themselves. In the US, after 1942, the tax exempt status of pensions was supposed to have been tightened up by insisting they had 70% of employees covered by any scheme. However, rather than curtailing the tax privileges this led to a massive increase as companies complied by extending coverage. Dobbin and Boychuk (1996) argue that despite management resistance, including efforts to protect their own pensions, trades unions had succeeded in getting private pensions for virtually all their members. Nevertheless, the fiscal benefits to the highest earners remained more generous, and were arguably even more regressive. The net effect, according to Sass, was to create a two-class system of pensions. On the one hand, a class of pensioners who would only collect the social security pension, and on the other, a class of pensioners with far more generous incomes who had benefited from their occupational and fiscal privileges (Sass, 1997).

In Australia the Age Pension is the safety net and is subject to both means and assets tests, but the federal state has, since the 1992 Superannuation Guarantee, required employers to pay a contribution into an occupationally-related pension fund. As of 2002 employers should pay a levy for each employee equivalent to 12% of their annual salary. At present there is no requirement for employees to contribute. In practice, however, the vast majority of full-time employees in Australia do contribute to their own 'super' fund due to employment and wage award agreements, and the preferential tax treatment of these. In marked contrast to the UK, however, the tax subsidy has been the focus of considerable debate. Newspaper headlines queried 'the gravy train' (*The Australian*, 16 June 1992), and the 'double dipping' (that is, getting the tax subsidies and then arranging their finances so they can claim the Age Pension), pointing out that the lower paid will get smaller tax breaks (*Sydney Morning Herald*, 16 June 1992, 19 June 1992). Even government figures showed that for those earning twice the average weekly income, the tax subsidy would be ten times greater than that paid to someone on 50% of AWE (Mann, 1993). Their retirement incomes will also be very different with the former high paid employee getting double the retirement income of the latter. The long-standing antipathy to compulsory saving in Australia, combined with a pragmatic egalitarianism, has ensured that fiscal welfare has at least been debated, if not resolved (Mann, 1993; Olsberg, 1997).

Despite the existence of a supposedly 'universal' system of public pensions, the pattern in the UK is harder to detect but clearly unfair. The combination of tax privileges, trades union pressure, employer labour market strategies and wage restraint policies encouraged the growth of company, and public sector, pension schemes (Green et al, 1984; Hannah, 1986; Mann and Anstee, 1989).

In the UK the crucial difference between most occupationally-related pension schemes is whether the pension is based on a proportion of former earnings with DBs derived from the final salary (usually an average of a number of years), or simply derived from the contributions made and invested DCs. In final salary schemes the pension is usually based on a formula that uses the number of years of service combined with a specific percentage of former earnings. A simplified example that illustrates the general principles would be: a pension of 60% of annual earnings is payable (based on an average of the previous 10 years' service) after 40 years. Thus 20 years' service would only generate a pension of 30% of former earnings. The level of tax free contributions paid in by the employee and employer will vary a great deal but normally – particularly in the public sector where such schemes are common – the employer contributes more than the employee.

As in the US, access to occupationally-related pensions increased greatly in the 1940s and 1950s, and among full-time employees was relatively stable until the 1980s. Consequently people retiring today in the UK also fall into two broad classes of pensioner, with the most recent retirees getting twice as much income from occupational pensions, in real terms, as they would have in 1979 (Walker with Howard, 2000, p 266). The two divisions within the retired population are clearest between younger retirees, who 'earned' their pensions in the post-war period, with the poorest and older pensioners much more likely to rely on the public pension. Fiscal welfare in the UK, as in the US, has subsidised this trend.

In 1955 Titmuss (1958, p 51) estimated the cost of occupational pensions to the Exchequer through lost tax revenue to be £100 million. Throughout the 1990s the tax relief on occupational schemes was between £7,300 million and £9,900 million. This may well be an under-estimate and it could be that a further £2,000 million per annum was doled out (Field and Owen, 1993, p 11; Inland Revenue, 1998).

Furthermore, because tax rates are graduated with income, the better-off get a disproportionate subsidy. The more tax a person is liable to pay the greater the tax subsidy from paying into a pension. This also encourages anyone close to the higher tax band to commit more of their pre-tax income to other tax privileged savings funds, such as AVCs that allow extra years in the fund to be purchased on retirement. This then enables the better-off to retire earlier if they so wish. The injustice of the UK system is compounded by the fact that, while private, stakeholder and occupational pension fund contributions qualify for tax relief, employee contributions into the state NI scheme do not. Thus the poorest pay tax on their savings and get the lowest pension.

Reductions in employer NI contributions, introduced by the Labour government, have cut the annual income to the NI fund by £1 billion (*Hansard*, Columns 772-3, vol 337, 11 November 1999). Employees, however, saw their contributions to the NI fund increase, in real terms, by 68% between 1979 and 1994 (Walker, 1999, p 516).

It has to be remembered that fiscal welfare is extremely difficult to define or measure accurately, but there is little dispute over its significance in promoting some forms of welfare rather than others (Kvist and Sinfield, 1996). Employers, professional groups, high earners, managers, trades unions and governments have used fiscal welfare to maintain and promote privilege. Without an extensive knowledge of accountancy and considerably more access to Inland Revenue data, it is difficult to judge the true value and significance of fiscal welfare. Disentangling the tax allowances, rebates and exemptions that are woven into the multitude of retirement savings schemes – let alone considering the tax status of assets and savings such as property, antiques, homeownership, funds overseas, and so on – has only been touched on here. Clearly, though, fiscal welfare is a key component within the SDW. When comparisons are made between the different elements of the SDW it is also plain that while each addresses similar welfare goals, they pursue them very differently and with very different outcomes. Hopefully, and as Titmuss intended, the concept of a SDW will continue to dispel the myths about 'the burden' of public welfare when discussing retirement incomes.

Summary

For any student of social policy the SDW continues to have a strong appeal both as a descriptive and polemical tool. It allows us to compare the different mechanisms by which welfare is provided and ensures that all forms of welfare dependency are acknowledged. It is, therefore, 'Not only the poor' (Goodin et al, 1987) who are welfare dependent, and it turns our attention to the various ways in which the state, the market, industrial relations, and informal socially established arrangements can all promote welfare. The strengths and weaknesses of the SDW can be seen as follows.

Main strengths of the SDW

- Adaptable, embracing mid-range theory.
- Firmly grounded in social policy.
- Challenges narrow stereotypes of public welfare.
- Acknowledges winners as well as losers.
- Recognises the complex relationship between welfare and social divisions.
- Rejects reductionism – that is, does not reduce all forms of welfare to public welfare, nor all social divisions to one factor.
- Has considerable potential for development.
- Reconstructed versions show problems with Titmuss's account can be resolved.
- Can make visible questions of power and influence.
- Has the potential to be a useful comparative tool.

Weaknesses of the SDW

- Has to be revised and developed from Titmuss's model.
- Titmuss under-valued the market as an innovating force.
- Titmuss under-estimates the political as well as economic power that vested interests have.
- Titmuss misrepresents the bases of social divisions.
- Tries to embrace too much and potentially strays into eclecticism.
- Bedded in, and therefore wedded to, social policy, and is therefore rather sociologically narrow.

- Not always clear about the key variables and major lines of social fragmentation.
- Can neglect consumption, desires and aspirations.
- Has a normative bias and can privilege public welfare over other forms of welfare.

Two versions of political economy: ease and plenty or immiseration and crisis?

Introduction

Two approaches to retirement and pensions are considered alongside one another in this chapter. Both take the political and economic context as their starting point but they reach very different conclusions. Political economy has a long tradition within the social sciences and two basic forms are identified. For the sake of clarity these will be referred to as 'orthodox' political economy and 'radical' political economy. Orthodox political economy is traced to Adam Smith, the figure whose shadow is the longest, with Karl Marx the major figure in developing radical political economy. These categories are complicated by the fact that radical versions of political economy can appear quite orthodox while orthodox political economy has been quite radical in some respects. The easiest way of thinking about the two schools of thought is to recall that orthodox political economy has the longer tradition and is often associated with the political Right, whereas radical political economy was developed by the political Left in the latter part of the 19th century. Both versions are quick to identify their respective political allegiances and their roots. Thus, for example, on the first page of their book, the Friedmans (1980) nail their colours to "*The wealth of nations* ... the masterpiece that established the Scotsman Adam Smith as the father of modern economics" (p 1). In contrast, Deaton (1989) makes it plain, in the first sentence of his study, that he is "using the approach of Marxist political economy" (p 1). Orthodox accounts will be considered first, with some examples from the UK between 1979 and 1997 provided to illustrate the approach. Radical political economy follows, with the discussion focusing on occupational pensions.

Ease and plenty: orthodox political economy

Adam Smith and Thomas Malthus are the two figures that are most significant in the development of orthodox political economy. Smith often appears to be the optimist and Malthus the prophet of doom and gloom. Smith asserted that a capitalist market benefited everyone in society, including the poor. Provided governments could resist the temptation to interfere, a capitalist market would generate goods and services to meet demand. Markets must operate within legal boundaries but if the market allows free and fair competition, then the 'invisible hand' of supply and demand would reward hard work and enterprise. Likewise, Smith argued that it was in the interests of employers to have employees who were fit and healthy to ensure a more productive workforce. In the context of retirement he argued that if workers were well rewarded, they would be able to put something aside for the future, thereby "ending his [sic] days perhaps in ease and plenty ..." (Smith, 1976, p 737).

In the context of 18th century Britain, Smith had a generous view of the poor, although today he is usually associated with conservative thinkers and welfare cuts. Smith was not a purist, his political economy was imbued with a moral economy, and he accepted the need for a safety net of public welfare. Although he believed individuals should be responsible for making welfare provisions of their own, he recognised that this was not always possible. Smith wanted to encourage saving for the future and he thought that labourers would do so if they were paid a reasonable wage. Residual public welfare measures would always be necessary, however, because the economic forces of the market were too tremendous and unpredictable for individuals to anticipate. For example, during the 20th century no individual could reasonably be expected to predict the financial crash and crises of the 1930s, or of major banks closing (as they did in 1998 in Japan), of massive fraud (as in the Maxwell case), the effects of two world wars, or numerous company closures taking their occupational pension fund with them. It seems likely that in these circumstances Smith would have seen the honest labourer, whose hard earned savings had evaporated, as deserving of public welfare. Some advocates of his approach might argue, however, that charities, family or friends would be more appropriate sources of assistance before the public purse is opened (Seldon, 1996).

Central to orthodox political economy is the desire to promote self-reliance and market-based solutions to social problems, whenever possible. The example that is often cited, of how 'the invisible hand of the market' works to good effect, is that which Smith gave when he pointed out that shopkeepers sold their goods without being told by anyone that they should do so. We take it for granted that the baker will have bread, the butcher meat, and so on. These services are efficient, with supply and demand balancing one another and the trader adjusting provisions according to their knowledge of the market. The efficiency of these services is guaranteed by each trader's desire to maximise their profits and to extend their market share. Supporters of orthodox political economy argue that many forms of welfare can also be left to market forces. With higher disposable incomes the potential for retirement saving is much greater and, therefore, there should be little need for the state to intrude in the market. If the individual is free to shop around for the welfare provisions that suit their needs and their pocket, then the market for welfare services will improve, along with consumer knowledge of these markets. State provisions and interference blunt the incentive to make provisions and the consumer's proper desire to understand the services they are buying. So the prospect of a life of 'ease and plenty' in older age ought to depend on individuals making adequate retirement plans. For anyone who expects to retire from paid work – that is, the vast majority of people in the developed capitalist economies – the need for welfare is predictable. Anyone failing to anticipate this only has themselves to blame if they do not make suitable provisions. With more people expecting to retire, the number and range of service providers ought to increase. These providers need not be profit-making organisations, for example, mutual and friendly societies offer retirement pensions, as they would still provide more market choice. Competition between pension providers should in turn promote efficiency and innovation (Seldon, 1996; Littlewood, 1998).

The net effect will be significant differences in the value of retirement income between various individuals, but these should simply reflect a person's success in the paid labour market and their spending priorities. Inequalities are inevitable and they serve as a spur to achievement and a reward for prudence. If the labour market is meritocratic, and rewards are not artificially manipulated, then access to welfare will mirror ability and achievement. Self-interest provides the motivation and consumer preferences will encourage providers to innovate and enhance market performance. However, if an individual chooses not to make provisions of their own, but to spend their income, then hopefully they will enjoy their consumption but will not subsequently complain about their lack of welfare provisions. Compulsion distorts the market and only when individuals are 'free to choose' (Friedman and Friedman, 1980) do goods and services, including provisions such as retirement pensions, respond to markets.

Malthus provides a more pessimistic analysis, and his ideas are only touched on here because they have been echoed in more recent analyses that stress population changes and dependency ratios (Johnson et al, 1989; OECD, 1998a). Where Smith believes people behave in economically rational ways, and that they will restrain themselves in anticipation of future benefits, Malthus believes this only occurs when the cost of unrestrained behaviour is extremely high. Likewise any improvements in wages would not necessarily encourage retirement saving unless the penalties for not doing so were blatantly apparent to the working classes. Malthus claimed it was far more likely that labourers would prefer to consume than save, and without some natural checks on population growth any improvements in living standards in the short term would simply produce 'misery and vice' in the longer run. Without famine, war or pestilence, the population would grow faster than food production. Providing welfare to the aged poor would simply diminish the resources available to all (Himmelfarb, 1984). His was an argument for the abolition of all forms of assistance to the poor. Malthus was writing at a time when family planning meant quite simply delaying marriage and/or not having sexual intercourse. Food production was only just beginning to adopt scientific methods, and so it is hardly surprising his predictions were dire, but wrong. However, concentrating on Malthus's food to population ratios alone misses the point that has endured – the numbers of dependent people has to be seen in relation to the resources available. Fears that the ratio of retired people to those in paid work will make pensions too expensive, or that the total number of public welfare recipients, combined with those who are not active in the labour market (children, students, retirees, and so on), will become unsustainable, have been heard on numerous occasions (Phillips, 1954; Walker, 1996; Budd and Campbell, 1998; OECD, 1998a).

Fortunately war, pestilence and starvation are not currently policy solutions with any support in the developed economies. Like Adam Smith, even the most strident advocates of orthodox political economy acknowledge that public welfare benefits cannot be scrapped overnight. "We need some way to ease the transition from where we are to where we would like to be" (Friedman and Friedman, 1980, p 119). The aim of late has been to incrementally reduce the relative value of public welfare while also encouraging individuals to make provisions of their own. Raising the age at which public pensions are paid to women to 65, and proposals to scrap the fixed age of retirement are also designed to address the 'dependency ratio'. In countries like the UK, where the public pension is paid from revenues raised from current workers (pay as you go), this dependency ratio is often seen as crucial. The picture across the developed world is one of an ageing population and declining participation in paid work for the over-50s, particularly men (OECD, 1998a). The data and demographic trends are open to dispute and the language of 'dependency ratios', 'burden of an ageing population' and demographic 'crisis' has been heard, and rebutted, before (Titmuss, 1958, pp 56-74; Walker, 1996, p 2; Vincent, 1996, 1999, pp 104-7). Nor are politicians too keen to be seen to cut benefits to a 'deserving' category. The logic of Malthus's approach would be swingeing cuts in public welfare provisions but to date politicians have been reluctant to grasp this nettle. However, low unemployment rates in the UK in 2000 witnessed a Labour Cabinet Office report that proposed, among other things, that even the over-60s should prove they were looking for jobs or lose their benefits (PIU, 2000). This does not chime with what younger people appear to want for themselves, nor does it seem likely that significant numbers of the over-60s will be drawn into paid work. The reasons for, and significance of, early exit will be revisited in subsequent chapters; for now it is important to note that the focus is primarily on public welfare recipients. The irony is that 'dependency' on other aspects of the SDW appears to promote early exit, and thereby increases the 'dependency ratio'. Greater retirement saving, increasing rates of owner-occupation and widening access to employers' occupational pensions – all facilitated by fiscal (tax) benefits – have enabled many older workers to consider retiring early (Walker with Howard, 2000). It might be thought that orthodox political economy would enthusiastically applaud these developments, even if they do have an impact on the 'dependency ratio', but occupational pensions in particular have not always been warmly embraced.

Occupational pensions: the golden chains?

Orthodox political economists have an ambiguous attitude to occupationally-related pensions. On the one hand, they demonstrate Adam Smith's point about all sharing in the profits of market success. They are also largely free from state interference, although orthodox political economists usually advocate the scrapping of the tax privileges that underpin occupational schemes in many countries (Green, 1996; Littlewood, 1998). On the other hand, occupational pensions can be seen as 'golden chains' (Rubner, 1962), binding employees to their employers for decades, and thereby interfering in the operation of a free labour market. This second claim hinges on seeing occupational pensions as provided by generous employers rather than a part of the price they pay to compete in the labour market. Other forms of non-wage labour costs, for example, holiday entitlement, sick pay and company perks, rarely attract the criticism that they distort the labour market. If the occupational pension is treated as part of the wage/labour negotiation, it is difficult to see why the pension need be any more of a bind than the wage. The problem in terms of labour market mobility is that the pension is tied to a particular employer, and changing employers can affect an employee's subsequent pension rights. If orthodox approaches are to be consistent, they should promote pension portability and vesting, thereby protecting the value of the fund and clearly earmarking it as deferred wages for the individual. With certain guarantees to allow fund managers a measure of predictability, for example, a time lag between leaving an employer and transferring the assets, and even with some small charge for making this transfer – which today would be electronic and akin to moving bank accounts – such a measure would break any 'golden chains'. Of course many employers would complain that they set up their scheme precisely in order to retain valued staff. Thus despite a general decline in occupational scheme membership in the 1990s, it was widely reported that computer staff were being offered very generous pension packages (*Pensions World*, December 2000). Making occupational pension rights more mobile need not prevent employers competing for labour and using the pension as an attraction. It would certainly ensure that employees, who are usually making substantial contributions themselves, could weigh up the total wages, pension and perks package on offer. Thus occupational pensions would develop from further competition in the labour market and provide an alternative to personal private pensions, adding another layer of innovation and choice for individuals. Since orthodox political economists would shudder at the prospect of preventing employers from offering the wage deals they feel are appropriate, and since wages are still likely to be the principal way that employers seek to retain and attract labour, it is difficult to see the case against occupational pensions. In practice, however, orthodox political economists have tended to see private pensions, offered by financial institutions like insurance companies, as preferable to employer schemes. This is a view that informed the British Conservative Party's thinking during the 1980s and 1990s with scandalous results.

The state, the regulators, the politicians and the market

One of the most articulate advocates of orthodox political economy has been David Green, Director of the Institute of Economic Affairs (IEA), a free market 'think-tank' with many supporters in the Conservative Party. He has suggested that there are essentially three ways that retirement pensions could be reformed:

> The first requires payment of compulsory contributions but allows individuals a choice of pension provider.... The second approach urges free market provision but calls for the government to encourage locked-in savings by means of tax breaks.... The third approach ... prefers to put few, if any, limits on the methods by which people can provide for their old age and also opposes the use of the tax system to encourage particular types of provision. (Green, 1996, pp 88-9)

Green goes on to support the third approach, underpinned by a minimal safety net of public welfare and the scrapping of the retirement age. With the Conservatives in power for almost two decades (1979-97) it might be thought that the IEA would have been more influential and to have seen these policies tested. However, and without running through every development between 1979-97, it is surprising how little actually did change. Although Green may be wise after the event, his opposition to the state offering tax perks to promote private pensions indicates where he feels the policy went wrong.

Despite being the single biggest recurring item on the social security bill, neither Margaret Thatcher, nor her Conservative Party successors, introduced widespread reforms to the retirement pension system. Cuts in public welfare benefits were introduced and some commentators have seen these as 'major', but the fundamental structure and costs remained unchanged (Phillipson, 1998, p 71). By and large the policy was to nudge people towards private, insurance-based, pension funds by gradually making the public pension schemes (NI and SERPS) less attractive, and offering the carrot of tax incentives for private pensions. This was a strategy that had appeared to work in respect of public housing (Forrest and Murie, 1989). Instead of slashing and burning, the Tories whittled and chipped at the state schemes. The SERPS, which had only been fully operational for a few years, was undermined by a combination of breaking the 'best year's earnings' rule, which effectively cut 20-30% off the future value of the scheme, unannounced reductions in widows' SERPS entitlement, and opt-out clauses for those who transferred to a private pension. Previously the basic pension had increased in line with average earnings, but this was replaced by a link to the retail price index, which lagged behind wages. The effect was to see the public pension fall to approximately 14% of AWE by 1997 from about 22% in 1979 (Budd and Campbell, 1998, p 3). Despite this, the cost of state pensions to the Treasury remained fairly static. The main development was the promotion of private pensions underpinned by fiscal welfare/tax handouts. This generated a 'personal pensions stampede' with roughly six million people, at a cost of £6 – £11 billion, taking out personal pensions (Disney and Whitehouse, 1992; Ginn and Arber, 2000).

It is now widely accepted that not only was the tax subsidy extremely expensive, but many of those who were advised to take out private pensions were misled (Ginn and Arber, 2000). Sales staff were working largely for commission and, not surprisingly, they were keen to stress the attractions to potential buyers. They also tended to over-state the future performance of private pension funds. The regulatory body, the Securities Investment Board (SIB), reprimanded numerous respected financial institutions for their sales techniques. In 1993 Norwich Union suspended 600 of its staff for 'retraining' but was still fined £300,000 for misconduct by the SIB. Premium Life was also fined £300,000, Legal and General £400,000 and Noble Lowndes £740,000 for similar 'deficiencies in advice'. Sorting out the mess has not been easy and the most recent furore concerns the time it is taking companies to compensate those who were misled or misinformed. Orthodox political economists accept that there was a scandal, but they identify six factors that were responsible for this:

- the various regulatory bodies set up by the state were inept;
- markets fluctuate and so they can, and do, go down as well as up;
- the government created a sellers market which undermined normal consumer scepticism;
- some sellers took advantage of a distorted market situation and were 'economical with the truth';
- product knowledge among consumers was inadequate – a legacy of the 'nanny state';
- government interfered in the market.

First, the failure of the regulatory system that the government had established was a major blow to consumer confidence and to the integrity of the financial services. The 1986 Financial Services Act (FSA) was meant to provide a bedrock of reliability, with the SIB reporting any concerns directly to the Treasury and overseeing the other regulatory bodies in the private pensions field. Reporting to the SIB was the Personal Investment Authority (PIA) which was established, as was the FSA, following the collapse of a couple of investment, and commodity brokers in the early 1980s. The PIA was supposed to devise rules for the selling process and to monitor compliance with those rules. However, Simpson (1996) argues that there are simply too many rules, too much regulation and interference, and therefore, too little competition in the pensions market. Of course the sellers of the policies and the companies they worked for bear a heavy responsibility, but Simpson (1996) argues that the regulatory framework aggravated the situation. Initially, and most importantly, the regulators were very slow to respond to warnings in the press and from industry experts. Then the SIB exaggerated the scale of the problem. Not only were there fewer people who had a legitimate claim against the industry than the SIB suggested, but also the amounts of compensation were always likely to be relatively small. For example, of the five million people who transferred into private pensions, Simpson estimates that only 4% may have a case for compensation, with £78 their estimated average loss. Subsequently the SIB has dithered in setting a timetable for compensation. Confidence has been eroded further because the press and public have blamed the industry for the delay. Therefore, instead of regulators, procedures, and rules, which are costly and bureaucratic, consumers need rigorous fair trading laws that are then monitored by a single regulatory body (Simpson, 1996).

Second, market fluctuations are a normal feature of any free market. Finance markets are no different. Unfortunately the investment markets did not maintain their rates of growth in the period shortly after the rush into private pensions occurred. When sales staff showed graphs of likely fund performance, these were often based on the recent past. They failed because markets can go down as well as up. Other goods and services will vary in price, and some such as houses can vary a great deal, but the purchaser does not expect compensation if the price falls. Thus the dip in the finance market was a normal feature of any market; it just happened at a bad time. Simpson (1996) is adamant that retirement pensions are long-term investments, and in the longer term the finance market can be expected to provide reasonable returns, but customers should not expect any 'quick bucks'.

Third, the government created a 'sellers market' by subsidising the purchases with tax handouts. Demand was artificially stimulated and much greater than expected because consumers were being offered pension products with a state funded discount. If the consumer is spending someone else's money – the general taxpayer's in this case – they are less likely to check on the quality of their purchase and to be in more of a rush to make the deal. Not surprisingly there was a 'stampede' into private pensions (Disney and Whitehouse, 1992). The sales staff were encouraged to sell by high commission rates and, because demand exceeded expectations, many of the sales staff were recent raw recruits. Their own knowledge of their product was often limited to the sales pitch they had learnt by rote in the previous few weeks. In fact, many relied exclusively on previous market performance graphs, videos of pensioners on golden beaches and on a standard sales presentation. They often knew very little about pensions, being unable, even if they had been willing, to advise on important questions such as opting out of SERPS, or transferring an occupational fund into a personal private scheme. What they knew was how to get a sale and what people wanted to hear, which was, in effect, 'The government is subsidising this scheme and if you get a private pension you can approach your retirement with confidence'.

Fourth, hardly surprising therefore that some salespeople misled and misinformed consumers. Some did so through their own ignorance; others deliberately misrepresented the truth.

For example, thousands of miners, teachers and nurses were persuaded to transfer from some of the most reliable and lucrative occupational pension schemes into personal pensions. Sales staff did not make it clear that transferring could be expensive and involved some risk. Many people claimed they were not told of the administrative, commission and other charges that were involved. These charges are usually 'front-loaded', meaning that the company takes them before anything is invested. It is not uncommon for the first 18 months or more of contributions to be consumed by administrative charges. Moreover, some companies appear to have moved pension accounts unnecessarily, imposing administrative charges each time, a process called 'churning' in the US (Simpson, 1996). Nor were the penalties of leaving the schemes, or of not being able to keep up the payments, adequately explained. By 1998 it was estimated that 2.5 million people may have been sold the wrong pension (*Hansard*, column 761, 1999).

For the low-paid, for anyone likely to take time out of full-time employment, most importantly women who might care for children, for older workers, or anyone in a public sector occupational scheme, private pensions rarely offered a good purchase.

Fifth, poorly informed buyers/customers were operating in a market they did not understand. Most private pension purchasers knew very little about retirement saving or the finance markets. It is likely that a more educated public would have been more cautious. A product that looks too good to be true probably is. But knowledge about pensions has, until recently, been regarded as unnecessary. The state provided for people and there was little reason for anyone to educate themselves. Orthodox political economists suggest that the transition to a more market-oriented system requires the state to educate people. While it is common for customers to lack perfect knowledge about any prospective purchase, pensions do have some peculiar features that demand more knowledge of the market if wise decisions are to be made.

For example, the long-term nature of the pension purchase makes it difficult to have a system of redress or refund, since by the time the pension matures it will be too late to select an alternative. Customers are committing themselves to recurring costs over a long period of time and their circumstances may fluctuate. It is very difficult for the purchaser to be familiar with the product (pensions) or the product market unless, and until, they are seeking a purchase, and no one, including the seller, can be absolutely sure that the product will perform as anticipated.

Finally, and most importantly, orthodox accounts blame governments for interfering and distorting the market. Events confirm the view that the state should leave the market to operate on its own. As Seldon (1996, p 67) points out, 'amateur' buyers were initially ill-informed and professional sellers thereby had an advantage, but this is a legacy of the state assuming responsibility for pensions in the past. There were no incentives for people to educate themselves about the market when one did not exist. Government then further distorted the market by artificially stimulating demand with huge tax subsidies. The private pensions industry had to quickly recruit and train new staff and, in the frenetic atmosphere created by several million new customers clamouring for advice, the normally prudent pensions industry got carried away. It is also likely that with the government sponsoring private pensions, false expectations were raised.

Many people had seen immediate benefits from previous policies, for example, from the privatisation of public utilities and the 'right to buy' legislation on public housing, and some may have had similar, but unrealistic, expectations for their private pension fund.

Rather than undermining orthodox approaches, as might be thought, the misselling scandal illustrates their central point that intervention in the market will have unanticipated and unhealthy effects. It is doubtful if Adam Smith, or any orthodox political economist, would have approved of tax handouts to stimulate market demand. Government intervention, as it often does, had the opposite effects to those that it intended. Since the early 1990s there has been a loss of confidence in the private pensions market and a fall in new business (Simpson, 1996, p 43). There was, however, a four-fold increase in market share, with roughly 16% of the paid labour force joining some kind of personal private fund by 1999 compared with only 4% in the mid-1980s (Goode, 1993; Walker with Howard, 2000). Nevertheless, Simpson complains that the fiasco has made it much harder to persuade a sceptical public that a move to market provisions is a project worth pursuing. Despite this, newspaper headlines continued to warn of: "Pension sharks who feed inside your living room" (*The Observer*, 13 April 1997). Most recently, following press releases about the new stakeholder schemes, some companies appear to be using telephone sales to promote their pension products. There have already been fears that another misselling scandal is waiting to happen (*Pensions World*, April 2000). Having been bitten by the sharks in the market it remains to be seen if people will be shy of entering the water again, and if so whether it will cost them an arm and leg before they can get out.

A final feature of orthodox political economy is the emphasis it places on self-interest, and how this affects politicians, welfare bureaucrats and the electorate alike (Friedman and Friedman, 1980). Teachers want smaller classes, doctors point to under-funding, social workers complain of ever-increasing caseloads and politicians want to stay in power. The electorate, however, behaves as consumers and continues to expect government to deliver their welfare goods. Like the proverbial turkeys who fail to enthuse over Christmas, people who rely on, or provide, public welfare do not call for cuts. By 1993 there were reports of proposals from the Treasury's chief secretary, Michael Portillo, to "axe state pensions for the better off" (*The Sunday Times*, 7 February 1993). He also appeared on television (BBC 2, *Newsnight*, 7 October 1993), proclaiming that some pensioners were 'undeserving' of the state pension because they had already been given tax subsidies to assist them with their private or occupational pension.

Portillo's stance in identifying fiscal welfare and 'double dipping' (as the phenomenon of getting both tax subsidies and subsequently the Age Pension is known in Australia), won very little public support in the UK. Telling pensioners that they had already had their cake sounded too much like Marie Antoinette urging Parisians to eat it instead of bread. By-election results in marginal seats with large pensioner populations suggested any further interference with the state pension was an electoral liability. With pensioners generally regarded as 'deserving', a peculiar antipathy towards occupational pensions, and public suspicion of private pensions following the misselling fiasco, the forces of inertia within the Conservative Party by the mid-1990s were greater than those of change. By 1995 public expenditure on state pensions was £28.8 billion, equivalent to approximately 5% of Gross Domestic Product (GDP) compared to £11 billion and roughly 6% of GDP in 1979 when the Conservatives came to power (Budd and Campbell, 1998, pp 1-4). If the money wasted on tax handouts for private pensions is added in, as it should be, it is difficult to see any savings, but there were cuts. The value of the basic state pension, in relation to earnings, had fallen by over 20%, one in four pensioners were having to claim means-tested benefits and at a cost of a further £7 billion per annum (Midwinter, 1997). If the period 1979-97 was an attempt at 'rolling back the state' it would surely have met with contempt from Adam Smith. Portillo could be seen as trying to sustain the Thatcherite project by reasserting some of the central tenets of orthodox political economy, but without offering any perks or Thatcher's ability to engage with a populist agenda. Thus by 1997, in a symbolic moment in British politics, Portillo again reminded many of a haughty French aristocrat, but this time awaiting the guillotine when he lost his previously safe parliamentary seat.

Radical political economy

Radical political economy reaches very different conclusions to the orthodox approach, but there are some similarities. They share concerns over the operation of capitalist markets, the profit motive, the relationships between capital and labour, and the role of the state in assisting or obstructing markets. But it should not be thought that the two approaches share much more than a very superficial agenda. They are opposing teams even if they appear to play much the same game. Radical political economists embrace Karl Marx's critique, seeing the market as imperfect and believing it operates in the interests of one class, the owners of capital, not 'the general interest' as Smith declared. Capitalism is neither willing, nor able, to provide a life of 'ease and plenty', but instead is constantly trying to minimise costs, which includes social costs such as retirement pensions, and to maximise profits. Wealth and privilege are protected by the state and competition in the labour market promotes social divisions. Competition between capitalists, and between different sectors of capitalism, can also generate problems that the state must resolve. For example, finance and industrial capital may hold different views on monetary union in Europe or the appropriate level for interest rates. Globalisation now means that even political parties committed to social reform must put the needs of a capitalist market above the needs of people and social justice. However, capitalism is always on the edge of crisis because of inherent flaws in a market economy and tensions between capitalism and labour. There is a need, therefore, to legitimate the system and to damp down opposition by offering minimal reforms, but this can undermine the need to restrain social expenditure. Balancing these contradictory objectives is the task of the state. These claims will be illustrated below by looking at how retirement fulfils certain needs for capital, how public pensions can generate a crisis for the state, and how the alternatives, private and occupational pensions, contain the seeds for further crisis and conflicts (O'Connor, 1973; Gough, 1979; Deaton, 1989).

The needs of capitalism

The state occupies a central place in radical political economy and the welfare functions it performs are especially important. The state must manage capitalism, in much the same way as a Board of Directors might run a large company with many different departments and a diverse range of products. As Gough explains, "the state requires a degree of autonomy from the economically dominant class(es) in order to adequately represent their interests" (1979, p 41). The task is complicated by the fact that long- and short-term interests may not correspond, but the state must weigh these up and, allowing for particular pressures and political expediency, facilitate the most favourable outcomes (Miliband, 1973; Gough, 1979).

The crucial point for radical political economists is that when the state introduces legislation regarding retirement pensions, it does so with a keen eye on the interests of capital. There may be political pressures from trades unions, social movements and pressure groups but the history of social reform shows that the needs of capitalism are paramount. Thus a state-defined age of retirement was introduced in virtually every industrialised country at around the start of the 20th century. Changes to the labour and production processes at this time meant that many older workers either had to be retrained or made redundant (Braverman, 1974). Investing in retraining older workers, when there were plenty of younger ones, was not an attractive proposition. However, sacking older workers at a time when socialist political parties were gaining support by highlighting the injustices of capitalism was also seen as problematic. In the UK the 1908 Pensions Act established an expectation that older workers would quietly depart the labour force and without stigmatising the respectable workers, who would otherwise have had to apply to the hated Poor Law along with the undeserving 'residuum' (Mann, 1992). The legitimacy of capitalism was maintained by this apparently generous reform, but it did so at very little expense to employers. The cost of supporting 'the aged poor' (Booth, 1892) was simply transferred from local (Poor Law) taxes to the central state and later, via NI, to workers as a whole. Thus capitalism creates dependencies and needs but one of the great ideological tricks it performs is to present these as either, the consequence of the individual's failure to plan, or the state's responsibility. Radical political economy argues that over time the social costs of capitalism – education, health, and pensions, for example – are invariably shifted onto the working population at large. Thus the insurance principles that underpin many public pension schemes are a type of regressive tax, redistributing resources within the working class as a whole. Capitalism therefore pays a small price for attaining its labour market objectives. As Nesbitt observes of the 1948 pensions reforms in the UK: "... the cost of providing the basic pension was effectively 'socialised' perhaps in part because it served the interests of capital, and what was in the interests of capital was in the interests of the state" (1995, p 17).

The needs of capital for labour can vary and although a fixed retirement age allowed employers to dispose of older workers, they could still be called on during acute labour shortages to serve as a 'reserve army of labour' (Gough, 1979), as they were during both world wars. Furthermore, the knowledge that there are reserves waiting on the sidelines can restrain those who are in full-time work. Trades unions and professional groups are usually in a stronger bargaining position when there are labour market shortages. Employers may, therefore, offer inducements to retain older workers, or press government to tighten the rules to restrict early exit. But when unemployment rates are high and employers want to 'restructure', older workers are often encouraged to take 'early retirement'.

For example, in the UK during the 1980s unemployment rates were high and industrial 'restructuring' saw older workers forced out of employment. By 2000 unemployment rates were low, and falling; in response the government pressured older people to take jobs and wanted to discourage early retirement. Prime Minister Tony Blair pleaded, "So we need as a society to learn to recognise and use the huge talents of older people" (Foreword to PIU, 2000). In the 1980s it was stated by the then Prime Minister Mrs Thatcher, that "there is no such thing as society". It would seem that the needs of capitalism and 'society' fortuitously coincide once again.

Inherent contradictions and fiscal crisis

Capitalist societies are not, however, functionalist, but riddled with contradictions and prone to crises. Capitalism is a class system that asserts the 'freedom' of workers but ensures that everyone is a wage slave. Labour and capital do not meet on equal terms and any individual worker trying to negotiate a price for their labour is in a much more vulnerable position than the individual capitalist with whom they are expected to negotiate. By collectively negotiating, in trades unions and professional associations, employees gain more influence, and historically this has been seen by many millions as the best way to improve wages and conditions. But this brings them into conflict with employers. Capitalists want to keep the price of labour, including social costs such as retirement pensions, low so that they can remain competitive and make a profit. Thus, the interests of employees conflict with capitalists from the moment that the market begins to operate. O'Connor (1973) claimed that welfare and public spending are at the heart of the difficulties that the state confronts when trying to facilitate a profitable market (accumulation), while maintaining social harmony (legitimation). Keeping the lid on the potential conflicts and managing capitalism is, therefore, a vital task and welfare provisions play a major role.

A good example of how radical political economists see the contradictions inherent in capitalism being played out, and of how retirement pensions are implicated, is provided by events in Britain in the 1970s. Following a period of intense industrial conflict between 1970-74, the newly elected Labour government agreed a deal with the Trades Union Congress (TUC) that, in return for wage restraint and cooperation, public welfare spending would be protected, unemployment would not be allowed to rise and the government would attempt to enhance 'the social wage', including pensions. In 1974 the basic state pension was increased by 28% and it kept pace with manual workers' wages throughout the 1970s. This seems, with hindsight, quite remarkable given that, along with price inflation, wages rose significantly (Johnson and Falkingham, 1992). Academic research into pensioner poverty and campaigning over pensions in the 1960s and 1970s had also increased the pressure for the state schemes to be improved (Abel-Smith and Townsend, 1965; Phillipson, 1998, pp 69-70). The introduction of SERPS in 1975 (but coming into effect in 1978) heralded a commitment to increased social expenditure in general and retirement pensions in particular. Phillipson (1998, p 69) sees this period as 'on the cusp of the welfare state' because the 1980s were to mark an end to the optimistic feelings of many reformers.

From a radical political economy perspective the state had intervened to legitimate capitalism and to achieve this, welfare spending was necessary.

Social expenditure, however, requires taxes to be raised and whatever the TUC and trades union leadership may have agreed to with government and employers, their members were increasingly disgruntled. In 1975 the annual inflation rate hit 24%, its highest ever, and 23% the following year,1976, when personal tax rates also hit a record high. This was not socialism but income redistribution within the working class. It needs to be remembered that in 1975 a single person on the average wage paid twice as much in taxes to the state as they did in 1955. For a couple with two children, again on average wages, the tax bill was seven times greater over the same period. A complex web of income-related benefits could even make the household worse off when wages rose slightly, because they would lose these benefits if they went just a few pence above the qualifying line (Mann, 1992, pp 92-3). This was the fiscal crisis identified by O'Connor and it meant that the government had to go cap in hand to the International Monetary Fund (IMF) who were unimpressed by Britain's economic situation and Labour's social policies. The long-term costs of SERPS were emphasised by orthodox political economists and it is unlikely SERPS would have gone ahead if the IMF had intervened earlier. Indeed every effort was made, both before and after 1979, to restrain the impact of SERPS on expenditure (Lowe, 1993). Compelled by the IMF to cut public spending in order to qualify for further loans, the Prime Minister told his party that the Keynesian option of spending their way out of the crisis was no longer available. Having constructed a 'social contract' with the trades unions in an attempt to reconcile the irreconcilable interests of capital and labour, the state was forced to renege on the original deal. In effect the IMF believed that the price of legitimation was too great because it had begun to erode accumulation. Public sector unions felt the brunt of the cuts and mounted a series of industrial actions, culminating in the 'winter of discontent' in 1978/79. And as O'Connor predicted, workers in the private sector did not align themselves with recipients of public welfare or with public sector workers defending their jobs. Thus the fiscal crisis also promoted sectionalism and self-interest, thereby fragmenting the labour movement (Coates, 1980; Mann, 1992).

With the end of the 20th century pensions are once again to the fore and the state, currently being administered by 'New' Labour, has to wrestle with the same contradictory elements. How, on the one hand, to ensure a flexible labour market that can compete in a global economy – the accumulation functions – and on the other, meet the aspirations of workers approaching retirement – legitimation. For radical political economy no system of public welfare within capitalism can resolve these contradictory tasks. Nor, however, are occupational and private pensions the answer, as the following discussion ought to show.

Controlling capital and creating savings

Deaton (1989) provides an account that addresses the political economy of pensions in general. Using Britain, Canada and the US as his main examples, Deaton claims:

> ... these three countries are on the verge of a crisis which can be explained by four structurally determined considerations, or motor forces, which converge in the future: first, the inadequate level of retirement income of the elderly results in their immiseration; second, the increasing proportion of the elderly in the population and the costs associated with supporting an ageing population; third, the general and specific limits of the employer based occupational pension system; and fourth, the appropriation of the occupational and state pension systems by the corporate sector and the capitalist state as a source of investment and social capital to meet their financial requirements. (1989, p 1)

Each of these 'motor forces' has a specific impact, but the potential for a more profound crisis arises if they occur simultaneously. Deaton argues that this possibility is very real and that retirement pensions may be the focus of intense conflicts because it is an arena in which "capital, labour and the state collide and simultaneously affect all interests of all key segments and institutions of society.... " (1989, p 2).

The first three 'motor forces' can be covered quite briefly but a little more space is required to explain the fourth. First, the immiseration of older people and the inadequate incomes they get is apparent from the persistence of means-tested payments in the UK. Public pensions are kept low to keep costs down but also to avoid competing with private pension providers. Although access to occupational pensions and savings have raised most pensioners above the level at which means-tested benefits are paid, this has had the effect of widening the gap with the poorest 20-30% (Walker with Howard, 2000). Thus the relative position of those dependent on public pensions has deteriorated over the last 10 to 20 years (see Chapter One). With the drop in occupational pension membership since the 1970s, the relative decline in manual workers' wages, mass unemployment for nearly two decades and entrenched patterns of social exclusion, the retirement prospects for the poorest are bleak. The impact of these patterns will only be fully appreciated in 10 to 20 years time when the casualties of the 1980s come to retire. It will be the working class, and especially working-class women, for whom the experience of older age and retirement will be one of poverty (Ginn and Arber, 1992a). Although it might be asked why women are more likely to be impoverished, the key issue for Deaton is one of class. Male mortality rates mean more working-class women survive to collect means-tested benefits, but state policies have also ensured women would take on care responsibilities which in turn has left them with very few pension rights of their own.

The second reason Deaton gives for the immiseration of the pensioner population is that their numbers will rise and the labour force to pensioner population ratio, the dependency ratio discussed earlier, will increase. However, any crisis that arises in this context is not simply a question of ratios or income per se. Rather, Deaton argues that it is the social and political marginalisation of older poor people that accompanies their exclusion that will promote new political movements of pensioners and political conflicts over pensions.

Third, a measure of exclusion is built into private and occupational schemes due to the way the labour market and pension funds operate. Among these inherent limitations are, for example, actuarial assumptions based on length of employment, contribution records and age of retirement, access to the sort of paid work that provides a pension, discrimination within, and the imperfections of, the labour market, employer demands for a more flexible work force, more part-timers and less people on permanent contracts. Most significantly, of course, occupationally-related pensions and provisions predicated on labour market access offers nothing to those whose work is unpaid, again affecting mainly working-class women. The inability of the poorest to make worthwhile contributions, and the greater risk of claims against life assurance policies, means the private pensions market has also been reluctant to cater for the poorest 20-40% of the prospective pensioner population (Glennerster, 1991, p 54). Simultaneously, private providers are actively opposed to the state competing in the market.

Deaton's fourth force in the impending crisis is directly related to the part pension funds now play in the corporate and finance markets. The sheer size of the funds, persistent queries and contests over their ownership and control, the contrasting functions they must perform and the impact of institutional investment strategies on the finance markets, are seen as the key features. However, these points require a little more elaboration to be fully appreciated.

Investment funds or welfare saving?

Retirement savings world-wide amount to "a sum bigger than the combined worth of all the world's industrial, commercial and financial corporations quoted on the three largest stock exchanges" (Olsberg, 1997, p 163). Given this, it seems incredible that these phenomenal sources of welfare and capital are so often neglected in debates over retirement pensions (Minns, 2001).

How much bigger can the funds get?

In the mid-1990s Diana Olsberg (1997) estimated that pension funds world-wide held over Aus$12,000 billion (equivalent to roughly £5,000 billion). This was equivalent to ten times the total GDP for Brazil in 1996. Just a few years later Richard Minns (2001, pp 26-7) estimated that pension fund assets amounted to 43% of the planet's GDP! In Britain in 1963 pension fund assets were 7% of all equities but this had risen to 29% of all equities by 1983. By the 1990s estimates of UK fundholdings ranged between 30-35% of total capital assets (Schuller, 1986; Goode, 1993; Budd and Campbell, 1998). The Myners Review, undertaken on behalf of the Labour government, stated that: "UK institutional investors own more than £1,500 billion of assets – over half the quoted equity markets" (Myners, 2001, p 4). A figure that is more than double the size of the US's GDP for 1998. Between 1990-1995 the annual rate of growth was 8.9% - 11.3% (Minns, 2001, p 26). A vital question here is whether such growth rates can be sustained, assuming that it is environmentally and economically desirable to do so, and if not what the implications are for future retirees.

In Australia the growth of the funds has been quite incredible. In the early 1980s Australia had one of the lowest per capita savings of any OECD country, but the development of occupationally-based superannuation schemes, culminating in the introduction by the Labor government of the Superannuation Guarantee Charge (SGC) Bill in 1992 has changed that. In March 1999 the Australian 'super' funds had assets of Aus$387 billion (Scheiwe with Katter, 2000). Australia's former Federal Treasury Minister, Ralph Willis, stated: "Importantly for the future of Australia, retirement savings are providing an increasing pool of patient capital to support the productive investment that is crucial to sustaining Australia's economic growth and prosperity" (cited in Olsberg, 1997, p 161).

The sheer scale of the pension funds is likely to promote crisis and conflict, according to Deaton, because: "The pension system under advanced capitalism has assumed a structurally strategic and pivotal macro-economic function" (1989, p 186). Contests over fund control will intensify because the activities of the funds pose ethical and political questions that some members will raise. Likewise, Minns (2001) suggests that the pension funds are the focus of a new 'cold war' that hinges on the demands of finance capital versus the welfare functions of the funds. Responsibilities toward members will often clash with the pension funds' role as a source of investment capital. Furthermore, under UK law the trustees must seek to maximise the investment potential for the benefit of current and future retirees. That can result in funds being invested in competitor companies, often overseas, and where wages and conditions are more favourable to capital. This was highlighted in October 1992 when the Conservative government announced the closure of 31 coal mines. The Mineworkers Pension Scheme had enormous assets of £8 billion and the government was proposing to cream off some of the surplus. Simultaneously the prospects of getting access to these assets made the miners' pension fund, but not their industry, an attractive prospective acquisition (*The Financial Times*, 21 October, 1992). There is, to put it mildly, a perverse irony of having, on the one hand, an industry with a huge fund of capital with overseas assets (some in competitor companies) and, on the other hand, closure and redundancies confronting the employees and members of these funds. Such ironies may well promote contrary views of who ought to control pension funds and poses the question of 'whose money is it anyway?' (Olsberg, 1997). Exceptional events like the Maxwell scandal in the UK have added to the view that members need to be better informed, and more closely involved, in what their pension fund is doing.

Moreover, the requirement since 2001 that trustees in the UK produce a Statement of Investment Principles (SIP) will add political fuel to debates over control. Although a survey by the National Association of Pension Funds (NAPF) concluded that SIPs would not influence investment decisions, 30% of fund managers felt it would. And as yet fund members, trades unions and trustees are only slowly realising the implications of SIPs (*Pensions World*, February 2001). When some of the more powerful lobby groups (for example, Greenpeace, advocates of animal rights, opponents of the arms trade, groups opposed to child labour, and so on) begin to appreciate the opportunity for raising their concerns, the debate could get much hotter. Simultaneously, employers expect their company pension fund to support their human and industrial relations strategies. Whether they want to retain or dispose of older workers means they require some measure of control.

Trades unions, on the other hand, invariably see the funds as deferred wages, and may contest both employer and lobby group interference. Compulsory superannuation in Australia was explicitly presented to the electorate and trades unions as part of the wage/labour negotiations (the Accords) throughout the 1980s and up to the 1992 SGC Act (Mann, 1993; Olsberg, 1997). Likewise in the UK occupational pensions were frequently offered by employers, and demanded by employees, during wage negotiations. Workers, therefore, regard the funds as deferred wages and as a form of welfare that they expect to collect in the longer term.

Fund managers operate with a rather different agenda and are generally more concerned with showing a reasonable return in the short term. The way fund managers behave is considered further in Chapter Four, but for now it simply needs to be noted that the conservatism of the funds is a recurring criticism, and the 'pool of patient capital', described by Willis, may be too patient, thereby distorting the finance markets and producing a lower rate of return than other investments. This too will mean that those charged with managing the funds will come under increasing scrutiny. Olsberg seems fairly confident that any conflicts over control and ownership can be handled by the Australian system.

> Australia is unique in having established a system of ownership and control of superannuation funds in which employee members are directly and equally represented on the boards which manage the funds and control the investments. The trustee boards must by law comprise equal numbers of employer and employee (or their union) representatives. These trustee boards legally own and control the funds, manage their day to day operations and allocate their investments. (Olsberg, 1997, pp 173-4)

However, this optimism is not shared by all, and some have suggested that fund members, employers and trades unions could become embroiled in litigation in the near future (Scheiwe with Katter, 2000). Likewise, trustees in the UK will have to tread very carefully when designing their SIPs, to avoid being sued by individuals who do not share their ethical stance and who are aggrieved at their fund's failure to maximise returns by not investing in, for example, countries known to rely on child labour (*Pensions World*, January 2001). In these circumstances governments are tempted to introduce regulations and statutory requirements to try and maintain balance and avoid crisis. However, in the UK the pension fund managers now feel they are "burdened with a mass of red tape" that is "counterproductive in terms of achieving the Government's objective" of shifting the cost of retirement pensions from the state to the market. (*Pensions World*, February 2001). Thus Deaton's (1989) points about the welfare and investment functions being in conflict appear to be well founded.

Furthermore, pension funds have impacted on finance capital itself in a manner that, irrespective of any pressure for reform, is likely to promote crises in the near future.

For example, in Australia and the US, fund members have been able to use their future pensions rights as a form of equity release. In the short term this can generate competition within finance capital. Olsberg reports that some of the large industry funds in Australia have introduced schemes that allow fund members to take out home loans, at rates better than the banks can offer. Along with initiatives to encourage longer-term investments in the Australian economy and in smaller business ventures, the industry funds in Australia are credited with having: "put pressure on banks and other lending institutions, effectively forcing them to reduce interest rates on home and business lending" (Olsberg, 1997, p 165).

Thus, initially, there is welcome competition in the market, but in the longer term, and within the finance sector as a whole, competition is likely to be reduced as the overlapping and interlocking pattern of ownership and control increases the institutionalisation of pension funds.

The growth of institutional investment funds as a proportion of all investment funding is significant because it changes the balance of power within finance capital, as a consequence of the concentration and centralisation of pension fund assets. Although concentration and centralisation are different processes, both have the effect of reducing the options for those who seek capital for investment purposes and as such distort the money markets. They are likely to steer investment into areas that are perceived as 'sound', and are unlikely to commit much of their portfolio to entrepreneurial projects (Deaton, 1989, pp 235-60). Competition in the finance market is reduced and the impact of investment decisions can then distort other features of the economy. The concentration and centralisation of investment funds, mirrored in the money market as a whole, means that key decisions over savings and investment are institutionalised. Ultimately, the impact of the pension funds and the finance markets will have profound "implications for economic policies designed to encourage the growth of the UK economy" (Goode, 1993, p 157). The widespread view presented to Goode was that pension funds are distorting the British economy by their 'short-termism'. As the Goode Committee made plain:

> Those who identified this as a problem saw it as making long term investment decisions in research and development or capital projects impossible for company managements to pursue. Any short term disappointment in profit performance was thought to invite the attention of corporate predators, who found pension fund managers anxious to realise short-term gains on the take-over of under-performing companies in their portfolios. (1993, p 159)

As such, the pension funds' control of the industrial sector is increased and simultaneously their fortunes are tied to the performance of that sector globally. The temptation and tendency for these institutional investors to directly intervene in the strategic decisions of the industrial sector is, therefore, also likely to increase, with the concomitant reduction in any 'real' market forces influencing events. Indeed, the Myners Review recommended that government should consider legislation similar to that in place in the US that places a duty on "... managers to intervene in companies – by voting or otherwise – where there is a reasonable expectation that doing so might raise the value of the investment" (2001, p 14). In these circumstances, investment decisions increasingly look like political decisions, reflecting the ability of the powerful elites to mobilise support or agreement for their preferred policy, but once again they raise the possibility for challenges and conflict (Deaton, 1989, pp 300-5).

Of course, so long as the funds reconcile these conflicting aims and interests, and deliver worthwhile retirement incomes for their members, it will be possible to keep the lid on the simmering pot. However, any stock market crash, prolonged crisis, or intensification in the internal contests and conflicts that the market is trying to balance, could be disastrous. Retirement savings now occupy such a key place in the investment and finance markets, in affecting patterns of investment control, the type of investment decision that is made and in corporate decision making, that their welfare purpose appears to be peripheral. Nevertheless, there is still a welfare function and a constituency of potential recipients whose rather different interests may conflict. For radical political economists there are inherent limits associated with the massive concentration of capital in institutional hands. The prospect of immiseration is therefore very real, and the dreams of many people currently approaching retirement could easily turn into a nightmare.

Reform or crisis?

Pension funds are now major players in the finance markets and consequently any reforms are likely to pay careful attention to what they say. Their centrality in the finance market bestows both economic and political power at a macro level. It would be folly for any government to neglect this power even if they were inclined to do so. For radical political economists the effect is to relegate social and political objectives to the economic requirements of the market. The state will invariably give a higher priority to the needs of the private and occupational pension funds than to the needs of retirees who rely on the public pension. But, again, there are contradictions and potential crises in store. In order to retain legitimacy, the state has to appear to address the needs of older people. However, any improvement in public pensions will reduce both the incentives for people to join occupational or private schemes and the investment funds available to the corporate sector. Quite simply, radical political economists assert that the interests of the market and the needs of retired people cannot be reconciled (Deaton, 1989, pp 228-31).

The scope for reform within capitalism is often keenly debated within radical political economy. Comparisons between capitalist countries appear to show significant variations in how retirement and pensions are managed. Social divisions are greater in some countries than others, and this would suggest that there is scope for genuine reform. Success, however, will depend on a number of variables, but vitally important is the ability of organised labour to form "political class coalitions" (Esping-Andersen, 1990, p 1) that can influence the state. Thus the political strategy pursued by organised labour is crucial, and a divided working class is likely to promote divisive social policies, including retirement and pension policies (Mann, 1992). For Esping-Andersen, meaningful reforms require class-based mobilisations that ensure social democratic control of the state and the development of generous, universal, public pension schemes that are provided as a right. This suggests that there can be no room for occupational or private pensions. Deaton, however, accepts that retirement funds are here to stay, but favours an explicit contest over their ownership and control, in effect 'socialising savings'. Thus demands for improvements in the public pension have to run alongside calls for the accountability of occupational and private funds. He feels that the state will have to intervene in the finance markets due to the inevitable and impending pensions crisis. The consequences go beyond retirement pensions and, as Deaton's concluding sentence asserts, "Relating the political economy of pensions to the coming pension crisis and to strategies for social change may therefore promote, and ultimately facilitate, a socialist transformation of society, liberating both workers and the elderly" (1989, p 351). This last point is very significant and indicates one of the weaknesses in Deaton's approach. Waiting for the impending crisis and the complete transformation of society to socialism before any real improvements can be made could be a long wait. The alternative criticism is that when the transformation has been attempted in countries claiming to be socialist (for example, the former Soviet Union), it has hardly provided an attractive alternative to capitalism.

Summary

There is a common agenda that both versions of political economy accept. They are both concerned with the functioning of capitalism and the obstacles the market confronts. Of course they have polar opposite views of this. Whereas orthodox political economy maintains that the market operates smoothly in the absence of any interference, radical political economy stresses the inherent obstacles and contradictions of the market. The part played by the state is crucial for both approaches to political economy. Like a football referee the state is accused by both sides of being biased. Whereas the orthodox 'team' protests that the referee is spoiling the game by constantly blowing the whistle, with hard tackling and a fiercely competitive edge vital for the future of the game, the radicals see it differently. They believe that the referee is ignoring fouls and that the rules are twisted to suit the opposition's players. Worse still, the referee/state allows the orthodox team as many reserves as they like and even steals the oranges from the radical kit bag to keep them going at half time. The orthodox response is that capitalism is not just a beautiful game, it is the only game that works. Thus orthodox political economy favours the absolute minimum of state interference and regulation. This will in turn promote better pension policies that are more able to address the needs of consumers. Radical political economists advocate the socialisation/nationalisation of pensions by the state. The dreams of the radical political economists are then the nightmares of the orthodox school and vice versa. The main strengths and weaknesses of both political economy appraoches can be summarised as follows.

Main strengths of the political economy approaches

- They are firmly 'grounded' and can be empirically tested and observed.
- They have specific proposals for retirement and pensions policies – albeit reaching very different conclusions.
- They stress the significance and power of the market and the state.

Additional strengths of the respective versions are as follows:

Orthodox accounts:

- Capitalism is the only economic system that works and ensures individual freedom.
- Only capitalism allows people to retire – other systems force everyone to work.
- People in general are rational actors (that is, intelligent), and markets respond to their demands.
- Markets have promoted diversity enabling many more people to approach retirement with the prospect of enjoying it.

- Private and occupational pension funds are almost always 'better' than public/state schemes – they are more generous, they allow more individuals greater flexibility and choice (for example, over retirement ages) and have been more reliable.
- Market solutions can respond to rising expectations more quickly than public/state schemes.
- Markets enable people to choose to spend rather than save – the state forces even the poorest to save thereby making them poorer.

Radical accounts:

- Only socialism can deliver social justice and eradicate social divisions. Capitalism relies on inequality and social injustice.
- Markets aim to make profits and cannot meet people's needs.
- Meaningful choice for most people is illusory – only the wealthy have options.
- The state favours market solutions and deliberately makes public welfare less attractive.
- Real control and choice requires the socialisation of occupational and private pension funds.
- Capitalism is inherently unstable and unreliable – pension funds are therefore gambling with people's future well-being.
- State intervention is required to redistribute resources otherwise the poorest workers will inevitably be the poorest pensioners.

Weaknesses of the political economy approaches

Rather than set out their respective weaknesses, as in other chapters, it is possible to simply point out that the strengths of one approach are seen as weaknesses by the other. Clearly the two versions of political economy are incompatible and despite any similarities should not be confused. Nevertheless, there are features of these approaches that are significant for the SDW.

First, it needs to be recalled that Titmuss rejected both versions of political economy and in so doing under-estimates both the potential for diversity and innovation that markets can promote and the power they can exert when resisting reform. Second, the flaws in both these approaches need to be highlighted at this point. As numerous feminist critiques point out, a focus on markets, the economy and production neglect the gendered features of retirees and the gender dynamics of capitalist societies (Rose, 1981; Groves, 1987; Williams, 1989; Lewis, 1992; Arber and Ginn, 1995a). Among other questions we might ask of both approaches would be:

• Why is it women rather than men make up the bulk of the poorest pensioners? Why is caring so undervalued by the market and why do both versions say so little about informal welfare?
• What part have employers and the organised labour movement played in excluding women?
• Why have state pension policies favoured male breadwinners over female carers?

Moreover, and in the same vein, other patterns of exclusion and disadvantage are frequently overlooked by both approaches to political economy. Racial discrimination (Blakemore and Boneham, 1994; Modood et al, 1997) for example, is treated as a 'market imperfection' according to orthodox accounts. In radical versions the idea of a reserve army of labour is usually invoked with racism serving capitalism's needs. Yet there is ample evidence of employers and organised labour operating racist policies and practices contrary to their supposed and respective class interests. Pension policies and practices that discriminate against same-sex relationships are similarly difficult to reconcile with analyses that place so much emphasis on class and markets.

Finally, both approaches assume economic concerns govern behaviour and that welfare can be assessed by measures of economic independence. Yet some people will assess well-being in terms that are more complex and ambiguous than this. For example, the reasons given for retiring can vary a great deal and, as subsequent chapters will show, these are not easily reduced to economically rational criteria, or the needs of capitalism.

THREE

Consumption, consumers and choice

Introduction

In the midst of the Thatcher years Featherstone observed, "pre-retirement planning today is presented as the management of life-style and consumption opportunities to enable retirement to be a progressive set of options and choices" (1987, p 134).

The central concern of this chapter is with consumption processes, consumption patterns and the difficult issue of 'choice'. Although consumption accounts need not be in conflict with production-based perspectives, they are often portrayed as such. Marxism, it is thought, deals with production, whereas it is tempting to portray consumption-based accounts as in some way essentially Weberian. However convenient such a contrast may be it would be misleading. There is certainly a Weberian wing among those who use consumption approaches. Life chances, understood broadly to include, among other things, education, status, housing, work, credentials and the opportunities that these provide for some sort of social mobility or 'choice', are clearly features of consumption that would be amenable to Weberian sociologists. The degree to which consumerism conforms to, or confronts, the 'Protestant ethic' (Weber, 1976) of hard work, deferred gratification and thrift would also be a task suited to Weberians. There is, however, another wing in the consumption camp that points toward lifestyle, identity and choice with, for example, Baudrillard (1975, p 144) claiming that people are "mobilised as consumers, their needs become as essential as their labour power" (cited in Smart, 1992, p 121). Between Weber and Baudrillard might seem (like the proverbial rock) a hard place to be, but there are numerous and different approaches pressing for their account to be given primacy (Warde, 1990). Nor should the reader think in terms of a linear development of consumption theory, from Weber up to Baudrillard. They occupy different places on the sociological map, not points along a continuum. Given the various features associated with consumption approaches it is, in many respects, easier to address these rather than identify core theoretical components. Any common ground they share derives from their insistence that consumption is significant in its own right, rather than in how they subsequently analyse its significance.

This chapter begins by briefly tracing the history of consumption-based analyses with those versions that emerged in the UK in the 1970s and 1980s seen as the most significant. Although they often took housing as their example, there are features of these approaches that could be applied to pensions. A crucial issue in this literature has been the degree to which consumption patterns reflect consumer preferences, or whether these are initiatives by the state intended to restructure public welfare provisions. Similarly, the impact of the advertising media, particularly the emphasis on lifestyle and choice for prospective retirees, is examined in relation to pension products. These can be seen as promoting what Laslett (1989) calls the 'third age'; a time when we can expect to fulfil ourselves, free to consume and free of the demands of work. However, such ideas confront a reality that for many pensioners is much more constrained. Thus, there is a brief consideration of the spending and lifestyle options that currently exist in the UK and these are related to the SDW. Finally, the chapter considers how consumption can promote a different approach to the rights and needs traditionally associated with welfare.

Consumption versus production

Consumption-based approaches are often contrasted with production-based accounts, but this dichotomy is difficult to sustain. Usually the key question is the balance between consumption, as a demand process that encourages the provision of specific goods and services, and production processes offering goods and services that are then in demand. This is like asking which came first, the chicken or the egg, and misses the point that consumption patterns, and consumers, appear to be more significant than in the past. "Consumption is now seen as one of the ways in which society is structured and organised, usually unequally, sometimes incredibly so" (Hearn and Roseneil, 1999, p 1). For Harvey (1994) consumption and production interact, with consumption patterns and processes used as a tool for exploring social change, albeit given a measure of independence from the economic requirements of the production sphere. Consumption patterns can also be used to highlight social divisions

(Harrison, 1986; Rex, 1971), to identify political pressures and processes of welfare restructuring (Dunleavy, 1986), or to assert a correspondence between both of these and consumers' own aspirations (Saunders, 1986; Saunders and Harris, 1990). Changes in consumption patterns and a growth of 'consumerism' can also be seen as disturbing trends fragmenting society and undermining social solidarity (Bauman, 1997, 1998). For others it is a mistake to overstate the social and political implications of how consumers see themselves as a consequence of their consumption patterns. The eclectic, almost chaotic, consumer rather than the 'heroic consumer' may nevertheless influence perceptions of different forms of welfare (Warde, 1994a). The implications for the accountability of welfare provisions is, as we shall see, particularly relevant in the case of retirement. Consumer pressure, expressed in terms of service users calling for a more responsive pattern of provision or through market preferences, provides a further feature of consumption approaches. Again, the general picture is one of ambiguity in which a new 'managerialism' attempts to both reflect the diversity of consumer demands and direct it in ways that can be managed (Williams, 1996; Clarke, 1998). In order to weave our way through this particular maze it is useful to cast our eye over the sociological map, taking in some important historical landmarks on the way.

Although consumption-based approaches were reasserted in the 1980s, they have been applied in, and to, earlier periods, most notably to the 'labour aristocracy' in mid-Victorian Britain and the 'affluent workers' of the 1960s (Goldthorpe et al, 1968; Bauman, 1972; Crossick, 1978). What distinguishes much of this work is a concern with forms of consumption that segregate or divide what might otherwise appear to be unitary social classes. The focus has largely been on intra-class divisions, with contrasts made between certain types of working-class households, masculine cultures and lifestyles.

For example, it was the ability of some male workers in the 19th century to make welfare provisions of their own through Friendly Societies and savings societies that distinguished them from many within their own class. The divisions of welfare that arose as a consequence of the ability of these male 'labour aristocrats' to make provisions of their own, combined with their access to a generally higher standard of living, meant that they were regarded as politically conservative. The contrast is usually made between the skilled and unskilled in relation to exclusion within classes and the resultant patterns of consumption, but ethnicity, 'race' and gender have also been recurring and significant features (Bauman, 1972; Best, 1972; Mann, 1992).

A recurring theme is the idea that certain types of consumption promote particular political attitudes. When working-class households access goods and services that were previously the preserve of the middle classes, it is often implied that they will also adopt middle-class values. Class-consciousness and cultures are seen as being undermined by 'bourgeois' consumption patterns. Thus in the 1960s, it was suggested that Britain was witnessing a new more 'affluent worker' (Goldthorpe et al, 1968) emerge with a shift in lifestyle, culture and political outlook that appeared to mark a break with traditional working-class attitudes (Mann, 1992).

In contrast to this affluent, usually male and white, worker, Rex (1971) pointed to types of housing and tenure to identify a number of 'housing classes', and identified 'race'/ethnicity as a key factor in the resource allocation process. Housing was also the basis for a number of consumption-based approaches that developed in the 1980s in response to government policies promoting owner-occupation. Again, the focus in the UK was on the growth of owner-occupation among working-class households. As home ownership grew, it appeared that consumption cleavages were emerging that served to segregate and marginalise local authority tenants (Forrest and Murie, 1983, 1986). These divisions in housing tenure patterns prompted an interesting debate over the degree to which this reflected consumer desires, shifts in traditional class allegiances, or whether this was deliberately manufactured as a consequence of a grander political objective involving the restructuring of welfare provisions and the creation of a 'property-owning democracy' (Dunleavy, 1986; Saunders, 1986). Without running through the debate in detail, it is worth highlighting some of the key features because these have a bearing on the analysis of retirement and pensions policy.

Constructed consumption or acknowledging aspirations?

The specific insights that consumption-based approaches provide are best appreciated in contrast to radical political economy (see Chapter Two). Put very simply, radical political economy claims that the Thatcher government had a pivotal role to play in resolving the fiscal crisis of the state in the interests of capitalism as a whole. Public sector housing was a target for cuts because it was an expensive social expenditure item, administered by local government, and occupied by 'natural' Labour voters. The sale of council housing to the sitting tenants 'saved' the central government money and served to divide the working-class vote by 'buying them off'. By giving some tenants the 'right to buy', and thereby become part of the property-owning democracy, while simultaneously recreating a spatially segregated reserve army of labour in the remaining public housing sector, the Conservatives resolved the crisis and split the working-class vote. This process also enabled the state to privatise a formerly public welfare service and promoted an ideological agenda of individualism that made further privatisation and restructuring more acceptable (Forrest and Murie, 1986, 1989; Forrest et al, 1990; Byrne 1995).

In contrast, consumption theory places very little emphasis on the ideological effects, and queries the causal assumptions that are often implicit in accounts that see the state as the key player. Rather, consumption theory regards those who exercised their right to buy as consumers who were, in general, competent and capable social actors. Simply because capitalism is in crisis (assuming it is) and needs to restructure, does not, in itself, lead millions of people to vote for political parties committed to this end. Dunleavy (1986) rejects assumptions that portray the electorate as ideologically manipulated or, alternatively, politicians as responding to the economic requirements and interests of capital. This credits politicians and the state with considerable political and economic abilities and presumes working-class voters were easily misled. Instead, the trend towards owner-occupation and the drift away from council housing had begun long before any 'crisis' could be identified. Consumption patterns were already producing social cleavages with the more affluent workers embracing homeownership in the 1960s. These developments, Dunleavy argues, have to be explained in relation to genuine aspirations and not dismissed as a mere function of capital in crisis. The shift from one form of welfare consumption to another occurs because, by and large, what is being offered is preferable to what currently exists. Consequently, the growth in, for example, private and occupational pensions as well as homeownership, are defensive actions taken by those who realise that if they rely on the public pension, or remain in rented accommodation, they will suffer in the longer term. There may be difficulties and costs in the short term, but their intention is to access the 'better' services and to avoid the worse. If they are encouraged to pursue the 'better' services with tax handouts – and both pensions and housing policy in the 1980s were underpinned with fiscal supports – the stick of declining public provisions should be sufficient to engage their aspirations. This pragmatism need not involve a break with the idea of supporting public welfare, as surveys often demonstrate (Walker, 1996), but unless and until 'better' public provisions exist, consumers take advantage of the most favourable provisions that they can afford. Nor do individuals necessarily make calculated and rational market choices. For example, many people will be members of occupational pension schemes without expressing a choice at all, but will, nevertheless, appreciate the benefits.

The crucial point is that patterns of collective consumption are not a straightforward response to economic imperatives that the state may, or may not, identify. Thus, for example, the 'respectable' working class embraced both owner–occupation and occupational pensions for much of the 20th century. Mrs Thatcher may have promoted policies that reinforced the existing trends, but neither owner–occupation among the working class nor occupational pension membership were initiated by her government. In general, government policy during the 1980s responded to and reinforced existing patterns of welfare consumption. The policies certainly enhanced and hastened existing trends and hardened social divisions, but they did not create them (Mann, 1992). Political alliances do change, but this reflects a declining reliance on particular welfare services. When sections of society that were previously relying on public welfare are able to access occupational or fiscal provisions, the political constituency for public welfare will decline if it fails to offer them any tangible benefits. This bears out Titmuss's (1958) fear that a widening division of welfare and the pursuit of sectional interests would promote social exclusion, unless the state promotes social cohesion through universal provisions. Furthermore, the social cleavages formed by consumption may provide politicians with a constituency for further reductions in state intervention in social/public welfare. As Dunleavy observes, "the most important consequence of the partial realignment of political parties and conflicts around sectoral issues is to crosscut social class divisions, and to undermine unity of the class-based electoral coalition which initially constituted the political driving force behind welfare state growth" (1986, p 142).

Consumption is still organised by the state and the costs may be borne by the Exchequer, but it increasingly appears that individuals make choices, which they do within defined parameters. The incentives for those who can access occupational and private pension schemes have been enhanced by the tax system, while the public/state schemes have driven people away from a service that is increasingly seen as residual. 'Others' may have to rely on public welfare, but those who can afford to do so are driven towards private and occupational welfare. The state, therefore, is portrayed as responding to and attempting to engage with, social processes, aspirations and attitudes that often cut across traditional class boundaries.

Arguably, it was the failure of the Labour Party in Britain to appreciate these shifts that left them in the political wilderness during the 1980s and most of the 1990s (Giddens, 1994). Hence, too, the current obsession with focus groups and surveys that enable politicians to put a populist spin on their proposals.

Other commentators perceive more or less correspondence between consumption patterns, the political projects of the state and social class than Dunleavy. Preteceille (1986) suggests that social divisions based on consumption show a high degree of fit with social class. On the other hand, Saunders (1986; Saunders and Harris, 1990) rejects the claim that there is any significant link between consumption patterns and the representation of class interests. Rather he sees consumption choices, social class and cultural identities corresponding. The state and production-based concepts of class are fairly meaningless in this social milieu.

Although changes in housing tenure in the 1980s provided consumption theorists with their empirical base, it should be clear that very similar issues arise in respect of retirement pensions. How far the pensions market now reflects consumer aspirations, or whether it is responding to state led, and class-based, interests that reflect changes wrought in the arena of production, is crucially important.

> For example, the desire to retire early may be a widely held aspiration. It is also the case that there is an apparent trend towards earlier exit, and more retirees appear to be enjoying part of their retirement (Dwyer, 2000; Kohli et al, 1991; Unikowski, 1996). But the correlation of these facts does not mean that they are unrelated to production-based classes or state policies. The restructuring of the labour market in the 1980s witnessed hundreds of thousands of manual workers in the UK being made redundant, or strongly encouraged to take early retirement. Some would have been pleased to leave work, but for others early retirement was enforced. Any consumption patterns as a consequence of 'golden handshakes' and early retirement deals must be located in this context (Phillipson, 1998, p 7). A context in which government policy was clearly to promote the 'shake-out'.

Likewise the ability to make consumption choices is restrained by factors closely related to social and economic class (Taylor-Gooby, 2001). An obvious example is the fact that committing resources to a private pension requires some 'spare' income over a long period of time. A significant proportion of the population simply do not have any spare money or the sort of employment security in the future that would enable them to choose a private pension. However, the fact that social class prevents many people accessing certain forms of consumption, and that the state may promote retirement when it suits production-based interests, does not mean that the aspirations are in some way *false*, or dismissed as socially constructed.

However, the argument over whether consumption simply mirrors production-based class interests or not, overlooks the possibility that other interests may be at play. Historically women's consumption patterns and access to welfare have been restrained by assumptions regarding their 'proper sphere', care responsibilities and access to an income of their own (Rose, 1981; Walby, 1990; Arber and Ginn, 1995b; Ginn and Arber, 1996). Moreover, these restrictions have profound implications for most women when they retire. A weak retort might be that women choose to take on responsibility for domestic labour and welfare, preferring part-time employment, and clearly some women do (Hakim, 1996). But this downplays the history of social closure, exclusion, state legislation and discrimination that frames many women's choices (Williams, 1989; Walsh, 1999). Given that consumption approaches have the potential for considering various restrictions imposed on life chances it is disappointing, to put it mildly, that more attention has not been paid to gender. It might be thought that a comprehensive review of consumption sectors and the different spheres in which these are significant would lend itself rather well to an account of the pension penalties women incur (Groves, 1987; Ginn and Arber, 1993). Of course this neglect is not peculiar to consumption-based accounts. However, it is important to note it at this stage because any discussion of how pensions policy is likely to change, and whether these changes reflect consumer aspirations and engage with their lifestyle, needs to acknowledge what it is changing from. Interestingly, the private pensions industry appears to have responded to changes in gender relations and women's aspirations.

The bride, the Virgin pensioner and the man with the Harley-Davidson

Consumption does not simply consist of people who buy goods and services; these also have to be promoted and the advertising industry exists for that purpose. Although consumers may seem susceptible to the seductive sirens of consumption (Bauman, 1998), it is still worth considering how their 'fancies are tickled'. In this context, advertising can provide some interesting insights into the way particular consumers and services are represented (Midwinter, 1991). The images and ideas used to convey the products cannot simply be read at face value since irony and ambiguity are frequently built into the message. Indeed, the rather earnest approach of the 1960s is often parodied in advertising and the way that retirement and retirees are presented to the observer can be illuminating. Thus the rather sensational heading above draws on three advertising campaigns for pensions that ran regularly between 1996 and 1998. The first example comes from Australia, the other two from the UK.

> The bride, who is in a traditional white wedding dress with family and friends gathered behind her in the church, is asked by the vicar, "Do you Maureen, take Bruce Bloggs to be your lawful wedded husband? To love, cherish and obey, in sickness and in health? Knowing that in 10 years' time he will abandon you for a younger woman with a Saab convertible. Leaving you without a pension or any savings of your own?"
>
> Maureen looks at her prospective husband and the congregation with a mixture of disbelief and anger at her own naivety.
>
> This TV advertisement exposes, and exploits, the risks associated with contemporary social life, stressing the greater economic vulnerability of women to changes in family and domestic circumstances, and offers women insurance against these risks. The product being sold is a private pension and it is clearly being aimed at younger women who should, so the advertisement suggests, be sceptical about committing themselves to a life of economic dependence on a man. Many Australian feminists must have chuckled at this stark, but realistic, message.

Increasingly private pension plans emphasise their flexibility, allowing for variable contributions during periods out of the paid labour force and are designed, so they say, to meet the needs of women. Whatever the advantages and disadvantages of the private pensions market, there is certainly a clearer identification of the potential consumer (and of their needs) than has been the case in the past from the state or occupational pension providers.

> The second advertisement is for the Virgin company whose boss Richard Branson appeared in a series of TV adverts promoting pensions, among other financial

services. The advertisements were a spoof on the sort of documentary that uses investigative journalists to track down fraudsters and shysters. The joke being that nice Mr Branson could be relied on to fulfil his promises. Here was someone to trust in a world of baffling complexity and bad practices. The smiling former record company owner, a man a generation of baby boomers had grown up with, was also the one to trust with your pension. He may have been a 'hippie' in the past but we all know – the advertisement implies – that he has been an astute businessman too. He used to sell us our records, now he flies us away for our holidays and offers a reliable pension product. Given Branson's credentials as someone who is known to the viewer, the advertisement uses an ironic but sober style to persuade us of his prudential financial record.

Third, and in contrast to the former hippie who had to behave like 'the man from the Prudential', it is perhaps not surprising that 'the man from the Pru' – Chairman Peter Davis – presented himself as a bit of a hippie.

The Prudential advertisement made it clear that Davis was ultimately responsible, not just for our investments, but also for our desires. He is presented as a sort of benign godfather or indulgently rich uncle. Reliably overseeing investments to ensure that we (the observer) could in our retirement indulge in those dreams that the daily grind of work destroys. The advertisement informs us that we could run a cheese shop, write a novel or sail the oceans, provided we are prepared to place our trust and money with him. The advertisement tails off with a man, 55-70 years of age, wending his way through the static commuter traffic on that icon of masculine independence, a Harley-Davidson motorcycle – 'born to be wild', with a few wrinkles.

The images used to sell private pensions rely on two contrasting models that make it easy for the observer to know which one they should choose. On the one hand the world is full of risks, including the risk of selecting a reliable pension provider. However, if the right choice is made, 'freedom' can be anticipated. The wrong decision is to delay, to anticipate that the state will adequately provide. Whether it is a model/actress playing the part of a Scottish Widow, again clearly aimed at the growing number of women taking out personal pensions, or executives in the washroom singing "there may be trouble ahead", the promotion and presentation of pensions stresses the flexibility of the pensions product and the reflexive qualities of the customer. A further feature of the presentation of pensions is the idea that a complex issue is presented clearly.

> As the Scottish Widows advert reads, 'Pensions Made Simple'.
>
> In Australia, BT Funds Management ran double page spreads with the following banner headline:"Superannuation scares most people. As always, Fortune favours the brave".

Here both the complexity and the risks are highlighted, but the observer is asked to consider whether they are 'brave' or not. Presumably the poor suffer from cowardice and clearly a lack of bravery will not be rewarded. In fact the first line of text stated, "How would you like to have hundreds of thousands of dollars set aside for the day you start Not Working?" The answer to that question should be fairly easy of course and all sellers in the financial services market lead the potential customer to the inevitable conclusion that they would be foolish not to buy the pension product. One mutual society even had a feature in their advertising brochure that reflected on the way they had constructed their advertisements. They used a talking baby, but as they pointed out: "the use of children in advertising is nothing new.... For us a talking baby is a good way of getting over hard financial information in a light and amusing way.... James [the baby] brings alive the subject of financial security" (Standard Life, 1998). It also emphasises that it is never too early to think about a pension and conveniently avoids any images of older people (Midwinter, 1991; Vincent, 1999).

With viewers increasingly aware of how advertising is trying to engage their attention, and advertisers that their audience is TV literate, ambiguities and paradoxes abound. None of which makes it any easier to disentangle the sales hype from what might eventuate. According to Aldridge (1997), even the UK Consumers Association struggles to keep up with the range of products and services on offer. Nevertheless, there are now a host of consumer guides produced, with advice geared to every income bracket and with a more diverse set of consumers in mind.

> For example, in the US, Berkery and Diggins (1998), among others (Berkery, 1996; Larson, 1997), provide advice on 'Gay finances in a straight world' to assist with retirement planning. Similarly, the Internet has been used to promote

financial services and products that challenge both government and private market providers (see www.pinkfinance.com).

Every newspaper in the UK has a pensions 'expert' and the Sunday papers invariably feature advice, articles and responses to readers' letters addressing the problems to be encountered when 'Sorting out a scheme that will give you that little bit extra' (*The Guardian*, 26 February 1998).

However complicated pensions may seem, the message is clear: a private pension ensures the consumer is anticipating and planning. Pension products, like other commodities, have to engage with the lifestyle and identity of those that they are aimed at. As Giddens claims, "... lifestyle choice is increasingly important in the constitution of self-identity and daily activity. Reflexively organised life-planning, which normally presumes consideration of risks as filtered through contact with expert knowledge, becomes a central feature of structuring self-identity" (1991, p 5). Thus people with private pensions want to be in control of their own lives, not dependent on others. Self-reliance is good, dependency bad. Pensions have been repackaged, made 'sexy', ironic and accessible. They are part of our life-planning project, sold by engaging with both our current lifestyle and those we hope to enjoy when retired. The customer must therefore approach retirement as a truly 'heroic consumer' (Warde, 1994a, 1994b).

The visible face of the current pensioner is only occasionally used to sell pensions. More often the models and actors are the same as the target audience; attractive, fit, young looking, thirty something's. The people appearing in the advertisements are therefore defying the ageing process, possibly to enable the viewers to identify with them without being confronted with getting old. When retirees are seen in advertisements, they are lively and vigorous souls hiking across the Yorkshire Moors, touring the US, wandering beaches with Champagne cooling in the ocean and generally indulging themselves, free of care responsibilities, work or money worries. This may be a reality for some, but media images, no matter what they are selling, are rarely truly representative. Indeed, the under-representation of older people in advertising, and the rather narrow stereotypes within which they are confined, is itself noteworthy (Midwinter, 1991; Vincent, 1999).

There is an ambiguity in the way that pensioners are being portrayed that needs to be highlighted. On the one hand images are more positive, less likely to portray frail, childlike characters who are incapable of looking after themselves (Hockey and James, 1993; Featherstone and Hepworth, 1995). There are also more diverse lifestyles and images being presented. In many respects such images might be applauded. On the other hand it presumes that everyone is capable of making rational choices about complex goods and services. These images make the private pensions 'carrot' appear irresistible and the prospect of living on the state pension a sharp 'stick' prodding us towards the 'obvious' choice. However, the 'choice' between a carrot and a stick is one that even the poor donkey can make. The advertisements also reinforce the idea of the 'heroic consumer', as Warde (1994a, 1994b) puts it. But the assumption that consumers construct their own lifestyles, that they embark on a lifetime project that involves the presentation of themselves to the world, cannot be taken at face value. It may be that the pensions industry wants to try and persuade everyone to plan their lifestyles as consumers, and to flatter the consumer with images and examples that promote such reflexive identities. Some people may even buy products and services because they identify with the images that they are presented with; that is after all the objective of the advertisers. However, as Warde (1994b) makes plain, there are other ways of considering the consumer and the presentation of consumption.

Many of the claims about consumption generalise from a very specific example. A certain type of middle-class person might well behave as the 'heroic' (Warde 1994a) model suggests, but many others will not. Some people may have a strong sense of self-identity and set out to plan their lives accordingly, from the type of car they buy to when they will retire. Many other people will be inconsistent, eclectic or contrary, consumers and lifestyle project managers. Others will simply lack the resources to make meaningful choices and some are understandably sceptical about the claims advertisers make. A scepticism that was borne out by the misselling scandal which saw Peter Davis's Prudential company singled out for criticism (*The Guardian*, 10 July 1997).

Nevertheless, the response of the private personal pensions industry to a more diverse market provides a good example of how consumption patterns may develop. Although a more critical view will be outlined in subsequent chapters, at this stage it should be noted that private pensions claim to provide flexibility and to be capable of engaging with different and diverse groups, reflecting their identities and preferences. Of course, such claims still have to be fully tested and will take many years to assess. They also appear to tie into a further feature of a more consumerist society by promoting their products as facilitating the aspirations of people.

Rather than pensioners being a burden, or promoting crisis and setting off 'demographic time bombs', they promote the idea that retirement should be a time for leisure and pleasure. This is a theme that underpins one of the more optimistic and refreshing approaches to retirement; the idea that it is a 'third age' to be enjoyed.

Exit to the 'third age'

In the context of Dunleavy's model, in which the carrot of private provisions are compared with the stick of a declining public service, the option of early exit from the paid workforce is clearly a major attraction. Trying to persuade people that long-term planning for retirement is necessary is not easy, but one tactic is to try to reduce the time horizon. Consequently private pensions often offer the prospect of retirement before the statutory pension age. By suggesting that 50 or 55 would be a good time to retire, the pension purchaser can see themselves enjoying their retirement. Moreover, many more people are retiring early, and at an earlier age in virtually every OECD country (OECD, 1998b). Consequently, the degree of choice that people have over when they leave paid work and the impact of early exit on their incomes, lifestyle and quality of life are significant issues. On the one hand it might seem that early retirement enables retirees to "depart for a life of sunshine" (Unikowski, 1996), confirming the promises held out by the private pensions industry. Thus, early retirement would bring forward and extend our 'third age' (Laslett, 1989). Alternatively, such 'choices' may be made under pressure, they may not be made with a full appreciation of the consequences, or they may be choices that are denied to specific sections of society.

Laslett's (1989) normative model of the third age provides a useful starting point for exploring the question of early retirement because it emphasises the positive aspects of this. He provides a 'fresh map of life' and brings a refreshing optimism to a topic too often dominated by important but depressing accounts of poverty and social isolation. By using his account as a benchmark of what retirement *should be* like, we can contrast this with other experiences. Laslett stresses changes in demographic data that show more people live out their full natural lives, with many more younger and fitter pensioners. The meaning of old age is being transformed as a result and it holds out the possibility of a time for us all to enjoy. He begins by suggesting that the populations of most developed economies can be divided into four 'ages' – the first is characterised by dependency in childhood through to leaving education, the second age is typified by independence severely restrained by responsibilities for children and the yoke of paid work, the third age allows independence from responsibility and opportunities for creative self-fulfilment and precedes the fourth age when frailty and dependency begin to restrain opportunities for enjoyment. He acknowledges that these 'ages' are not fixed by actual birthdays, but by a combination of the physical and social features of ageing. For example, some people may experience the third age from as young as 50 years old and remain active for 30 or more years. Others may retire from work and very quickly become frail, effectively moving from the second age to the fourth. His point is that a growing proportion of the total population will, in developed economies, consist of people in the third age. These demographic trends, combined with more people taking early retirement, require a shift in social and individual attitudes. Planning for the third age in terms of both pensions and lifestyle becomes more significant as the choices that confront people become a reality. Social attitudes to the younger retiree will need to change, as will the arrangements individuals make for their third age. The third age is, therefore, one in which consumption and lifestyle choices are crucial. Do we want to write a book, ride a Harley-Davidson, sail the seas, open a cheese shop, take a degree in art history, or depart for a life of sunshine?

Laslett's account poses many possibilities and the trends he identifies have important implications for anyone approaching retirement and for consumption sectors/cleavages in the near future. But despite its considerable attractions Laslett's account is not without its flaws. The normative approach blurs the distinction between what he believes *should* occur and the trends he is trying to track. Similarly, his enthusiasm for a lifestyle of self-fulfilment in the third age tends to highlight a particular type of retiree and distracts our attention from other types. Many of the examples he gives of a fulfilling retirement reflect the values of a middle-class person pursuing middle-class aspirations. These often require resources and services that are stretched or non-existent. Public services are increasingly either handed over to private, for profit, providers, or subject to cuts. Public transport in rural communities is increasingly unreliable and car ownership is not an option for everyone. The ability to enjoy the third age is, therefore, often restrained by income, geography, social class, and most frequently, gender. Although he acknowledges that women will form the bulk of those in the third age, he under-estimates the resources that they would need if they are to be full and active participants in their third age. There may also be calls on women to sustain their traditional caring roles, for their spouse, older relatives or for grandchildren. Laslett's response might be that they must resist these pressures, but this neglects how deeply entrenched gender expectations are in our society (Bury, 1995, pp 22-4). Consequently, and despite the importance of asserting the idea of the third age as a challenge to ageist stereotypes and prejudices, Laslett's model remains at best a useful template.

The danger of assuming that everyone can make plans for their retirement is that it comes to mean that they *should* do so. In reality, retirement is socially constructed and the opportunities for enjoying it are uneven. Extending the more privileged features of the SDW (for example, lump sums on retirement that allow cars to be purchased and early exit that provides time when still fit) is an attractive proposition, but it also seems unlikely for those who rely on public and informal welfare. Worse, it may be that the ideas surrounding his model of retirement can be misleadingly associated with freedom, options, economic considerations, choice and calculations of 'efficiency' (Kingston, 1997). Instead, whether it is to fit in with a spouse or to avoid the stigma of unemployment, even the decision to define oneself as retired may be the least unattractive option in a situation where real choice, for example retaining a job that provides some satisfaction, is felt to be unrealistic. As Arber and Ginn state:

> ... the assumption in most of the US literature that retirement is voluntary, giving couples freedom to decide on how they time their exit in relation to each other, is less applicable in Britain; the majority of labour market exit is non-voluntary and its timing is therefore relatively constrained. (1995b, p 72)

In Laslett's defence, however, it might be argued that the US provides the model that will soon become more common in Britain and Europe (see Chapter Six). We may well see many more people negotiating their exit from the labour market and consumption expectations are likely to be influenced by this. That is clearly what the private pensions industry would like to happen; invest now and you too will be able to ride into the sunset on a Harley. The crucial question is how many others will be left behind to manage their lifestyle projects with incomes that effectively exclude them from any such fantasies.

The gap between Laslett's hopes, and those of many retirees, and the reality for a significant proportion of the population has to be acknowledged. Whatever aspirations and desires retirees may have, these will be constrained by existing social structures, labour market location, particular domestic/household arrangements, existing patterns of discrimination and exclusion, processes of change within the paid labour force, employer strategies, state policies and, it has to be remembered, a large slice of luck.

Consumption patterns and cleavages

During the 1990s, evidence of consumption cleavages between different types of retiree began to attract some attention. Most apparent was the difference that a good occupational pension could make (Walker with Howard, 2000, p 265).

As Midwinter (1997, pp 66-70) points out (see Figure 3), for those who rely on the public pension their weekly personal expenditure will be approximately 40% of that available to the average non-retired person. In contrast, the average occupational pensioner has a personal weekly expenditure that is roughly 70% of the average non-retired person. Given that consumption relies on disposable income, and that some forms of expenditure are essential, it should be plain that a lower income will generally mean less spending choice.

For example, in 1999/00 the median net income of the richest 20% of couples among the retired population was more than three times that of the poorest 20%, £462 and £134 respectively (Cousins et al, 2000, p 53). Of course this means that once the poorest have done their essential shopping they often have only a few pounds to spare. The richest 20% of households, even if they spend more on essential items, can have as much as £300 per week of additional disposable income (see Figures 3-6).

Despite the divisions and differences there is still a much flatter distribution of incomes and expenditure between pensioners as a whole than among the non-retired population as a whole. However, a range of hidden benefits and assets complicate the picture, and these need to be considered. For example, in addition to a pension, occupational pensions can also provide a handsome lump sum on retirement. This is often worth tens of thousands of pounds and is usually tax free. Moreover, richer people tend to have more assets and these too provide more possibilities for 'lifestyle choice'. Assets acquired prior to retirement can be translated into cash and can serve as a useful pool to be dipped into when necessary.

Figure 3: Average weekly spending for poorest and richest deciles* by household categories (1994/95)

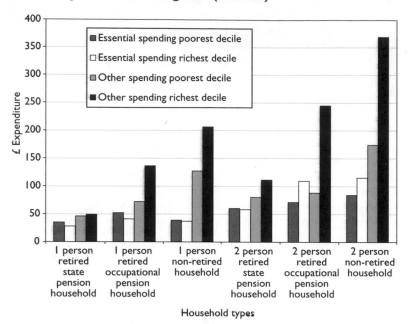

Note: *poorest state pensioner decile taken as less than £65, richest state pensioner decile as more than £85. All data is at 1994 values.

Source: adapted from Midwinter (1997, pp 66-7); CSO (1995)

Trading down in the housing market, for example, is not uncommon following retirement and can generate considerable resources. Furthermore, it is an open secret that the possibilities for concealing income and assets, for avoiding tax, for generating income and maximising the benefit systems are greatest for those with the most resources (Henry, 1978; Cook, 1989). Even the national press urge retirees to exploit every tax-avoiding, benefit-maximising opportunity (for example, *The Observer*, 18 March 2001). Overseas bank accounts and property, accountants that can promise tax savings, building society and savings accounts in the names of relatives, combined with a lenient policing of pensioners by the tax and benefit system because pensioners are perceived as 'deserving', all provide more options for those with resources than those without. The point is that opportunities for consumption in retirement and the patterns this produces vary significantly depending on geographical location, social class, gender, age, previous (paid) occupation, care commitments, employment history, and which element within the SDW the person is dependent on. To add more depth and meaning to this brief sketch some hypothetical cases studies may help to illustrate the significant trends.

Figure 4: Median income of pensioner couples (1996/97)

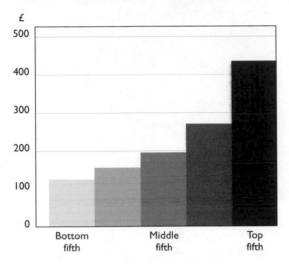

Source: Adapted from Walker with Howard (2000, p 264)

Figure 5: Average weekly income of single female pensioners (1999/00)

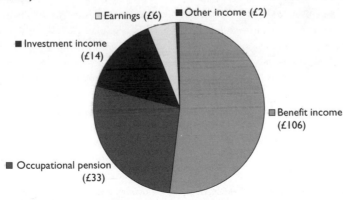

Note: gross income = £161
Source: Cousins et al (2000, p 37)

Figure 6: Average weekly income of single male pensioners (1999/00)

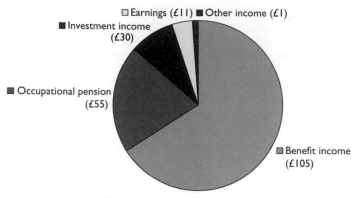

□ Earnings (£11) ■ Other income (£1)
■ Investment income (£30)
■ Occupational pension (£55)
■ Benefit income (£105)

Note: gross income = £202
Source: Cousins et al (2000, p 37)

Keeping up with the Jones's

It is possible to illustrate the points above by taking two hypothetical households, the Jones's and the Smiths, both recently retired couples, based on averages outlined by Midwinter (1997) and Walker with Howard (2000) whose work has been relied on heavily here (see Figures 3-6).

The Jones's get an occupational pension (worth on average £78, but for those who retired recently it is closer £90), plus a return of £10-15 per week on the retirement lump sum that they invested, plus of course the universal basic NI public pension. Bear in mind that the Jones's are not in the richest 20%, who get nearly three times as much from their occupational pension and ten times as much from their savings, as the Jones's. Then there are the Smiths, who have to rely on the basic public pension, but are not so desperate that they have to claim means-tested benefits, like the poorest 20% of pensioners.

As Warde points out, the Jones's are "a much maligned couple with an irritating habit of exposing their newly acquired consumer goods to neighbours currently bereft of such items (which) caused epidemics of envy in Britain during the long boom" (1994a, p 227). Maligned or not, in the mid-1990s the Jones's had twice the spending power on leisure goods and services as the Smiths. Mr Jones could purchase a new car with part of his retirement lump sum but the Smiths had to keep their old car, even though it was a bit difficult for Mrs Smith to get in and out of when her arthritis was playing up. The Jones's enjoyed regular trips out to visit friends and relatives and could afford to spend more than two-and-a-half times as much on motoring as the Smiths. The Jones's also spent 50% more on household goods and services than the Smiths. In total, expenditure by the Jones's would have exceeded that of the Smiths by nearly £100 per week. On average the Jones's consumption expenditure was 75% higher than the Smiths. Even in retirement it would seem that 'keeping up with the Jones's' was not a serious possibility for the Smiths. The only small crumb of emotional comfort for the envious Smiths may be the fact that the Jones's themselves found it increasingly difficult to display their consumer goods with confidence since they were 50% worse off than the average non-retired household (see Figures 3-6).

However, it needs to be repeated that these averages conceal even greater inequalities in consumption patterns and quality of life, both among pensioners and between all pensioners and non-pensioners. By averaging expenditures the inequalities at either end of the spectrum appear less stark than they actually are because the poorest and richest are, respectively, averaged up and down. The poorest are thus even worse off than these figures suggest and the wealthiest are considerably richer (all data taken from IDS, 1999; Midwinter, 1997; Walker and Howard, 2000).

To clarify what these consumption patterns mean for the average single pensioner, in contrast to the average single non-retired householder, two further hypothetical examples are useful (see Figure 6 and Table 1).

Table 1: The proportion of pensioner units (households) with income from means-tested benefits (1994/95 to 1999/00)

Proportion in receipt of income-related benefits (%)

	1994/95	1999/00
All pensioner units		
Total	38	34
Pensioner couples	23	18
Single pensioners	47	44
Recently retired pensioner units		
Total	26	23
Pensioner couples	17	13
Single pensioners	41	38

Source: Cousins et al (2000, p 45)

Ms Green, who lives on her own with only the public pension for support can be compared to Mr Brown, an average single non-retired householder. Because Ms Green is an example of the average it means that we are still not discussing the poorest of the poor. Likewise, Mr Brown is not one of the richest but an average of single person households; others will be much richer. Nevertheless, Mr Brown spends three times as much as Ms Green on drink and tobacco, nearly four times as much on clothing and footwear, three times as much on leisure and, overall, spends three times as much on non-essential items as Ms Green. Even on essential items – housing, food and fuel – Mr Brown spends twice as much as Ms Green (Midwinter, 1997, p 68). The actual process of consuming/shopping will also involve Ms Green and Mr Brown in very different activities. Ms Green will either have to shop locally, which is often more expensive, or catch a bus and carry her bags home, probably trying to negotiate with other passengers for a seat that will enable her to keep an eye on her purchases. Mr Brown will more usually have a car, buy his produce from one of the major supermarket chains, at lower prices than at local shops, pop his bags in the car and be indoors before Ms Green has got out of the rain.

Out of town shopping centres, poor public transport systems, a pattern of car ownership that means older women are less likely to have cars, shopping environments that often seem to be geared to the young and alien to older people, and most significantly, a low income, all conspire against Ms Green and the poorest pensioners in a consumer society.

These examples also illustrate the likely trends. For the next 10-20 years the proportion of retirees receiving an occupational pension will continue to rise, but this will slow down, in line with the dip in membership from the mid-1980s onwards. Personal/private pension membership from the early 1990s, if sustained, will however, probably match any fall. More significantly the value of occupational pensions for those who get them will, in conjunction with top-ups from AVCs and Free Standing Additional Voluntary Contributions (FSAVCs), see the income and consumption gap widen between the richest 40% and the poorest 20% of retirees. The retirement experience of those who have a good occupational pension, or could afford the contributions to a private pension, will be very different to that of the public pensioner.

The proportion of pensioners in the poorest fifth of the total population fell dramatically in the last quarter of the 20th century. In the late 1970s, over 40% of pensioners were in the poorest 20% (before housing costs) of the total population of all households in the UK. By 1994, this had fallen to roughly 25% (before housing costs and 19% after) of all pensioners in the lowest income quintile (Budd and Campbell, 1998; Cousins et al, 2000, p 61). As Walker and Howard point out:"the average income of pensioners is known to have increased by 70% between 1979 and 1997, which is considerably faster than average wages" (2000, p 263). However, the increases have not been evenly distributed across the pensioner population. Richer pensioners and recently retired pensioners have seen their incomes rise most rapidly (Cousins et al, 2000).

The crucially important point is that, as more pensioners escape the trench of public welfare dependency, those who are left behind are in a deeper hole. The current trend is clear, with a majority of people retiring on incomes that are taking them above the poorest 20% of the population in general. But for the poorest pensioners the gap between themselves, their fellow retirees and most of the general population is widening. Pensioners in the lowest income quintile will be those without any worthwhile income from an occupational or private pension. The great majority will be women. Very few are likely to benefit from the current stakeholder scheme and they will still be relying on means-tested benefits. They will usually be living alone, relying on public transport, older pensioners (often over 75 years of age), and they will be effectively excluded from engaging in the patterns of consumption that the rest of society regards as 'normal'. Any suggestion that retirement is a period of fulfilment and achievement may well produce a hollow laugh from such pensioners. They will be non-producers and non-consumers and as such their social, political and economic position is likely to be one of marginalisation.

Lesser consumers and heroic consumer citizens

Of course for those who are not in the poorest 20-30% of the population there is another side to the coin. Retirees with sufficient resources may feel it is not their fault that others are poor and, quite reasonably, they will expect to enjoy their retirement. A consumer society contains many promises for those that can afford to consume, but there are potential pitfalls, as Bauman explains:

> The dismantling of the Welfare state is essentially a process of 'putting moral responsibility where it belongs' – that is, among the private

concerns of individuals. It spells a hard time for moral responsibility; not only in its immediate effects on the poor and unfortunate who need a society of responsible people most, but also (and perhaps, in the long run, primarily) in its lasting effects on the (potentially) moral selves. It recasts 'being for others', that cornerstone of all morality, as a matter of accounts and calculation, of value for money, of gains and costs.... The process ... leads inevitably to the relentless deterioration of collective services ... which prompts those who can to buy themselves out from collective provisions – an act which turns out to mean, sooner or later, buying themselves out of collective responsibility. (1993, p 244)

The processes promoting consumption that concern Bauman are similar to those outlined earlier by Dunleavy (1986). As the safety net of public welfare shrinks, so the social and political constituency that is required to sustain public welfare programmes also declines. Individuals pursue their best interests and in this pursuit the poorest, most vulnerable groups are left behind.

Against this backdrop four further features of a consumer society need to be drawn out.

- First, there is the prospect of some retirees being defined as lesser or discounted consumers in respect of goods and services.
- Second, other retirees may have greater consumer power and be able to influence the provision of goods and services.
- Third, the formal rights of the poorest consumer citizens may be restrained, or conditional.
- Fourth, there is the prospect of a heroic consumer citizen emerging who can exercise their rights and has the potential to disturb both government and market providers.

The rest of this chapter will explore these four scenarios.

Discounted consumers

The idea of some retirees being defined as lesser or discounted consumers derives from the way specific goods and services are aimed at pensioners. Concessions on a variety of products and services may discount the pensioner as a consumer. Cheap pub lunches, discount afternoons for DIY centres, cinema tickets and hairdressers, SAGA holidays and coach trips, through to special deals on timeshare apartments in Spain, cheaper car insurance and afternoon bingo sessions, all cater for and patronise the pensioner. Many retirees are of course thankful that these discounts exist, but there is a danger that they will be offered a poorer service or shoddier goods disguised by concessions. Often the best deals are off-season, when business is slack, using trainees or providing 'end of the line' goods, with providers very conscious that their consumers are 'on a budget'. In an age when the power of the consumer is heralded as sovereign, the pensioner may be perceived and treated as a lesser consumer. Concessions may acknowledge the reality of pensioners' weaker economic status, and perhaps a continuing commitment to the idea of pensioners as deserving, but they also diminish their influence as consumers.

Consumer power

On the other hand, the demographics of the market and the increasing purchasing power of many retired people may influence the provision of goods and services in a positive manner (Featherstone and Wernick, 1995). Retirees are being targeted by sections of the market, but they rarely feature as models or consumers in advertisements, unless these are aimed very specifically at the older person. As we have seen, even advertisements for pension products tend to favour younger lifestyle images, but this may change once retirees are a major sector of the market. The power of the 'grey pound' may generate a more vibrant market and cultural milieu for retirees in much the same way as the 'pink pound/dollar' is supposed to have for the gay communities of many cities. Questions of cultural identity may then enable different and diverse representations of older people to emerge that might challenge ageist stereotypes and promote services geared to their specific needs (Hall and du Gay, 1996; Williams, 1996). Rather than consumer services being aimed at an undifferentiated population of 'older people', niche marketing, for example for older gay men, retired African Caribbean women or for specific cultural events and traditions, might promote more diverse and responsive services. Vincent (1999, p 133) illustrates this when he explains how he enjoys travelling around Europe to various jazz festivals. He also reminds us that cultural identities can be vital in promoting agendas of resistance and change, issues that will be revisited in Chapter Five. For now it should be noted that consumption processes may witness something akin to Laslett's third age developing. If so, tensions between consumption sectors, service providers and production spheres may assume increasing significance. Consumption requires a market, in this case retired people, but instead the British government is stressing the need for labour and the economic costs of retirement (PIU, 2000). Any sweeping restraints on early exit, for example, would undermine one of the major sales features of private pensions. Since it is also government policy to promote private pensions it is difficult to see these tensions (Harrison, 1990) being easily resolved, unless the right to retire and any idea of a universal retirement age is scrapped. In which case there are profound implications for the formal rights of the poorest.

Conditional consumer citizens

No rights without responsibilities has been a recurring theme of the Blair government and there is no reason to believe that this will not apply to retirement pensions. The idea of retirement as a citizenship right, fixed by age and underpinned by a universal benefit, may not survive much longer. There are already powerful voices being raised against the idea of a fixed age of retirement (see Chapters Five and Six). By diminishing the rights of citizens and enhancing those of consumers the stick driving people towards the private market takes on a sharper point. Amid the chatter of reflexivity, diversity, identity and consumerism it can be hard to hear the voice of the poorest. Extending meaningful choices to the poorest can only occur if welfare provisions exist to cushion the effects of the wrong choices. The fear is that talk of choice and moral responsibility ignores the obstacles the poorest sections of society confront in trying to address these. The prospect of compulsory retirement saving being imposed on households that already struggle to make ends meet is very real (*Pensions World*, October 2000). Obligations and responsibilities are increasingly being imposed on those who rely on public and informal welfare that do not apply to the more privileged features of the SDW (Dwyer, 1998). A society that makes retirement conditional on engagement with full-time paid work and private pension providers for 40-50 years – which is what would be required to generate a pension for the poorest – is likely to be an authoritarian society. Consumer choice in these circumstances would be reserved for the comfortable majority and compulsion reserved for the poor (Deacon and Bradshaw, 1983; Deacon, 1997).

Heroic citizen consumers

It has to be recognised that the drift towards a consumer society and the creation of consumption sectors contains the seeds for new social and political agendas to emerge. Some of these might derive from the way the market responds to the diverse consumer demands mentioned above. Another possibility is that consumers will press for more rights, more information and more accountability. Harrison (1990) has observed how the structures of organised consumption can generate claims and entitlements related to forms of savings and accumulation. He suggests that these will, in turn, promote calls for more accountability and transparency from consumers and their representatives. If pensioners become active consumers, exercising rights, then the decisions of both market providers and government are likely to be closely scrutinised. Indeed, this is already a factor according to Frank Field, a former Labour government minister and long-time campaigner for improvements in pension provisions. He identified "the drive towards greater individual consumer sovereignty" (1996, p 26) as a major influence on both politicians and welfare service providers in the last two decades of the 20th century. One way that consumers might pose difficult problems for both private and occupational pension providers, hinges on the investment decisions of the funds. This is tackled in more depth in the next chapter, but for now it should be noted that the ethics of fund investment are already being raised by some fund members. The requirement that the funds provide SIPs is simply one of the first indications that consumers and members will seek much more information in the future. Likewise there are already pension providers who claim to be ethical, avoiding the arms trade, environmentally damaging developments and so on. In the past consumer boycotts and pressures from shareholders have persuaded numerous companies to change their activities. Similarly if the state is urging, and probably very soon compelling, people to save for their retirement, even more clarity and accountability can be anticipated. The stakeholder pensions are, therefore, likely to be scrutinised very closely and any whiff of unethical investment, let alone dip in fortunes, will surely attract attention.

Information is also seen as vital by pensioner lobby groups and will clearly impact on how the private market behaves. Private pension providers in the UK have been operating in a market where the purchaser has very often relied on the seller to explain what it is they are buying. Thus the National Pensioners Conference has stated:

> We believe, however, that serious consideration should be given to the creation of a centrally funded, genuinely independent, highly trained and salaried financial advice service. It could be financed in part by a

statutory levy on financial service providers and in part by fees, at an affordable level, paid by users of the service. There would be a case for establishing such a service, even if stakeholder pensions were not to be added to the array of savings and investment schemes on offer, but the introduction of stakeholder schemes would greatly strengthen that case. (Cited from National Pensioners Conference website www.natpencon/ org/uk, February 2001)

Even ardent advocates of the free play of market forces like Simpson (1996, p 78) accept that the purchaser of a private pension is in a very different situation to that of other consumers. He suggests education is required, with consumers learning quickly it is to be hoped, about market volatility. But information and education will provide very little comfort if, after 30-40 years, the funds have not performed as expected. The unpredictability of the market and the long-term nature of pensions means that they cannot be, and increasingly are not, guaranteed. The Goode report (1993) acknowledged this and the fact that saving for a pension is unlike other forms of saving. Thus many people will save for Christmas or a holiday (Goode, 1993, p 137), but unlike Christmas, retirement only comes once in a lifetime. Consequently we cannot learn from the previous year in order to save more or spend less. By the time we collect our retirement pension it will be too late to adjust.

Nor is it clear that consumers and retirees, in general, want to behave like the citizens of ancient Athens. Constantly trawling through information packs, scanning the broadsheet newspapers, educating themselves about investment returns, deciding between active or passive fund management, ensuring their savings are in socially responsible investments, comparing administration charges, looking for balanced portfolios and keeping a watchful eye on the financial markets, among many other tasks, assumes consumers are tremendously heroic. Only a certain type of consumer is likely to invest their time, resources and energy campaigning for information, letter writing and so on. The rest of us might applaud their activities but would not take part. Moreover, like Laslett's model of retirement, it assumes a high level of competence and commitment. As Warde (1994a) notes, it would be a mistake to generalise from examples based on the most capable consumer, particularly when it comes to something as complex as pensions. Consumer pressure, therefore, is likely to focus on particular themes that emanate from specific consumer constituencies. Some may not care where their pension is invested, so long as it generates a good return. Consequently, political and managerial agendas in the future may be more concerned with organising and managing opinion than in the past. Ensuring customer satisfaction, or at least compliance, could prove to be as important as fund management itself (see Chapter Four). A failure to manage consumer interests, to respond to calls for information and accountability may be bad for business, much as it is in other areas of consumption. However, not everyone can be, or will want to be, consumer citizens. Many will be excluded because they lack the necessary resources, while others will be content for their future well-being to ride, quite literally, on trust. They might prefer to just head off for a life of sunshine on a Harley-Davidson, always assuming their pension fund performs as promised.

Conclusion and summary

Approaching retirement as a time for consumption and looking at retirees and pension fund members as consumers is an attractive proposition. Clearly 'consumption matters' (Edgell et al, 1996), and consumption approaches can provide some important insights into the social and cultural forces that shape welfare and society. And vice versa; the approach can acknowledge the divisive effects of welfare itself, and how this may influence life chances and society. Indeed, Dunleavy's account of consumption sectors is compatible with the idea of a SDW and illuminates the way that 'choices' are structured and constrained without denying that these preferences are significant. Nor can we ignore the way consumption influences attitudes to retirement, with ideas, culture and lifestyle key components in the sales pitch of the pensions industry and the expectations of their target audience. This can serve as a sharp reminder of the inadequacies of the existing provisions, and an indication of how difficult it might be to resurrect a commitment to a universal public welfare system to which all sections of society feel able to subscribe. However, because some forms of consumption are preferable to others, those who can afford to do so effectively unsubscribe, and social divisions in retirement are reinforced. The prospect of enjoying a 'third age', as Laslett described, is what many consumers want. Although Laslett's account was criticised, it needs to be emphasised that he was challenging the ageist prejudices that serve to exclude older people from being active and vibrant consumers. Furthermore, the possibilities for new forms of political mobilisation and challenge arise from the consumption processes and cleavages that a consumer society generates. It will be interesting to see how financial institutions and welfare bureaucracies respond if they do become the focus of political mobilisations. Their ability to address consumer politics and ethical issues is likely to be a severe test in the near future (a point explored further in Chapter Four). Critics sometimes suggest that a focus on consumption and 'choice' neglects the way these are socially constructed, but hopefully it has been shown here that this need not be the case. On the contrary, and as Bauman (1998) demonstrates, a society of consumers is one that excludes the poorest from meaningful choices and makes their rights conditional on unrealistic responsibilities (Dwyer, 1998).

Nevertheless, consumption approaches can, like the pensions advertisements, conflate image and reality. As we have seen, most retired people have incomes and consumption patterns that are well below those in paid work. Too often the consumer is equated with the most well-informed and self-conscious customer. They know what they want, what they are entitled to expect and how to get it, but this model of the heroic consumer is difficult to sustain in reality. Many people, particularly when confronted with complex products and services such as retirement pensions, are confused, erratic and impulsive consumers. Furthermore, the market for welfare services, arguably best illustrated by pension policies, is very different to that for consumer durables. Nor is it always clear why one form of consumption is any more significant than another, for example housing rather than food or transport, when analysing consumption patterns. This in turn poses the possibility that some sort of consumption index, embracing a range of goods and services, would be more appropriate. However, like the criticisms of deprivation indices (Piachaud, 1987), a great deal then hinges on what the observer counts as a consumption good or service. The possibilities for constructing and classifying different items and the weight each should have is endless. The final critical point to bear in mind is that despite the politics of lifestyle and culture that supposedly typify contemporary consumer society, many retired people are excluded from making choices and are often discounted, and therefore, lesser consumers.

This is not to suggest that things will remain as they are. The demographics of the market place may well see the consumption patterns of retirees becoming more significant.

I was reminded of this when walking along the promenade at Manly Beach in Sydney. A group of about 20 men and women, all I would guess between 55 and 70 years of age, approached on mountain bikes, loaded down with camping gear and clearly heading for a cafe or bar. In the front was a man with a silver-grey beard, pink face, pink cycle helmet, pink shorts and a pink T-shirt with the slogan across the front '*Retired at last*'.

Perhaps the most important feature of consumption-based analyses is that they engage with people's aspirations, which in turn provide such a massive challenge to social policy in the future. Thus the strengths and weaknessess of consumption approaches can be summarised as follows.

Strengths of the consumption approach

- Retirement can be viewed as an age-related period of consumption.
- Consumption patterns can fragment society.
- Desires and aspirations are acknowledged.
- Recognises that consumer rights may relegate or replace citizenship rights.
- Increasing consumer sovereignty may harden consumption cleavages and thus public welfare becomes reserved for the poor.
- Consumer sovereignty may promote accountability and in turn impinge on the pensions industry.
- Consumption approaches can be reconciled with the SDW.
- Treats retirement as a time to be enjoyed, not endured.

Weaknesses of the consumption approach

- Unclear which form of consumption should be measured.
- Can conflate consumer images and reality.
- Can promote normative models of what retirees should be like.
- Not always clear how consumer goods and welfare services differ.
- The focus on consumption can overlook other sources of social power.
- May promote misleading ideas of consumers 'freely' expressing choices.

FOUR

Post-work and post-structuralism: first past the post?

Introduction

This chapter looks at retirement and age-related pensions from the perspective of post-structuralism. It draws on the work of Michel Foucault and other scholars who identify with his approach. Although Foucault is often associated with post-modernism, his approach needs to be distinguished from such accounts. Post-modernism and 'post-traditional' perspectives pose a rather different set of questions that need to be acknowledged, and these are addressed in Chapter Five. Trying to locate Foucault's work alongside that of post-traditional perspectives, such as Beck (1992) or Giddens (1994), might have muddied the waters and obscured their respective features. By drawing such boundaries, however, there is the danger of constructing the sort of distinctions that are rejected by post-modernists and post-structuralists alike. However, a mitigating factor here is that these are theoretical models that may appear alien to a social policy readership. Initially the chapter is concerned with the key concepts drawn from a broadly defined post-structuralist analysis. Knowledge, power and discourse are outlined in turn, and examples provided of how these are manifest within retirement and pensions policy. The significance of the terms power/knowledge/discourse will be fully explored throughout the chapter, but a brief initial explanation may assist the reader.

Power is understood as a feature of all social relationships and although it may discipline clients, consumers and subject groups, it does not necessarily mean that they are forced to comply or that their interests are offended.

For example, medics clearly have a great deal of power in their dealings with patients but this will usually be framed by the patients desire to get better. It is assumed that the knowledge the medical profession has will be used benignly,

> but this knowledge is itself framed in such a way that the patient (or subject category) is excluded from engaging on anything like equal terms with the medical practitioner. Moreover, the discourse – the way of thinking, talking and dealing with illness – is structured by the medical profession and the patient/subject is expected to either engage with this discourse or, quite literally, be 'treated' as a sick being (Davis, 1988).

Foucault considered knowledge, discourse and power as integrally related and regarded them dispassionately. That is, he is reluctant to blame or to applaud the experts and the professions which construct their specific claims to knowledge. He also wanted to avoid any hint of reductionism and did not tie his analysis to specific class or organised interests. Thus, in this approach, power is addressed in relation to fund managers, actuaries and other pensions experts who promote certain technical and scientific means as the way to manage and control populations. The populations they deal with are current pensioners and members of retirement schemes. How experts understand and discuss their clients, customers and members promotes a 'discursive frame' that reinforces their claims of authority. This in turn has an influence on retirement and pensions policy because it legitimates some claims to knowledge and excludes other voices. Likewise, the technology and 'modes of information' (Poster, 1984), and mechanisms of communication in structuring legitimate 'knowledge', along with the potential for alternative discourses, will be explored in this chapter. Finally, the impact of a more widespread shift in the discourses that surround welfare is considered. A shift that has "tried to wean people off dependence on the state pension" (*Pensions World*, August 2000), and to encourage the vocabulary of ethical investors, informed consumers and discerning customers.

Knowledge

The way that knowledge is defined, articulated and generated, the way it enables or excludes, is a central pillar of post-structuralism. Put most simply, the effect of knowledge is to reinforce the position and power of those who orchestrate the 'tunes' to which retirees and prospective retirees must 'dance'. Like medics and other groups whose claims to knowledge are predicated on their status in law and their rational scientific discourse, pension fund managers, actuaries, consultants and accountants call the tune. They may feel hemmed in by legislation and regulation, but that reflects their pivotal location in a system that cannot operate without their expertise no matter how complex they may regard their task (*Pensions Administrator*, October 2000). Indeed, it is because pensions are complex that we need experts to manage our funds and advise us on the best retirement options. Unlike medics, who have found that their subjects/patients increasingly query the 'hierarchy of knowledge' (Smart, 1995, p 72), experts in the pensions arena have only recently begun to be questioned regarding the assumptions behind their claims to knowledge.

An attractive feature of Foucault's approach is the way it can turn our attention away from public welfare recipients and taken-for-granted ideas about dependency to make visible the experts and their 'truths'. Examining the experts' claims to knowledge involves establishing the assumptions they work with and the context that frames their *modus operandi*. Competing and contradictory claims may be asserted by different experts in the field, but all will declare that their knowledge is based on rational scientific criteria. This does not mean that the experts' knowledge *is* rational or scientific but that such claims are made. Indeed, knowledge itself will be defined within specific disciplines – accountancy, fund management and so on – and may be marshalled by each of them to support their claims to knowledge and power. Like a map that defines where we are and what we know of the landscape around us, including the routes we might take to other places, our knowledge is restricted by what has been written down. Whoever has a say in what the map covers – what information/knowledge is deemed valid – has a more privileged place in the hierarchy of knowledge, and therefore power. Caution is called for here because it should not be thought that this mapping is necessarily a conscious or conspiratorial process, designed to exclude. Exclusion occurs because the layperson is unable to understand or engage with the discourse undertaken by the experts. Knowledge is best defined in terms of control over information and what information is collected and deemed useful. What counts as knowledge is still subject to scrutiny and criticism within the field of expertise and it will change over time to incorporate new modes of information and forms of knowledge. The crucial point is that only those experts whose knowledge is deemed to fall within the legitimate boundaries of the field of study will have the possibility of 'authoring a statement' (Poster, 1984; Bauman, 1992, p 71). Thus it is important to consider which voices get heard and who is engaged in the powerful discourses, and which voices are ignored or excluded.

Experts and retirement knowledge

Demography, pensions and trust law, actuarial calculations, investment modelling, fund management and accounting are among the sciences that form the factual, objective existence of the pensions experts. An expert in one area may not be familiar with other aspects of the pensions arena, and like medics or lawyers, specialisation is commonplace. Hardly surprising therefore that many people regard pensions as complex, part of a technical world that is alien to them. The need is for good expert advice; professional independent knowledge that will make the mysterious world of pensions understandable. Financial advisors in most newspapers act as interpreters of the experts' language and communications experts are the latest recruits to the industry (*Pensions World*, January 2001). Interestingly, the increase in DC schemes has motivated many more experts dealing with occupational pensions to feel that they need better communication with scheme members. Moreover, the chair of the pensions board at the Institute of Actuaries, Peter Tomkins, fearing that his profession would shrink in size following the trend to DC schemes, suggested that actuaries ought to take up other expert tasks "forming businesses and becoming advisors in other areas" (*Pensions World*, October 2000). Thus it is important to recognise that changes occur in the hierarchy of expert knowledge and that they are closely related to the development of new techniques, sciences, alternative discourses and 'modes of information' (Poster, 1984).

The discursive formation that maps the boundaries of retirement pensions is not fixed and has changed over time. In 19th century Britain, the respectable working classes often relied on mutual and friendly society membership to provide minimal unemployment, widows and sickness benefits. Towards the end of the century sickness benefits were sometimes serving as a type of retirement income for skilled workers who were effectively redundant. By the 1860s, the middle classes had adopted the language of 'self-help' and advocated the principles of mutualism and cooperation as a solution to the social problems industrial capitalism had generated. Working men, and this address was overwhelmingly concerned with respectable working-class men, were urged to pursue their individual interests through thrift and the discipline of saving for the future. But this was not necessarily how many of those who saved through friendly societies saw this activity. Like trades unions, cooperatives and other mutual societies, their concern was more pragmatic and predicated on collectivism. The discipline they feared was the workhouse and their response was a collective one, intended to protect both their families and other mutual society members. At the beginning of the 20th century NI was introduced to fund unemployment and sickness benefits, but in Britain, Australia and many other countries, the labour movement was often ambiguous about such state intervention. Better-off workers often resented redistribution within the insured population and some socialists argued that the insurance systems were getting workers to pay for the social costs that capitalism produced. Others argued that state intervention would undermine the collective ethos of mutualism and witness a redrawing of the deserving/undeserving distinction (Mann, 1992). All of these fears have proven to be well founded.

Knowledge, for Foucault, is not an artefact of power, nor power a product of knowledge; they are inextricably intertwined. In *Discipline and punish* (1977), Foucault shows how all concerned with punishment operate within a particular discourse and that over time this has shifted from punishing and controlling the body to a more insidious form of discipline, one in which, despite ourselves, we often collude. Science, experts, professionals and managers survey and assess the subject. In penal policy it is of course the offender, the criminal, the inmate, who must be scientifically addressed and observed. As Stephen Katz (1996) shows, the 'disciplining of old age' and the development of public welfare went hand in glove with the emergence of social exploration, social research and social engineering. In respect of pensions it is the prospective pensioner and the pensioner population that must be scrutinised, counted and disciplined. The keyhole through which insurance companies, actuaries and demographers peer allows them to observe every aspect of their subjects' lives, and then to assess them. Knowledge is engineered through the measurement of populations; their available spending, their desires and lifestyles, previous insurance claims, geographical location, whether they are married, divorced or single, HIV positive or not, male or female, previous and current occupations, whether they might live for five or 20 years on their pension, and when they will die. Insurance principles, whether they are applied by the state, insurance companies or occupational pensions necessarily involve various techniques of surveillance and specific forms of knowledge (Ewald, 1991).

Ewald (1991) has provided a useful guide to the techniques employed by insurers and he illustrates the way that knowledge, discourse and power can combine to discipline populations. Ewald identities three economic and financial techniques that developed to enable 'risks' to be insured at a time when the Church prohibited usury:

- the techniques have to be rational and scientific;
- the techniques impose moral regulation;
- the techniques rely on reparation to imply a system of social justice.

Taking these in turn: first, the techniques had to be rational and demonstrable, thereby disciplining the providers, regulating the market and ensuring a 'level playing field'. "Second, insurance is a moral technology. To calculate risk is to master time, to discipline the future" (Ewald, 1991, p 207). Prudence, providence and planning impose a severe discipline on many people who feel that they must defer pleasure today for security tomorrow. Governments may pronounce their belief in 'choice', but they have been quick to compel compliance among those sections of the population who make the wrong choices. State compulsory 'saving' is complemented by insurers who penalise behaviour they have identified as 'risky'. (This has led to the situation where when asked, and we are all increasingly asked, on insurance forms, "Do you engage in any social, sporting or leisure activities that might put you at risk of an accident?". A Norwich Union respondent allegedly stated, "I promise never to leave the house and only watch game shows on TV".) The appearance of control over fate is possible for those that plan and save and the prudent are therefore defined as deserving.

Those who save for their retirement through insurance schemes also rely on Ewald's third 'technique' of reparation and indemnification. Insurance operates as a system of justice that purports to share risks and redistribute resources according to equitable rules. He states, "The combination of these different dimensions makes insurance a *political technology*.... Insurance makes it possible to dream of contractual justice.... Insurance makes it possible to envisage a solution to the problem of poverty and working class insecurity" (Ewald, 1991, p 207).

The net effect is profoundly misleading; creating a sense of security, whether that is real or not, defining some forms of behaviour as undeserving and therefore potentially subject to being disciplined, promoting retirement dreams that cannot be realised and creating an illusion of equity and justice when this only applies within the insured population. Although writing of insurance schemes, Ewald's points also apply to the different forms of retirement pension. Moreover, the populations that make up the constituents of the SDW are rarely aware of their respective subject identities and how these are framed by the technologies applied to them. They are, however, increasingly made aware that their behaviour – their ability to conform to a prudent lifestyle –

will enable some to enjoy richer dreams and a better retirement deal than others. That is why the rich do not join schemes populated by the poor, if they can help it, because they would simply get a poorer deal.

Whose funds and whose knowledge?

Writing of the US, Drucker notes: "Instead of the old-line capitalist, in developed countries pension funds increasingly control the supply and allocation of money.... Pension funds are run by a new breed of capitalists, the faceless, anonymous, salaried employees, the pension funds'; investment analysts and portfolio managers" (1993, p 5). He goes on to describe how 'pension fund capitalism' no longer hinges on labour or capital, but on knowledge. In the future, access to, control over and what we understand knowledge to be, will be vital. Drucker is not, however, promoting a post-structuralist perspective, although the title of his book suggests that these changes have produced a 'post-capitalist society'. A central issue for Drucker is the part that pension fund assets will play in the new knowledge-based society of the future. Who, and how, will control and accountability be managed when the capital assets are already earmarked for retirement pensions? There are also questions of whether fund members, or their nominees, will take a different view of the knowledge and ethics involved in portfolio management. In effect, whose view of the world will control the retirement funds and whose money is it?

An interesting example that illuminates these questions of knowledge and control is the case of the SGC introduced in Australia in 1992 (Mann, 1993; Olsberg, 1997). In 1979, the Australian Council of Trade Unions (ACTU), which at that time represented over 40% of the employed population, launched a campaign for an occupationally-based superannuated pension scheme that would provide a fund managed by an ACTU controlled trustee company, with minority employer representation on the board. This was extended in 1985 when Congress resolutions called for the administrators of funds to be fully accountable to their members and for workers to have a say in how the funds were invested (ACTU/TDC, 1987; Plowman and Weaven, 1988). Two years later the ACTU advocated the establishment of a National Development Fund that would have access to 20% of 'super' funds to be used in a counter-cyclical fashion to stimulate the economy. When investment in the Australian economy was low the fund would be active and it would taper off its activities when investment picked up. There were further proposals to limit overseas investments, with the general

> logic of these reforms being to ensure that the Australian Labor government
> was not hamstrung by the need for investment capital. The example of the
> British Labour government in the mid-1970s having to curtail social spending
> and reforms was still fresh in many minds.

All this illustrates the ACTU view, circa 1987, that pension funds could
be seen as a legitimate source of national investment revenue. The ACTU
believed the funds were deferred wages that they, as the major representative
body for workers, should be able to use, even if this meant interfering in
the finance markets. Besides, the funds had a privileged tax status bestowed
on them by government and therefore all interested parties should have
some say over what happened to these privileged funds (ACTU/TDC,
1987, pp 16-23). By 1991, fund assets were approximately 5% of Australian
GDP and the ACTU was beginning to back away from its previous
interventionist stance (Mann, 1993; SSCS, 1992, pp 20-1). With an
economic slowdown in the early 1990s, with considerable labour market
restructuring, proposals for massive investments drawn from
superannuation funds failed to materialise. Instead, the ACTU called for
federal government spending and merely for further tax subsidies for
"funds invested ... in socially and economically desirable investment"
(ACTU, 1991, p 168). Inward and directed investment was no longer a
priority. Indeed, it was admitted that the ACTU lacked the necessary
expertise and by 1992 it was stated that: "We believe the key to promoting
investment in these areas [is] the promotion of a climate which encourages,
rather than compels, superannuation funds to invest" (pp 1-3). Inward
directed investment was effectively killed off because "to flood the area
with funds is to invite potential disaster" (ACTU, 1992). This was also
the year in which the SGC came into effect, providing an occupational
pension to virtually every employed person, funded by a levy on employers
(see Chapter Six).

Fund management and control in a global financial market is now
accepted by the ACTU as requiring knowledge and expertise that it
lacks. Confronted by the possibility that they could be jeopardising
prospective retirees' incomes, the ACTU concluded that it was best to
leave fund management to the experts. Indeed, by the early 1990s they
took the view that there was more than enough capital within Australia.
Rather the problem had become what to do with the reserves that fund
managers were holding, without undermining the remaining industries
trying to compete in the Pacific Rim. Moreover, the fund managers

were able to persuade the ACTU that development and venture capital investments within Australia have a poor rate of return. The bitter irony is that the success of the ACTU in pressing for widespread superannuation membership, has witnessed both a growth in fund membership and a corresponding growth in economic conservatism. The intention of boosting the economy with investments from superannuation funds has been overturned by the desire to maximise members' retirement incomes, although "trustees should look at each investment on their merits" (*Superfunds*, May 1991). It now appears that the finance markets have to be the arbitrators of what is, and what is not, a sound investment prospect (ACTU, 1992; Mann, 1993; Olsberg, 1997).

Similar concerns over occupational pension fund control and the role of trustees arose in the UK following the Maxwell scandal in the early 1990s. The TUC advocated a majority of member trustees on fund boards in their evidence to the Goode Committee (1993) that considered how to avoid future scandals. Whether trustees could, or should, take a more proactive role is open to debate. There are some grounds for thinking they might do so now that ethical investment issues are higher up the agenda, but they start from a fairly weak position. It needs to be stressed that most trustees are not experts, but are nominated from within the schemes' membership. They are formally in charge of the funds but they must not touch a penny of these.

Among a growing number of responsibilities that trustees are legally responsible for are selecting fund managers, establishing investment principles and ensuring a measure of security for the fund. They must discharge their duties on the basis of only three to five meetings per year (IDS, 1999, pp 324-5). It is possible that they will not know any of the other trustees. They may even be based in different parts of the country and can often be working a long way from the organisation's pensions department. The Myners review found that:

- 62% of trustees had no professional qualifications in finance and investment;
- 77% had no in-house professionals to assist them;
- more than 50% of trustees had received less than three days' training when they became trustees;
- 44% had not enrolled on any courses since their initial year of trusteeship;
- 49% of trustees spend three hours or less preparing for pension investment matters. (Myners, 2001, p 5)

At first sight it seems remarkable that people with little or no expertise should be overseeing capital assets that often dwarf the sponsoring organisation. Again, the main fear among the experts seems to be not that trustees know too little but, like their Australian counterparts, what they think they know is too much. In other words, the trustee with a particular agenda, a mindset that knows the significance of the funds and how they could be used differently, is perceived as a far more dangerous animal than the half-hearted member nominee. There is, however, some ambiguity within the pensions industry toward trustees. For example, Alan Pickering (then chair of NAPF) stoutly defended lay trustees in his association's journal, but wanted to ensure that:

> ... security and technical compliance might be more properly the responsibility of appropriately qualified hired help. While training is essential, making it compulsory would be counterproductive. [And he concluded:] I spend much of my working life with trustees. They are the salt of the earth and meeting them is humbling. They respond so generously to challenges which may appear thankless tasks. They require a pat on the back, not a kick up the backside. (*Pensions World*, August 2000)

Earlier in the year he was more concerned that trustees might collude with specialist fund managers and pressure groups with similar interests. "Emerging market funds and third world charities may be a case in point. You must never allow commercial self interest and altruism to be confused" (*Pensions World*, June 2000). So they are the 'salt of the earth' so long as they undertake the thankless tasks, but taking an interest in ethical, political and socially responsible topics poses more of a problem. For post-structuralists the crucial issue is the framework within which some forms of knowledge are deemed valid while other claims are marginalised. Knowledge is ideally free of interests, being a matter of technical or administrative competence and ideologically neutral. Thus, the labour movement's attempt to assert an alternative has been compromised by their status as an interest group. The experts are deemed to be independent and, despite any interests that they may have, their claims to knowledge are therefore privileged. Similar claims have been voiced before and the mildly patronising tone that greets the layperson who queries the expert is also familiar. The expert, the professional and the technician invariably deride 'the punter', but they, in turn, have been confronted within other welfare arenas. Social work, criminal law, medicine, housing policy and a host of other 'complex' policy areas have all, at some point or other, been perceived as beyond the layperson's comprehension. But a feature of contemporary societies is that the expert's discourse can be interrupted and voices that yesterday were on the margins are today being raised (Beresford et al, 1999).

Modes of information and ways of knowing

For Foucault the techniques involved in collecting information are a fundamental part of how a body of knowledge develops and this information subsequently frames the way the 'social problem' is perceived. Poster (1984) has developed this point and suggests the 'mode of information', as he puts it, is increasingly significant in the management, surveillance and governance of populations. An extreme example would be the use of closed circuit TV for policing public spaces that not only enables police to identify rioters and muggers, but also 'civilises' the behaviour of passionate lovers, or anyone with a bursting bladder looking for a dark doorway. Information provides the means by which we learn to police ourselves. Information technologies and the exchange of information they allow have increased the scope, speed and potential for a high degree of surveillance, with numerous implications for pensioners and anyone who is approaching retirement. Some of the possibilities are only just beginning to be realised. Here the focus will be on three populations and possibilities. Although there are others that might have featured, these will hopefully suffice to demonstrate the significance of Poster's approach.

• First, the retired population, pensioners and future pensioners who, depending on how systems are set up, may either be marginalised or empowered by developments.
• Second, there are profound implications for those who currently manage these populations and how they do so.
• Third, the new technologies are likely to impact on the hierarchy of knowledge, with the possibility of actuaries and fund managers themselves becoming the subjects of the technician's gaze.

Enabling and controlling pensioners and future retirees

First, for the pensioner population and prospective pensioners there are countervailing possibilities. On the one hand, new modes of information could be used to enable greater access to data that relates to benefits and for individuals to keep track of their entitlements. With labour market flexibility increasing the number of employers with whom individuals have some pension rights, it is very difficult for many to plan for retirement. A system that kept track of one's pension rights would be attractive to many people.

> If the various contributions – for example, in the UK: NI, SERPS, occupational pensions, AVCs, stakeholder pensions, and so on – could be electronically transferred to generate one fund, that could then be invested in a suitably diverse portfolio. This too might enable individuals to feel that they have some control. The NI system previously managed something like this with a simple paper trail from one employer to the next and it is hard to believe that current technology could not refine it. If this were also linked to the tax and benefit system it would even be possible to have automatic transfers into an individual's fund, and in a progressive manner. Thus, maternity leave, childcare responsibilities, attendance allowances, elder care, and so on, might all witness transfers into a pension fund. The administrative costs associated with pension transfers might reasonably be expected to fall with an automated electronic system, thereby making it cheaper and easier to divide pension rights on divorce. More information might also allow scheme members to compare the costs and performance of their fund, thus increasing competition, as it appears to have done in Australia (Olsberg, 1997). If pension providers can give reliable, clear information it may also encourage some of those who are currently perplexed by the options to make suitable provisions, thereby extending the more privileged elements of the SDW to a wider constituency.

Fund managers and government in the UK are acutely aware that poor information, complexity and a confusing array of options deter many people from taking an interest in retirement saving (DSS, 1998a; *Pensions Administrator*, October 2000; *Pensions World*, January 2001).

Calls for clearer and better information are one of the mantras that everyone involved in retirement pensions repeats. For some observers, computer-linked multi-media technologies provide the answer to such prayers (IDS, 1999, p 364).

Pension providers in the US and Australia have been using the Internet for some time and the UK seems to be slowly appreciating the possibilities for service provision to be more tightly tailored to an individual's needs. The US government also has a more sophisticated (by UK standards) array of websites giving users access to information about social security entitlements, age-specific data and links to other relevant sources of information.

Using a computer from home allows for more detailed and personalised forms of communication between scheme members and administrators than 'information booklets' are capable of, and could ensure public welfare recipients are not exposed to the glare of the social security office (IDS, 1999, p 364). All of this could be done electronically without the need for intrusive inquiries or overt means testing. The optimistic scenario might even allow for diversity within a universal system.

On the other hand the individualising effects of information technologies could further isolate and divide the pensioner population. Paradoxically the potential for exclusion lies in the ability of the technology to be more precise, clearer and more tightly tailored to the individual.

For example, reliable information on employment history, contribution records, medical records, leisure activities and likely beneficiaries could be used to 'firm up' actuarial predictions. The information would ensure more accurate assessments of the risks an individual undertakes and the costs this may impose on the fund. Such information could be used to ensure that individuals are not classed with others of the same age, gender, sexual orientation, social class or income bracket when they, or their behaviour, differs.

On the face of it this would seem to be quite reasonable, until we note that the more accurate actuarial predictions are the more regressive will be the effects in terms of contributions and benefits. Instead of spreading risks within fairly broad bands across different population types, which has the potential for a measure of redistribution on the basis of need, the tendency is likely to be to identify high risk, low-contributing individuals. These would then either be excluded completely, as often happens in high crime areas where residents are refused contents insurance, or confined with others of the same type to a poorer scheme. Although the information itself is apparently neutral it is likely that it would be used to the disadvantage of particular groups. Discrimination, therefore, is a logical outcome of more reliable information and is not necessarily a result of prejudice or bigotry.

Managing 'risk' populations

Second, there are some crucially important implications of more reliable information for those who currently manage 'risk' populations.

> For example, in the late 1980s and early 1990s many insurance companies refused cover to people who admitted having had an HIV test, irrespective of the result. Other companies proposed to compel single men to undertake HIV tests and/ or medical reports before they would consider life assurance policies.

Genetic testing offers the prospect of potentially even more reliable data that could see pension providers offering a range of benefits tailored to the individual's propensity for illness, disability or death. The fund managers' journal *Pensions World* (December 2000) speculated that if testing became standard practice, occupational pension funds might wish to exclude certain 'impaired lives', and on this basis employers might also refuse them the job. In contrast, life annuity policies might be more generous for those who can be identified as at 'more risk'. As Mr Bullivant of Evergreen Assurance explained:

> With life assurance, ill health means increased premiums [because this information has to be disclosed, author], but with an enhanced life annuity it means more money. For example, with an ordinary annuity, you could have two people at retirement: one is Linford Christie and the other is a man who has recently had a heart attack. Traditionally, they would both get the same annuity, in which case Linford wins because he lives longer. What the enhanced annuity is about is ensuring the guy who dies early gets more money. Enhanced annuities are addressing one of the inequities of the insurance world. (*Pensions World*, December 2000)

Retirement saving is not, however, a sprint race and anyone advising Linford Christie ought to tell him to find a scheme that does not offer enhanced annuities but privileges the very healthy. This would simply accelerate the processes of individuation and, in the longer term, it is not clear that heart attack victims would 'win'.

There are powerful pressures to allow testing in the UK and reports of some insurance companies breaking the current restrictions amid government "fears they may create a genetic underclass" (*The Observer*, 8 April 2001). The implications of genetic testing, bearing in mind the overlapping histories of eugenics and social science, are particularly worrying for disabled people and people from certain ethnic minority groups (Dyson, 1999). However, in a global financial market it is not clear that current restrictions can be sustained.

For example, if someone is tested privately, and on the basis of these tests seeks out a pension or annuity provider who can tailor a package for them, the effect will be to raise contributions for those left behind. Contributions and premiums will increase across the board as those who can demonstrate that they are a 'good risk' seek out the best deal from a provider elsewhere. The 'bad risks', and those who cannot afford the tests or private provisions, will be either excluded or confined to a residual service that will demand disproportionate contributions and premiums and offer poorer benefits. Pension and life insurance providers are very aware of this fact; it is a fundamental feature of their business (*Pensions World*, December 2000).

Genetic testing, however, is only the most recent technology and existing modes of information already provide considerable possibilities for discriminating within populations.

For example, information gathering techniques based on spending patterns with particular companies, holiday destinations, supermarket 'loyalty cards' that reveal specific purchases, credit cards that say a great deal about an individual's behaviour, and so on; the potential for providers to 'load' and target individuals is considerable. Employers already discipline employees who undertake activities they feel are inappropriate. Medical checks, including the compulsory provision of blood, hair or urine samples, for alcohol and drug consumption are not uncommon in the US and have been introduced by numerous employers in the UK in the last few years. Sanctions, including dismissal, can be applied.

Similar information would clearly assist governments keen to promote responsible behaviour and to make welfare conditional on this being accepted by applicants. The tone and vocabulary of the British Labour government has shifted from one that stressed empowering and enabling the excluded, to one of cajoling and compelling. Changing the moral fabric of society and establishing the *third way* is a project that focuses attention on how individuals behave and distinguishes those who reflexively adapt from those who persist with their errant behaviour (Dwyer, 1998; Giddens, 1998; Hoggett, 2001). In terms of public welfare, current pensioners can expect to be cajoled into work or given a minimal income (PIU, 2000; see also Chapters Five and Six). The modernising project is, therefore, to induce subsequent retirees, current workers, carers and consumers to make their own provisions, to change their behaviour "... by finding new ways of *using* the state to impose the discipline of the market on its population" (Holden, 1999, p 538). Information technology would undoubtedly assist in this task.

Changing knowledge hierarchies

The third feature to be considered here is how the new information technologies might impact on the hierarchy of knowledge among the experts jostling for position. Information technology has already had a profound effect on how the various retirement savings, insurance companies and pension providers manage their respective populations. Competition between providers in the private insurance sector and with DB occupational schemes, along with legislation and regulations that have facilitated change, have encouraged an array of new retirement and savings vehicles. In the past DB occupational schemes were the main alternative to public welfare provisions: "A supportive tax regime for most of the last century was a major contributor to the virility of the UK funded pension system" (*Pensions World*, June 2000). However, fiscal welfare has been extended in the UK to promote many of the newer market-based savings products. While this has added further layers of complexity to a picture that many people already perceive as complex, it has also made it possible to compare the performances of the various providers. Previously, investment decisions and fund management were activities that escaped the public gaze; increasingly they are in the public eye. For example, advertising hoardings proudly proclaim the success of fund and investment managers, while the resignation of Equitable Life's chief actuary was national news (BBC Radio 5, 1 March 2001).

In terms of how we approach retirement it is important to consider these experts because: "Pension funds are part of the long-term investment institutions of the UK. Their purpose is to accumulate assets, the income from and capital values of which are used to pay for the pensions of retired workers" (Blake, 1992a, p 1).

Observing the experts

Foucault reminds us that if we want to understand how policy develops we must look at the sciences and experts that define it. Thus we cannot understand how penal policy emerged by looking simply at the prisoner, nor appreciate health policy by observing patients. Penal reformers and criminologists, psychologists and medics respectively have to be observed too; it is their claims to knowledge, their discourse and, of course, their power that frames the subject. Examining the claims to privileged knowledge of professionals and experts can be an illuminating exercise. According to David Damant, whose expert credentials include, among many other responsibilities, Managing Director of Paribas Asset Management, a subdivision of the 28th largest bank in the world, membership of the International Stock Exchange, former President of the European Federation of Financial Analysts Society and a representative on the Board of the International Accounting Standards Committee which establishes accounting standards on the world level (Cooke et al, 1992, p xiii):

> We are in the presence of [a] very definite revolution in investment analysis and portfolio construction.... [And] The change in the way the subject is viewed will be as different as the way in which the structure of societies was viewed after the French Revolution.... (Damant, 1992, p 7)

The key factors in this revolution, according to Damant, are:

• the globalisation of finance markets;
• new information technologies;
• the development of new theories regarding portfolio and investment modelling.

These are intimately connected and they are transforming working practices, concepts and assumptions within the hierarchy of knowledge of the retirement savings and fund managers' world.

Globalisation of finance markets

Globalisation impacts on the various investment fund experts in several ways and the following simply touches on some of the more significant points for this discussion. Share trading on the stock markets around the globe is much faster than in the past and it is now virtually a constant process of buying and selling, irrespective of when a national stock exchange is open, with a fragile balance between trust and risk (Boden, 2000). Computerised databases transfer stocks and capital at speeds that make it difficult for national accounting and regulatory bodies to ensure compliance with domestic standards without slowing down, and thereby disadvantaging, their domestic finance and investment market. The investment manager who fails to engage with computer databases "will simply be too late in the vast majority of instances; and there will be nowhere in the world where he [sic] can go to apply the more traditional and slower techniques" (Damant, 1992, p 17). The US has been to the fore, but following the 1995 Pensions Act in the UK, pressure is likely to increase from both within the finance markets, with fund managers lagging even further behind other investors unless they adapt, and from without as trustees seek lower charges and better performance (Myners, 2001).

Information technologies

In tandem, globalisation and information technology are likely to transform the way investment managers do their job. This will impact on even the most senior experts. But, like other industries where information technology has been introduced, much depends on who controls and designs the systems. Contests between expert bodies of knowledge are akin to contests over the labour process in other industries, with similar patterns of jockeying for control and influence (Edwards, 1979; Knights and Wilmott, 1986). Paradoxically, early retirement may be the fate of some senior staff who struggle to adapt or find that their particular skills have been computerised. Information technology is, after all, often about transferring knowledge from people to an 'expert system'. The administration of the funds, the records of members, contributions and so on, is also being transformed by information technology. These changes to the labour process throughout the fund management and financial services sector can be seen to be deskilling the traditional bodies of expert knowledge, but simultaneously 'enskilling' newer groups. Programmers, systems analysts and technical support staff, often with no experience of pension fund investment or administration, assume tremendous significance when change occurs, while established expert staff can view change as a 'nightmare' experience (*Pensions World*, March 2000).

New theories

Crucially important to this revolution are changes in the theoretical models that underpin the way information technology is used (Damant, 1992). The development of sophisticated investment and asset liability models can be seen as a discursive shift within the finance sector. However, these changes have not gone uncontested from within the industry. Blake (1992b), who provides some fascinating insights into the world of pension fund management, suggests that:

> As with many long term forecasting exercises, the predictions are only as good as the assumptions used to generate them. Some claim that the assumptions made about future investment returns are likely to be so unreliable that the modelling exercise provides very little value. Less sceptical proponents of asset liability modelling argue that the models are to be used and not believed, 'with the usefulness of the technique to provide a disciplined quantitative framework for qualitative discussions on investment policies'. (*The Financial Times*, 18 April 1991, in Blake, 1992b, p 75)

Skill and judgement regarding market trends are contrasted with the science of asset–liability modelling. Tensions between expert bodies of knowledge are likely to surface in this context.

> Another problem encountered with the technique comes from fund managers who are concerned that it gives an unwarranted role to actuaries in designing investment strategies, in particular asset allocation strategies. Actuaries have always had a role in determining a pension scheme's liabilities. But with the advent of asset–liability modelling, actuaries have begun to have a role in setting long-term asset allocation over, say, a 10-year horizon. Fund managers claim they are being reduced to the subsidiary role of determining short-term asset allocation and stock selection relative to this new long-term benchmark. (Blake, 1992b, p 76)

Leaving aside these demarcation disputes it should be plain that the ordinary fund member will usually be blissfully ignorant of the contested nature of these expert bodies of knowledge. Pension fund trustees, who in the UK have an inordinate amount of responsibility for little or no reward, are, however, expected to interrogate fund managers regarding their performance. Again, the task has been complicated by disagreements within the pension fund industry over how to assess performance and a tradition of anonymity for fund managers.

For example, passive investment strategies that simply follow market trends (indexing and tracking) are generally acknowledged to be 'less risky' than active fund management that can produce either a better, or worse, performance. But prior to 1995, fund managers in the UK were effectively protected from the prying eyes of trustees and members, and even the principles underpinning the fund managers' investment strategy were concealed (Blake, 1992a, p 79). The recurring criticism of pension fund managers is not that they jeopardise members' funds by their dangerous investment strategies but: "Most striking is fund managers' reluctance to stick their necks out. They prefer to stick to the consensus" (*The Observer*, 11 May 1997). As one advocate of active fund management put it in the fund managers' journal: "It is hard to think of another industry where the average is so willingly embraced as being the best option. It suggests that fear of under performance in the market is a more powerful force than hope of out performance" (*Pensions World*, August 2000). Similar concerns have been expressed in Australia.

Olsberg, who served as a trustee, concluded that fund managers had a 'herd mentality', took a short-term view of investment decisions and often did not achieve the sort of investment returns that might be expected (1997, pp 162-4). It is difficult to comprehend why this should be so, particularly if we recall the claims of orthodox political economy (see Chapter Two) that market forces promote competition and encourage entrepreneurial activity. Although members and trustees might be alarmed by more ambitious investment strategies, it is equally worrying that these highly paid experts adhere to such conservative norms.

Moreover, resistance to new theories of investment, to accountability and transparency in performance extends to information technology as well. Almost a decade after Damant (1992) heralded 'the revolution' that would transform investment management only:

> A few UK fund managers have made the necessary capital investment
> in the required technology to enable the settlement of large volumes of
> cross border trades in T+1 [the system adopted in the US]. Their
> continued over reliance on the manual processes means there is an
> intolerably high risk of failure. (*Pensions World*, January 2000)

Trustees are in an invidious position in assessing any prospective fund
managers. They are expected to inquire about the fund managers' strategies,
their technical capabilities, their performance and the fees to be charged.
In practice, the tendering process itself can often privilege the best sales
person over the best product. Fund managers will "fight like crazy" to
win a contract (*Pensions World*, June 2000). Thus prospective fund managers
with style and personality may be selected ahead of competitors who
have invested in the technology or offer lower fees (*Pensions World*, February
2000). This has been reflected in the growth in the number of consultants,
communications and public relations experts employed by fund
management teams. It appears that the management of information is
the latest 'expertise' and it may serve as a gloss that conceals traditional
practices and privileges within the industry. Alternatively, because the
task of the communications experts is to translate the technicians language
for the layperson, it may create opportunities for alternative, disruptive
and dissonant voices to be heard.

Discourse, dissidents and disruption

For Foucault the concept of discourse cannot be divorced from knowledge
or power. Simultaneously, knowledge is defined and ordered in disciplines
that have their own discursive frame, which is often seen as 'another
language' by the layperson. Various disciplines (for example, psychology,
sociology, economics) will often compete to 'explain' social problems,
but each will insist that its perspective and its vocabulary provide a more
accurate picture of the subject. Of course disciplines are not homogenous
and static but vibrant bodies of knowledge production capable of
embracing different opinions. Nevertheless, there are boundaries and as
Bauman (1992, pp 70-3) explains these are discursively constructed to
define the various disciplines' right to exist. Where these boundaries are
accepted by other discourses and disciplines they are elevated in the
hierarchy of knowledge. Thus, fund managers and actuaries will, sometimes
grudgingly, acknowledge the contribution and competencies of one
another, although there may be skirmishes over where the boundaries

are drawn – hence the analogy mentioned earlier with demarcation disputes. Where these discursive formations have more difficulty is when they are confronted with claims for recognition from outside the established disciplines.

Challenging and questioning expert opinion has been a feature of many social and welfare movements since the early 1970s. Medics provide perhaps the best example of experts who, until very recently, the layperson was just expected to defer to. Medics now acknowledge the importance of sociological approaches to 'illness', and while sociologists do not 'do' medicine they regularly pose questions and challenge the hegemony of the medical profession. So why should retirement pensions be different? Complexity is often cited as the main reason; however, given that medicine is far from simple, this is hardly a sufficient explanation. Furthermore, it is possible to see a number of pressures coming together since the late 1980s that are beginning to disrupt the discourse of the retirement pensions experts.

First, there are changes that derive, in the main, from within the discursive frame of the experts. Again it is worth recalling Damant's (1992) claim of an impending 'revolution'. Global markets and information technology have enabled the development of new theoretical approaches and methodologies in the management of pension fund portfolios. As we have seen, each of these factors has had the effect of interrupting the traditionally conservative discourses within the pension fund industry. In the UK the growth of private/personal pensions, along with the development of AVCs and a host of other savings and investment packages such as TESSAs and ISAs, promoted a more consumer-oriented culture within the industry. In the US consumers had for some time been asking awkward questions and in Australia the SGC, with the phenomenal increase in superannuation coverage from the mid-1980s, had a similar impact. Market competition has clearly encouraged providers to consider how best to present their product and to account for their activities. The promotion and advertising of pension products in the UK, discussed in the previous chapter and typified by the slogan "pensions made simple" (Scottish Widows), illustrated the industry's belief that they needed to make their products more accessible. In isolation these changes in the internal dynamics, market operations and activities of the pensions industry would probably have posed enough questions to have interrupted the complacency of the pension experts. Moreover, retirement pensions made front page news in the UK in the early 1990s and since then there has been very little complacency and a constant stream of interruptions for the experts to deal with.

A combination of the fiasco over the misselling of private pensions and Robert Maxwell's creative accounting with the Mirror Group Newspapers pension fund severely disrupted the pensions world. The misselling scandal was a clear case of poorly informed buyers confronted with sales staff with powerful incentives to sell. The need for consumers to be well informed was repeatedly asserted and the private pension providers were later named and shamed by government, but it was the newly recruited sales staff who were fired. In the Maxwell case the language of fraud and theft were shocking enough but the implications went much further, querying the experts' expertise and the science they were engaged in. The scale of events alone was remarkable with £453 million (in 1992) simply 'lost'. The Goode report that was commissioned to look into events following the Maxwell case identified poor accounting procedures, lack of monitoring, inadequate checks and balances, dubious decision making, insolvency and a general lack of clear reliable information that would assist members and their trustees. Nor was the Maxwell case an exception: "There were other major failures, if on a less spectacular scale" (Goode, 1993, p 361). The scandal went to the very heart of every pension fund and raised questions for anyone planning their retirement on the basis of getting an occupational pension. "The pensions promise" that Goode identified as underpinning the retirement plans of millions, if not most households in the UK, had been broken. Not surprisingly "some commentators have derided trust law as medieval and archaic, and having failed its purpose in the pensions field" (Goode, 1993, p 187). And for anyone looking for an example the 34-page glossary of terms provided in the report to make pensions 'simple' is a testament to the archaic and complex language of the pensions industry.

Following Goode, the Myners review (2001) has also called for more and better information to be provided to members. This has been interpreted by the industry as "getting members to read communications" they are sent, "getting the membership to pay attention and understand" and a "need to educate members" (*Pensions World*, January 2001). This reads more like a frustrated head teacher calling for silence in assembly than an attempt to engage with members. And these comments were supposed to be promoting the need for better communications!

The perceived solution is the appointment of 'pension communications specialists' and to encourage scheme members to develop a sense of ownership and control over their pension. However, to date, access to information is severely constrained and, in general, the trustees and fund managers are not obliged to explain how, or why, they reached a particular decision. There is a general presumption that discretionary powers are exercised in good faith and the basis for any decision need not be disclosed to members or their representatives. In practice the information provided usually consists of a summary of the individual members' accrued pension rights and a vague and general summary of the fund's performance. Annual reports usually say who the auditors were and provide the names of the trustees, actuaries, custodians and organisations that the fund has dealt with over the previous year. But information on precisely what these people did, how they invested the funds, or why they chose one option rather than another, is rarely disclosed (IDS, 1999, pp 313-5). Whether the Myners review (2001) will open the door on how the funds and trustees operate remains to be seen. For now it seems the experts' response is to pass meaningless notes out of closed meetings and then to complain that the readers were not interested in the contents.

Calls for ethical investment and the demands of the individual consumer provide further voices of dissent and dissonance for the experts' discourse. The requirement (since July 2000) in the UK that fund trustees provide a SIP can be seen as a first step towards members having more say over the funds.

> The recurring questions of whose money is being used by fund managers and how they ought to use it responsibly, are implicitly raised by this requirement. The relative success of sanctions against South Africa, which saw pension funds putting pressure on companies to withdraw or risk losing investment funds, has been a strategy adopted by other campaign groups such as Amnesty International and Greenpeace. Socially Responsible Investment (SRI) is heralded as "a way to combine ethics with financial and industrial concerns and the pensions industry is ideally situated to do this" (*Pensions World*, January 2001).

Ensuring that funds are not invested in child labour, experiments on animals, the sex industry, environmentally damaging developments or armaments, is not easy for fund managers. Goode reported that in many cases it was unreasonable to expect anyone, in any scheme, to be able to say precisely where funds were invested at a given moment (1993, p 364). The constant movement of funds, often using systems that follow market trends (for example a computer model that tracks the FTSE 100) makes it virtually impossible for trustees to know, or for fund managers to say, where the funds are. Those fund managers who rely on tracking the markets, with lower fees for the fund, will be tempted to simply screen out certain companies. However, this is a negative approach and can see investment returns dip, contrary to the members' best financial interests and the trustees' duties. The problems outlined earlier that the ACTU confronted in relation to directed investment are also raised by SRI. Trustees have to reconcile any SIP with the members' desire for a decent pension. If the SIP is open to debate among the membership (currently a rare event in the UK), it raises the nightmare scenario for trustees and fund managers of a political 'bun fight'.

For example, screening out from a fund portfolio a very profitable company based in Northern Ireland that is widely reported, but not proven, to discriminate on the basis of religion, would probably be contentious. It only requires one member who does not share the trustees' ethical stance to take legal action. Alternatively, fund managers may be asked by trustees to engage in dialogue with companies to promote change if there is a suspicion of unethical or irresponsible behaviour. But how much dialogue is it reasonable for fund managers to engage in? "Done properly, engagement is a time consuming process and requires a team of experienced staff dedicated to this role" (*Pensions World*, June 2000).

Fund managers are not ethical envoys and their expertise certainly does not run to resolving ethical and political debates. Extending the parameters of the discourse to include ethics may well see the voices of some of the excluded raised, along with the fees fund managers charge. Moreover, trustees are entering a legal minefield.

> Trustees must think very carefully about what their function truly is ... they must follow the legal requirements carefully. They can't have their own private political or moral agenda. There is a great legal risk for trustees who have not understood what their obligations to their beneficiaries really are. (*Pensions World*, January 2001)

Legal discourse is ranked high on the hierarchy of knowledge and this is likely to play a vital part in any redrawing of the boundaries within which ethics, fund managers and trustees must be located.

For individuals prepared to seek out a personal private pension there are more opportunities to exercise ethical and moral rights. A number of ethical funds exist that purport to offer investors a good return, even in dedicated areas such as global sustainability (see, for example, www.sustainability-index.com). Alternative experts, with a different discursive frame, have begun to emerge whose task is to make sense of developments for consumers. As we saw in the previous chapter media experts and lobby groups using information technology can provide a voice to challenge and query the market traders. Consumer law, media exposés and social movements that identify malpractice and unethical behaviour can also provide a dissenting voice. Unfortunately there is a time lag before bad practices, misselling and unethical behaviour are exposed, and even more time before this can seep into the popular consciousness.

Power, visibility and a wider discourse

The final feature of a perspective informed by Foucault's work is power. It should be clear from the previous discussion that power is embodied in discourse and knowledge. Power is manifest in virtually all forms of social interaction, but it is not necessarily used consciously or maliciously. It is because expert bodies of knowledge are seen as 'doing good' that clients, consumers and welfare subjects generally concede power to them. Welfare users, whichever form of welfare they rely on, are positioned within a framework of power, knowledge and discourse as *the* object/subject of the experts' gaze. The retired population, the pensioner and the fund member are the subject categories that are observed, measured and classified (Katz, 1996). The expert is the active data collector, while the subject of the gaze is expected to be passive. It is not that subject identities *are* passive or powerless, they frequently contradict any such idea, but they do usually and unwittingly collude in a socially scripted power game. But it is also a game that privileges some players and can cruelly expose the socially incompetent players. Failure to go through the 'proper channels' or an inability to voice a complaint, to, in effect, lack the necessary information about how the game is being played, is more common for the poorest, for minority ethnic groups and subject identities that are marginalised or stigmatised. Thus, retirees in general are stigmatised by association with 'the elderly', a subject category that is one step removed from the pensioner and one further step from death. Here it is important to recall the points made in Chapter One regarding the discourse of 'infantilisation' that affects older people (Hockey and James, 1993). This discourse equates old age with childlike qualities of dependency and vulnerability. It was suggested that the older person becomes the *other*, estranged from *us* – the younger observers. One effect may be to subdue the voice of the older person and to force the retiree/pensioner into a dependent category, silencing their legitimate voice. Such a discursive frame may be applied to all pensioners, but it is likely to have greater resonance for those who rely on the public pension. This is such a powerful discourse that many older people will themselves say that they "don't want to be a burden" (Warnes, 1993).

Moreover, there is wider discourse that affects welfare in general. In the UK, as in many other countries, public welfare for lone mothers, unemployed people and disabled people have all been subject to scrutiny and criticism. Pensioners, as part of this broader constituency who rely on public welfare, have been tainted with the stigma reserved for the poor. It should be recalled that Sinfield (1978) highlighted the visibility and relative powerlessness of those who rely on public welfare in comparison to those who can access fiscal and occupational welfare. Using the SDW, he stresses the uneven distribution of power among welfare recipients generally. Public welfare claimants will be less powerful than other pensioner groups because they alone are perceived as a dependent subject category, and like other dependent groups they will be stigmatised by their dependency. The deserving/undeserving distinction in the provision of welfare has often hinged on the idea that independence is a good thing; deserving of sympathy and support. The status of the dependent person is, in contrast, always suspect. Historically, those who have had to depend on public welfare are the subject of a stern gaze that queries their status as full citizens. Within this broader framework of power the public pensioner is singled out for further questioning, means testing and inquiries into their personal circumstances. Their failure to make adequate provisions for themselves has been a constant but insidious subtext since the 1980s in the UK (Bagguley and Mann, 1992; Dean, 1992). In contrast to the occupational pension and private pension fund member, the voice of the public pensioner can easily get lost. The categories of customer, client and consumer can provide more scope for querying the experts' claims to knowledge. For those who rely on the state/public pension, the scope for querying and questioning is, however, much more restrained. Reliance on public welfare serves, as Dean (1992) suggests, to define recipients as failures, portraying them as incapable of making 'better' provisions for themselves. When this is also overlain with socially constructed ideas about older people, particularly older women who are most likely to have to rely solely on the public pension, the effect may be to withdraw their status as adults. In so doing their visibility may promote the insidious idea that, like children in Victorian Britain, they may be seen but they should not be heard.

The crucial point is that the voices of some subject identities are more likely to be heard than others. Acknowledging the diverse constituencies that form the retired population may be fraught with difficulties (Bury, 1995). The possibilities for transforming the experience of retirement for the poorest 20–30% of the pensioner population may well depend on a further shift in the discourse, one that will hear the voice of the excluded. However, and like the concept of the heroic consumer in the previous chapter, there are limits to what is possible. The poorest pensioners are mainly women over the age of 75 for whom there are many material, not simply discursive, restraints on exercising their voices. Apart from any other considerations, time is not on the side of the poorest pensioners as they wait for the discursive shift to occur.

The post-structuralist response to the weakest voices is, it has to be admitted, rather ambiguous. It may be that all forms of welfare are "disciplining techniques" (Ewald, 1991), but some forms of discipline and punishment are less painful than others. The danger is that control, discipline and power – all of which operate throughout society and in many different contexts – are subsequently treated dispassionately and *as if* they are the same for all. But the meaning of power, the effects of control, and how these are experienced and felt by subject identities will vary significantly. In general Foucault was reluctant to discriminate between the plurality of discursive formations and locations of power; a position that makes any discussion of social justice, equity or interests very difficult. This in turn makes it very difficult to imagine how an unreconstructed analysis using Foucault's approach could engage with policy, since even the most tentative engagement turns the commentator into an "unwitting participant in the reconstitution of power" (Hillyard and Watson, 1996, pp 341–2).

Summary and assessment

Foucault clearly provides some important insights and his approach has the potential to illuminate some of the less visible features of the SDW. However, Foucault and post-structuralism have only recently gained an audience within social policy. As Hillyard and Watson (1996) noted there is a tension, to put it mildly, between an approach that interrogates the experts and queries their claims to knowledge, and the study of social policy which is founded on the idea of the expert. Unfortunately, this tension has enabled the pensions and retirement experts to promote their discourse and to ignore any dissident voices. Had this been deliberately orchestrated it would be a clever ploy. If the secret of power is to make it appear onerous or difficult to manage then retirement and pensions policies have succeeded in keeping their secrets. Given that legal and medical discourses, in general, are also tedious and inaccessible, the neglect of the pensions industry is significant. In part this neglect derives from the political agendas pursued in the last quarter of the 20th century. While women's experience of the medical profession and the law has combined with feminist scholarship to query the power, knowledge and discourse of the legal and medical professions, this has rarely been replicated by subject identities in the pensions arena (Donzelot, 1979; Sim, 1990; Smart, 1995).

Whereas other approaches discussed in this book assert a particular standpoint and stress conflicting interests, post-structuralism queries any claims to knowledge, interests or expertise. They do not believe interests, usually reduced to class but also linked to gender and/or ethnicity, provide the key to unlocking the door behind which the 'real world' can be revealed. Rather post-structuralists suggest there may be a number of doors and one key will not unlock them all. As we have seen, a strength of this approach is to turn attention onto those who claim a privileged place in the world of pensions. Fund managers, actuaries and advisors promote a power/knowledge/discourse that marginalises the voice of the pensioner and prospective retiree. However, their knowledge is open to question, their discourse can be interrupted and their power undermined.

The science and skill claimed by the pensions experts is profoundly suspect. Actuarial assumptions, interpretations of demographic data, risk assessment and fund management decisions are all framed by the boundaries of the discursive formation (Bauman, 1992, p 71). Once we step outside the boundaries we are able to query these knowledge claims, but simultaneously unable to engage in the discourse. Alternative experts are, within their own consumer-oriented arena of knowledge, capable of querying the claims of those who set the boundaries and, to a degree, asserting an alternative voice. Likewise the misselling and Maxwell scandals have required the experts to address a lack of confidence in the 'pensions promise' and the Goode report (1993) can be seen as one response. Another response might be to assert new modes of information, particularly information technology, that will be more scientific and less subject to human error. This has already begun with investment decisions, actuarial calculations and risk assessments increasingly relying on computer programs designed to ensure greater reliability. While there are possibilities for subject identities to assert their voices in the short term, this may simply witness a new group of experts emerge with more insidious means of collecting data, quantifying risk and calculating investment returns.

Alternatively, because the task of the communications experts is to translate the technicians language for the layperson, it may create opportunities for disruptive and dissonant voices to be heard. Thus as customers and clients, occupational and private pensioners may be able to engage with the experts on the boundaries. A more consumerist and consumer-oriented discourse may enable experts representing the subject identities a greater say. However, in conjunction with the wider discourse of welfare reform this may simply reinforce the marginal status of those who have to rely on the public pension. The example of the Australian trades union movement, which retreated from a position that was driven by political and social objectives, into a position where they conceded that the experts knew best, does not bode well. Arguably it was always a rather benign view to think that organised labour would articulate the claims of those it too has excluded (Mann, 1992). Increasingly it seems that responsibility is being devolved to the individual by an agenda that neglects and negates the discourse of social justice. Thus, the 'deserving' shall in future be those who were a good actuarial risk and the 'undeserving' those who could not afford the contributions.

However, in a world where scepticism is common, experts are scrutinised more closely and their claims tested. For example, in the US confidence in fund managers has apparently waned as a growing proportion of the population have become familiar with Internet share trading and are able to use their retirement savings for this purpose. In effect, individuals are being encouraged to become their own fund managers (*Newsnight*, BBC2, 31 July 2000). How long though before an 'unethical fund' providing better investment returns is available? Not everyone will do the 'right thing' or agree what that might be. Some will seek out the best investment whatever it is funding. Moreover, and as we saw in the previous chapter, the individuating effects of a consumer society may further reinforce the social divisions of welfare in relation to rights and responsibilities. Consequently, consumer citizens with private/personal provisions may seek expert advice and redress through consumer law; members of occupational pension schemes must trust trustees and fund managers to engage; public pensioners can ask for more but their voice is only faintly heard, while informal welfare draws a veil of silence over its recipients. The strengths and weaknesses of the post-structuralist approach can be summarised as follows.

Strengths of the post-structuralist approach

- A sophisticated and general theory that avoids economic reductionism.
- It draws attention to the experts and institutions such as fund managers and the funds themselves.
- It can easily embrace all forms of welfare and does not presume that only public welfare is worthy of our attention.
- Power is viewed as a complex component in social relations and is not simply 'read off' from vested interests.
- It recognises that exclusion from the 'discursive frame' can be significant.
- Social divisions can arise from the way knowledge is defined and promoted – highlighting the need for access to modes of information.
- It embraces social movements that form around 'subject identities'.

Weaknesses of the post-structuralist approach

- It can overstate the disciplinary potential of welfare.
- It can neglect economic power.
- It may assign discourses too much power.
- It is not clear how the hierarchies of knowledge and 'voice' arise.
- The failures of technocrats, experts, and discursive formations can be overlooked.
- It can underestimate traditional subject identities, such as class, 'race' and gender.
- It is unclear what the alternatives are, or what would be 'better'.

FIVE

Risk and post-traditional welfare

Introduction

The first task of this chapter is to try and clarify the key features of a post-modern perspective. Distinguishing this from accounts that observe post-modernity without necessarily subscribing to a post-modern frame and from accounts that are 'post-traditional' is equally important. The observer must not be confused with the enthusiastic participant. However, before doing so it would be reasonable to make the case for including a chapter on post-modern/post-traditional perspectives, since this could be seen as an unwarranted intrusion by some ill-mannered sociological neighbours who mock the cherished, but 'kitsch' possessions within the home of social policy (Mann, 1998; Soper, 1993).

Although a number of distinct and different insights are provided by observers of post-modernity (Bauman, 1992). post-scarcity society (Harvey, 1994), risk society (Beck, 1992) and commentators on post-traditional society (Giddens, 1994, 1998), the number and type of 'posts' alone can be confusing to the uninitiated. Here five themes are seen as significant and although some are peculiar to one 'post' perspective, others are shared, albeit with a few quibbles over the degree of consensus.

- First, there is a suggestion that a number of social changes have combined in a manner that means society is very different today from 50 years ago when the 'modern' welfare state was established.
- Second, these changes pose fundamental questions about the ability of any form of public welfare to address the desires and needs of the population.
- Third, some of the brightest sociological minds are persuaded that contemporary developed societies, like Britain, the US and Australia, are qualitatively different to their predecessors, wrestling by and large with the problems of success rather than failure. Such claims have to be taken seriously because they appear to have had some influence,

even infiltrating the vocabulary of politicians. The agenda set by those at the 'top table' can clearly be significant.

• Fourth, difference and diversity, part of the mantra of post-modernity, have also been key themes for specific welfare constituents. Thus there may be pressures and processes that are 'bottom up' as well as 'top down' that correspond with a post-modern/post-traditional perspective.

• Fifth, and finally, the central themes of a post-modern frame – risk, diversity, anti-universalism, ambiguity, desire and difference – have profound implications for the future of welfare in general and retirement pensions in particular.

Post-modernism and post-traditional responses

The first and least contentious point that post-modern/post-traditional approaches make is that developed societies are qualitatively different today to 50 years ago, but welfare provisions have not changed accordingly. Advocates of public welfare services are seen as stuck in a post Second World War of austerity, minimal universalism and traditions that no longer apply. Marshall's model of citizenship, along with the Keynesian economic policy that underpinned the New Deal in the US, Menzie's welfare model in Australia and Beveridge's blue print for Britain are simply out of step with the needs of people today. We now live in a world where classes are fragmented, families and households can be constituted according to preferences rather than patriarchal and parental pressures, gender and sexual identities appear to be more ambiguous than even 30 years ago, production relations are less important than consumption patterns, traditional political allegiances are less reliable, economic growth creates environmental problems and new social movements dare to challenge their assigned status as victims (for example, the disability rights movement). Simultaneously, finding solutions to the new social problems has become more difficult because faith in the experts seems to be less secure and national governments claim to be helpless in the face of globalisation. Amid the ambiguity and uncertainty that supposedly typify contemporary social life in the most developed economies the place of welfare policy is especially vulnerable. The social engineers and economists who constructed 'the' welfare state are, at best, portrayed as benign but misguided, at worst they are damned for their imposition of an all encompassing universalism that smothered difference and diversity. Social policy, therefore, has to 'rethink' itself (Williams, 1989, 1996; Giddens, 1994, 1998; Carter, 1998; Adam et al, 2000; Lewis et al, 2000).

By and large post-modernity heralds a future in which we can be less confident and less secure. Scepticism has replaced faith in the natural (and social) sciences claims to knowledge, with everyone prepared to question any claims to truth. Post-modern societies make redundant the old frameworks of analysis that promoted welfare reform and require a break with traditions of all kinds. It calls for a more sensitive approach to social divisions, social identities and diversity that does not reduce these to grander monolithic accounts or subsume them as subheadings. The contrast is often made between the confident and progressive ideas of the 19th century and the growing doubts and concerns that are supposed to typify the period since the Second World War. A crucial feature of all post-modernist accounts is their deep scepticism regarding the construction of the 'good society'. The 20th century, it is argued, provides a catalogue of social engineering feats that have been misconstrued, misconceived and mistaken. From Bentham to Beveridge the attempt at social engineering has been unsuccessful and since the Second World War faith in the idea of a 'good society' has been eroded. Thus, the very idea that we can promote social policies that try to engineer the future could be seen as in conflict with the post-modernists' approach (Taylor-Gooby, 1994; Thompson and Hoggett, 1996).

Despite the very real tensions between a subject (social policy) that is quintessentially concerned with promoting a better society and an analytic framework that challenges such claims, this does not necessarily mean they contradict one another. It is important to remember that there is a well-established critical tradition within social policy that has consistently expressed scepticism about the ability to engineer society. Likewise many of the newer social movements that are cited by post-modernists as examples of how politics have changed, have themselves focused on welfare issues. For example, identity, difference, agency and diversity, all now closely associated with the church of post-modernity, have been much debated within social policy circles and for some time (Titmuss, 1958, p 14; Mann, 1986, 1998; Williams, 1989, 1996).

Post-modernity might also be conceived of as the stage that follows modernity, but this implies that there is some line we can track from the past to the present and that is too deterministic a view. Instead what is significant is the break with tradition, the fragmentation of traditional social and political constituencies, and the loss of faith in solutions predicated on traditional analyses (Bauman, 1995). Consequently, and rather than clumsily referring to post-modernists and post-traditionalists, the concern here is primarily with accounts that emphasise the post-traditional (Beck, 1992, 2000; Giddens, 1994, 1998). For post-traditionalists the key to understanding contemporary societies is the constant whittling away of ideas that rely on, and simply appeal to, tradition. Thus the seeds of modernity contained ideas that were, it now seems, always likely to produce some exotic fruit. Sown in the West during the Enlightenment, the seeds of change germinated during the 19th century and came to fruition in the mid-20th century. Stretching the analogy further, industrial capitalism might be portrayed as the stake that held modernity while it was watered by the 'other' world of the empire. A free market, free choice and a free range of ideas, the inconvenient but essential fertiliser that accompanied capitalism's development in the West, all queried and questioned existing traditions. For Marx the freedom capitalism granted was always constrained by the overarching control of capital and in tension with the conformity the economy demanded. Capitalism nominally promoted individual independence (a 'free' labour market for example) and a questioning of traditions that could conflict with the operation of the market (for example, the need for 'wage' slaves). Initially such questioning of tradition was confined to the 'public sphere' – free speech, freedom of belief, free elections, free labour – but it has increasingly focused on traditions more usually linked with the 'private'. For Giddens the attack on tradition, associated with Enlightenment thought, has only really reached maturity now that a number of social life traditions – family, gender roles and sexuality – have begun to be questioned (1994, pp 5-6). The effect is fragmentation, individuation and uncertainty as communities, constituencies and categories that previously served to anchor identities no longer retain their grip. The loosening of traditional grips can, however, be both liberating and bewildering at the same time. Free to choose, we are also compelled to reflect on our choices: "Attempting to anchor our sense of self in this maelstrom of social life, to create ontological security in a world of rapid social change, we each as individuals face the task of constructing for ourselves our biographical narratives" (Roseneil and Seymour, 1999, p 4).

Consequently, with identities being rapidly reconstructed it makes no sense for politicians and policy makers to appeal to traditional constituencies. For retirees this uncertainty and disruption to what was previously taken for granted applies as strongly as it does for any other social category. Expectations have risen and many retirees, like virtually everyone else, do not see themselves, or the world, in the way pensioners might have done 30–40 years ago. Who in the 1940s could have anticipated the desire of pensioners to have, for example, televisions and cars, let alone holiday homes in the sunshine resorts of Spain, Florida and Queensland? The shift in what people expect from retirement has also been reflected in the way some retirees see themselves. Identities do not evaporate on retirement and how these will be articulated, interpreted and addressed will be discussed towards the end of the chapter. The evidence of change and the successes of the past in raising living standards and life expectancy are, however, used by some observers to suggest that traditional ideas of retirement and of pension rights need to be reviewed (Giddens, 1994, 1998). It is in this context that the meaning of concepts such as risk, exclusion and ethics assumes tremendous significance (Levitas, 2000). Despite the benign vocabulary of politicians the meanings may be very different, depending on whether we are looking from the top down or the bottom up. I shall return to these accounts shortly, but there is one other post-modern approach that, while related, merits consideration separately since it does not rest easily within the post-traditional school.

Performing policy

Some accounts of post-modernity can initially seem rather obscure to students of social policy who are usually more concerned with substantive issues. Even within the broad church of post-modernism there are sectarian spats with readers encouraged to "forget Foucault" (Baudrillard, 1987), or "forget Baudrillard" and simply "sod Baudrillard" (Rattansi, 1995, p 339; Rojek and Turner, 1993). In these circumstances anyone concerned with welfare might be forgiven for dismissing the histrionics of social theorists. However, that would be to overlook some interesting ideas and runs the risk of returning social policy to the days of "arthritic empiricism" (Taylor-Gooby, 1981). For example, the idea of 'performativity' offers a novel perspective on the presentation of policy, something that has come to obsess politicians and their press secretaries. This approach draws on the work of Lyotard (1984), who certainly demands much of a social policy audience, but Stephen Ball (1998) has shown that there are some fascinating insights for those who persist. Thus, Ball explores the confusing and apparently incoherent tensions in education policy using Lyotard's formulation of performativity.

The key features of this approach that might be applied to retirement pensions are the presentation of information and the management of social problems. As we saw in Chapter Three, presenting the prospective pensioner as an active consumer, enjoying their retirement, planning their lives and constructing their lifestyle identity is a key feature of the pensions industry sales pitch. The retiree as consumer is contrasted with the public pensioner as dependent. The presentation of potential market solutions, via private pensions, serves to fragment the prospective pensioner population. Citizen consumers have primacy over mere citizens (public pension recipients) in the hierarchy of legitimacy and claims (Ball, 1998). The citizen consumer has reflected on their desires and made appropriate arrangements. In contrast, the pensioner who relies on the state, who has not reflected on what sort of life they want in retirement, is at best a sad victim, at worst a burden on their fellow consumer citizens. Although other accounts can claim to address similar shifts in terms of discourse or ideology, the notion of performativity takes a rather novel approach. An important feature of this is the way the observer/viewer is engaged in the performance.

> For example, in January 2001 the British government advertised an information pack that was intended to promote the new stakeholder pension scheme. The advertisement began with two dogs, border collies – intelligent working dogs it should be noted – herding sheep and reflecting on the recent retirement of another dog. Using the techniques of films like 'Babe' – so the viewer has a cultural reference point that distances the advertisement from previously dry government information/propaganda material – the advertisement dubbed male voices onto the dogs. Throughout the advertisement it had a 'matey' feel to it, with an engaging scene of 10-15 dogs having a retirement 'drink' in a brook and being somewhat 'laddish', as if they were in a pub.

Leaving aside the anthropomorphism, the key message was that while the array of pensions options appeared confusing, the Department of Social Security (DSS) had an information pack that would clarify matters. Information is conveyed through performance, the observer is expected to identify with the performers and then to reflect on the appropriate response. In this case the viewer is meant to seek further information and then a suitable pension provider. The performance thus involves the observer as well – indeed, audience participation is the objective.

According to Ball (1998) performativity 'works' in three ways. It disciplines, transforms and has the effect of reframing the language of 'problems'. Television advertisements are particularly useful in exploring these themes because they have to engage the viewer without demanding concentration (Ball, 1998, p 197). Although the advertisement given in the example was much easier on the viewer than the drab presentation of government information in the past – often a male civil servant in a grey suit talking directly at the viewer with a headmaster's paternalistic tone – it has to be remembered that this was *not* an advertisement. It was a government information film intended to change behaviour. Although care is often needed when interpreting cultural representations, the scope for ambiguity in this case was severely constrained. Viewers were clearly meant to think about their retirement, to plan and to ensure they were informed. Men are the apparent target audience and a responsible, respectable working-class man (represented by the intelligent collies) ought to reflect on their future needs. This traditional message echoes Smiles' Victorian edicts on 'self-help' (Gosden, 1973), but it is presented in a non-traditional manner. 'Real' men, it is acknowledged, go to the pub and enjoy a few beers, but they must also take responsibility. The cultural ideal represented in this case is both 'masculine' and working class (Connell, 1995). It replays some familiar stereotypes, but simultaneously extends the prospect of reflexivity beyond the middle classes (Featherstone and Hepworth, 1989; Phillipson, 1998). A few weeks after the advertisement was released foot and mouth disease was widespread and the advertisement was dropped. The dogs, like many manual workers, were presumably all made redundant, having just started their stakeholder pensions. Irony, uncertainty, risk and performativity combined; an exemplar of post-modern times.

Traditionally government information that tried to change behaviour in this way might have been dismissed as propaganda, but because it lacks any hectoring tone such a charge seems ridiculous. And yet there certainly was, and is, a desire on the part of government to transform behaviour, to promote a 'reflexive' self-regulating individual and, in so doing, to shift the perception and language of the problems they confront (Rose, 1994, 1996). Educating the masses by rote, simply telling them what to do, has been a pedagogic failure. Populations must 'learn', they can no longer be 'taught' and in order to learn they need certain 'skills'. Skills require training and that is a 'hands on' activity (Smart, 1992, pp 169-76).

> For example, the US government was quick to use interactive websites that were designed to educate potential retirees about their pension rights. By clicking on birth dates and prospective retirement ages to 'find' their likely pension entitlements, there was a presumption that people would 'learn' from the exercise and not expect the same rights as previous generations because of population ageing. Thus their benefits are conditional and the conditions vary

according to 'objective' facts, such as life expectancy based on aggregate health data. Younger people 'learn' that they must choose whether to retire later or if not, to accept a reduced level of benefit or make provisions of their own. Thus, it was hoped they would also learn to be active, reflexive individuals in the process.

Rather than bureaucrats and bureaucracies constructing an iron cage that restrains us, as Max Weber suggested, we now have technocrats installing programs that are user/customer friendly. Application forms can be downloaded, information immediately accessed and 'rights' clarified, and all via the Web. Of course the need to meet claimants and their ability to press for discretionary improvements is also reduced by, what are in effect, distance learning packages. Contentious or speculative proposals can also be placed on the Web, putting them in the public domain 'for consultation'. But without any furore from a press secretary (telling journalists what to focus on), they can either remain buried, or dug up – once the possibility of a stench has subsided. As we saw in the previous chapter, 'modes of information' (Poster, 1984) are vitally important and post-modernists like Lyotard have done much to highlight them. An electronic Web now replaces the iron cage. Less obviously restraining, and with so many seductive strands of information, it appears quite 'open' at first sight. However, as was said of the old Poor Law, and despite the softer texture: "It is a prison, with a milder name" (Crabbe, 1810, cited in Thompson, 1968, p 295).

Performativity, as it is understood here, can also illuminate aspects of political theatre. Increasingly, content takes a back seat to style, as politicians use media experts and 'spokespersons' to release information on policy changes. If press releases can be timed to conveniently coincide with parliamentary recesses, public holidays or alongside bigger news stories, attention may be deflected from those policy proposals that would otherwise attract criticism. In Britain, 'New' Labour's proposals for pension reform in the late 1990s underwent a lengthy period of gestation and, it might be thought, were delayed to ensure that they could be presented at a time when they would be best received. In the interim there was a great deal of rhetoric about life-planning, stakeholders, clients, individuals with duties and citizen consumers that set the scene for the grander theatrical exercise of establishing 'new ambitions for our country' and a 'partnership in pensions' (Deacon and Mann, 1997; DSS 1998a, 1998b). The proposals were, as Alan Walker (1999) has illustrated, primarily concerned with shifting responsibilities in the future rather than addressing the needs of current pensioners. Again, the central message was educational – future retirees must learn to plan and not look to the state. The presentation of retirement policy corresponds with the way this is to be managed and in both cases the aim is to promote a more reflexive, market-oriented individual, prepared to undertake 'lifelong learning'. Politicians think as much, if not more, about how to present proposals for reform as they do about the policy itself, ambiguity and double-speak often being facilitated by previous statements aimed at massaging public opinion or the pretence of consultation. For example, in the UK the meaning and significance of 'stakeholders' was changed beyond recognition between the initial idea being floated in the mid-1990s and the tepid reforms that emerged (Field, 1996; Walker, 1999).

'New' Labour, with the 'new' being part of the rebranding exercise, were not, however, the first to use spin doctors to perform tricks with the presentation and language of social reform. Keating in Australia, Clinton in the US and governments in many other countries had already replaced economic management with economic rationalism, collective responsibility with social responsibility, the obligations of the privileged with the obligations of the disadvantaged, and the positive role of public welfare in maintaining social cohesion to a negative account in which it caused social exclusion (Pusey, 1991; Levitas, 1996; Jordan, 1998). Again, the example of the misselling of private pensions in Britain ought to serve as a warning to those who are now promoting stakeholder schemes. The sleight of the invisible hand working its magic in the finance markets only becoming visible when it was clear that there was no rabbit to pull out of the hat (Disney and Whitehouse, 1992; Ginn and Arber, 2000).

Beyond 'Left and Right' – or simply getting in the 'Third Way'?

To the fore in advocating a break with traditional approaches to welfare, and specifically retirement, has been Anthony Giddens. As Director of the London School of Economics and Political Science, an institution that has previously provided the Labour Party with some of its most noted intellectuals, Giddens is well placed to assess the prospects for welfare in the short to medium term. He was also on board the New Labour Party bandwagon before it looked certain to roll into government. Indeed, according to the dustcover of his book *The third way* (1998) he is: "Frequently referred to in the UK as Tony Blair's guru". Thus, when

Giddens asserts that: "We should be prepared to *rethink* the welfare state in a fundamental way" (1994, p 17, emphasis in original) it needs to be taken seriously. Moreover, he takes retirement pensions and the social construction of the pensioner as one of his main examples of how we might rethink our approach to welfare. In order to appreciate Giddens' account, and his influence, it is necessary to unpick some of the sociological strands from the social policy prescriptions.

Giddens is unashamedly eclectic, profoundly perceptive and, unlike 'true' post-modernists, adamant that social scientists should take a standpoint. That is, he rejects ideas that presume society is constantly improving and any idea of 'the evolution' of welfare (Fraser, 1984). Linear accounts of modernity and progress are flawed for numerous reasons, not least that the world consistently fails to conform to the anticipated outcomes. Neither Adam Smith nor Karl Marx, nor too many of their followers, can have predicted their respective successes and failures. Even the more modest efforts at social engineering associated with Keynes and Beveridge look overblown and underwhelming today. But if unpredictability and uncertainty typify 'the post-modern condition', this does not mean that we should adopt a Gallic shrug when confronted with "the rise of new totalitarianisms, the disintegration of the world's eco systems, a fortress society of the affluent in permanent struggle with the impoverished majority" (Giddens, 1994, p 253). "But nostalgia, indecision, and bewilderment do not exhaust the possibilities. Other more constructive responses are possible, responses which attempt to keep open the prospect of making progress by reconstituting a sense of what is possible, necessary and desirable" (Smart, 1992, pp 25-6).

Rather than uncritically celebrating the successes of capitalism – one of which is greater life expectancy for most people in the developed economies – or condemning the failures, such as ecological crisis, Giddens tries to set a new agenda for politics. He is not adopting the middle ground, a position that social engineering and social democratic politics has traditionally taken, but instead wants to go 'beyond Left and Right' (1994). We currently confront new political priorities and different social problems to those that concerned most social and political commentators for the bulk of the 20th century. For Giddens (1994) a central feature of these social changes has been the breaking down of tradition in various social settings. A post-traditional society might, therefore, be one characterised by the fragmentation of various established social categories and forms that were previously central to society and social policy. The massive increase in divorce rates, the increase in the number of lone parents, and a host of family forms that have step-parents, or do not have a clearly defined male 'breadwinner', highlights one feature of a less traditional, more diverse society. These changes have profound implications for social policy because it was traditionally assumed that households did, or should, conform to the male breadwinner model. As we saw in Chapter One, the assumption of a male breadwinner model of the family has had important implications for pension provisions, particularly in respect of women's access to a decent retirement income in their own right (Groves, 1987; Williams, 1989). With the possibility of pensions being split on divorce, uncertainty over the precise value of future retirement incomes is also increased. Turning the clock back to 1950 is simply not an option and predicating social policy on traditional categories that are no longer appropriate, assuming that they ever were, would clearly be a mistake.

Likewise, changes in employment patterns that point to a less secure future with more flexibility, periods of unemployment being experienced by more people and with higher rates of female labour market participation, all point to a break with mid-20th century expectations. Again there are implications for any pensions policy. Occupational pension schemes assume employees will remain with the same employer for many years, or decades if they are to accrue any reasonable pension rights.

Simultaneously, and despite the greater vulnerability of people in the labour market, expectations continue to outstrip the ability of the state to cope. Thus it seems there is a widespread desire for earlier exit from paid employment (OECD, 1998a; see Chapter Six of this book) and a belief that retirement income ought to enable retirees to enjoy their retirement. The slow but persistent decline in the value of the state pension, combined with a significant proportion of the population accessing occupational pensions in the 1950s and 1960s, means the consumption patterns of the retired population are diverging between 'the haves and have nots' (Bauman, 1998; Walker with Howard, 2000). Those that have any type of supplementary income via an occupational or private pension, or assets that they can realise, such as trading down in the housing market, will experience retirement very differently from those that have not. This in turn fragments traditional political allegiances and constituencies that supported universal pension provisions.

Universalism

Universalism itself has been a pillar of British social policy, ensuring there was a safety net for all. It was never entirely adequate and there was always an assumption that individuals ought to make additional arrangements if they wanted more than a basic income. However, for most of the 20th century pensioners were assumed (erroneously perhaps) to have rather modest expectations and despite the evidence of relative poverty there was an oft-stated commitment to a universal pension that would be funded by revenue collected by the state (Abel-Smith and Townsend, 1965; Townsend, 1979). So long as retirees appeared to be a deserving case, conforming to traditional views of them as needy, there was no problem. Once some of them appeared to be enjoying their retirement, taking holidays, running cars and apparently coping quite well on their pensions, the purpose of the state scheme began to be questioned. No one has doubted the need for a basic scheme, providing a minimal means-tested safety net, but there have been doubts about the need for universal coverage. The unfunded NI scheme in Britain (with the tax and social security systems in Australia and the US having a similar effect) involves a 'pay as you go' principle – with resources being transferred from the current labour force to fund current pensioners. Yet by the last quarter of the 20th century some retirees appeared to be quite comfortably off, while some (paid) workers were noticeably struggling on low incomes. There was, it seemed to some observers, something wrong with a system that took resources from people in full-time work who could not afford a holiday abroad to give to people who did not work, had a reasonable income and a holiday home in Spain (Seldon, 1996).

For Giddens the concept of a 'pensioner' and of a fixed age of retirement typify the rigidity of 'universalism' serving to identify and exclude older people.

> Old age at sixty-five is a creation, pure and simple, of the welfare state. It is a form of welfare dependency much more widespread than any of the dependencies noted by the rightist interpreters of the underclass. (1994, p 170) [And] A society that separates older people from the majority in a retirement ghetto cannot be called inclusive. (1998, p 120)

Thus he sees the state excluding older workers and discusses the marginalisation of older people, their desire to be fully active citizens and their potential contribution to society. He also feels that once they break out of their 'dependency ghetto' they may achieve greater political influence (1994, p 188). Unlocking the chains of welfare dependency is therefore a key feature of his account.

> The relief of dependency becomes a *generalized* aim in a post-scarcity society. Overcoming welfare dependency means overcoming the dependencies of productivism, and both can be combated in the same way. (1994, pp 193-4, emphasis in original)

Unfortunately, blocking the road to the 'third way' (1998) are some traditional obstacles, not least of which are the expectations of retirees and prospective retirees.

> Once established, benefits have their own autonomy ... expectations become 'locked in' and interest groups entrenched. Countries that have tried to reform their pensions systems, for example, have met with concerted resistance. We should have our pensions because we are 'old' (at age 60 or 65), we have paid our dues (even if they don't cover the costs), other people before have had them, everyone looks forward to retirement and so forth. Yet such institutional stasis is in and of itself a reflection of the need for reform. (Giddens, 1998, p 115-16)

Quite why pensioners and people looking forward to retirement should be so obstructive, given that they would be liberated from welfare dependency, is unclear. On the one hand he suggests 'entrenched interests' are the problem, although these are not specified and it is difficult to see any of the lobby groups representing pensioners as particularly powerful. Moreover, if marginalisation and exclusion typify the situation of older people, as he claims, it seems unlikely that they are simultaneously so politically powerful that they can prevent reform. On the other hand he claims his reforms would be in the interests of pensioners themselves. By claiming that he understands what is in the interests of pensioners, but that they are unable to appreciate this fact, Giddens reproduces one of the oldest and most negative political traditions. He does not say pensioners are suffering from 'false consciousness', but he certainly implies it. Worse still the fact that they dare to object to reforms is further evidence that reforms are necessary. Such authoritarianism sits uneasily alongside his suggestion that welfare reforms be underpinned by individuals with a more reflexive, thoughtful and contemplative sense of their own welfare needs, and of their 'selves' (1991, 1994, 1998). However, Giddens highlights two other features of a post-traditional and post-modern world that merit further attention: risk, identity and difference.

Risk

Risk, and how it is addressed, is significant for post-traditional approaches and social policy for four main reasons.

- First, it is plain that traditional responses to risk are no longer appropriate.
- Second, and a key factor highlighting the above point, developed societies are themselves less predictable. Change and flux typify society today. Faith in the ability of the state or scientific experts to manage risk on our behalf has therefore diminished.
- Third, and as a consequence of the above, people have to try to anticipate and address risk themselves. Whether this is best achieved by collectively sharing the responsibilities and costs of a risk society, or instead, leads to individuation, becomes a crucial issue.
- Fourth, traditional definitions of risk, premised on technical measures, neglect the social construction of these and of the risks themselves. This in turn poses fundamental questions about the way we define welfare and well-being.

These four features of a post-traditional society are difficult to disentangle and they combine to pose advocates of universal public welfare provisions a major challenge (Culpitt, 1999).

Public welfare provisions provide a clear example of how traditional perceptions of risk are inadequate and how difficult it now seems to find solutions. Responsibility for protecting populations against the risks of modernity was assumed by the state in most countries during the 20th century. For most of the 20th century, the insurance principle was a benignly authoritarian mechanism for redistributing the costs associated with the risks of a modern industrial society. Actuarial calculations loosely informed NI schemes and intergenerational transfers provided a safety net for predictable risks (Walker, 1996). Public welfare was aimed, primarily, at protecting men as wage earners and women as mothers until they retired. However, these narrow welfare categories were premised on a view of family and social life that is increasingly regarded as inappropriate.

Life expectancy has increased dramatically, fertility rates have declined, industrial restructuring means very few manual workers can expect a job for life, divorce rates have soared, households and 'families' no longer conform to the heterosexual 'nuclear' norm and many women's relationship to paid labour has changed (Lewis et al, 2000).

Moreover, contemporary developed societies have, as a byproduct of their successes, generated many new and different risks. For example, extending civil and social rights has enabled some women to escape from traditional authoritarian family forms. However, state run welfare schemes have inadequately covered the new risks associated with, for example, divorce or lone parenthood. The reconfiguration of 'families' that is often seen as a key feature of a post-traditional society is not addressed by traditional welfare solutions predicated on the (insured) male 'breadwinner'. As noted throughout this book, informal welfare arrangements bestow few rights and even those that do exist may be of little benefit.

> For example, pension-splitting on divorce will undoubtedly provide some middle-class women who currently lack a pension of their own with a much needed income in retirement. However, for working-class women who are likely to be the poorest pensioners, the value of their spouse's pension will be negligible. Bearing in mind that any pension rights women have in their own name will also be 'split', plus the lawyers and fund administrators will want paying for sorting out the liabilities – with the administration costs usually deducted first – it is not clear who the major beneficiaries will be (*Pensions World*, December 2000).

In their responses to change, governments have often added to the uncertainty that many people feel as they approach retirement. Changes to benefit rules, new types of benefits for specific groups, changing and even scrapping the retirement age, trimming entitlements that were 'earned' through NI contributions and tinkering with the tax liabilities of pensioners have generated further uncertainty, fears and insecurities. Trying to plan for retirement has become increasingly complex and not surprisingly only a minority in the UK feel able to do so with confidence (Boaz et al, 1999, p 17). It often seems that the rules change to suit whatever the economic situation demands, particularly the demand for labour and the level of unemployment. Even trying to plan when to retire is fraught with uncertainty in these circumstances and the constant moving of the goalposts is not peculiar to the UK. As Guillemard and van Gunsteren (1991, p 367) point out, "nearly everywhere, the same decision-making processes have led to drawing up, then doing away with or making changes in, early exit arrangements". This leaves actors trying to 'piece together' their responses and they have to try and anticipate the likelihood of a government, in perhaps 10-30 years time, changing the rules. Good luck, rather than prudent planning, is what the individual needs. This, in turn, creates situations where people with very similar work histories, of similar ages and with similar expectations, can find they have very different income levels due to the fact that one person may have realised an opportunity and another 'missed' it. Not surprisingly post-traditional societies have witnessed a loss of faith in the benign state.

Occupational pensions also began life with a male 'breadwinner' in mind and assumed transfers were from working husbands to dependent wives. For most of the 20th century the actuarial calculations they relied on assumed that the membership was male and on the death of the member any derived benefits would go to widows. Whereas widows are usually entitled to a proportion of their husband's occupational pension, typically in the region of 60% in a DB scheme, if the 'dependent' spouse of the occupational (DB) pensioner dies the pension is not reduced, since it 'belongs' to the person who 'earned' it. This apparently benign method of calculating benefits is one reason why women currently have lower incomes in retirement than men, even when they are not relying solely on the state pension. However, because women outlive men by several years the cost of transferring 100% of the pension to widows would impose severe strains on the pension funds. These assumptions have had to be revised in the light of women's increased labour force participation in the last quarter of the 20th century. Many more women have accessed occupational pensions, particularly in the public sector, and they will be claiming their full pension for longer than their male colleagues.

For many employers in the private sector the prospect of not being able to meet their future pension commitments, in part because they were premised on misplaced assumptions, has encouraged a move to DC schemes. This change means employers carry little or no risk because the fund will usually be operated by an insurance company. Although employees may be offered terms that are slightly more favourable than if they purchased a private pension policy themselves, because administrative charges or risks can be shared, the logic of risk calculations is to individuate risks. In addition to the changes to public provisions and the development of DC occupational provisions, private market-based schemes also serve to disaggregate rather than share risks.

Risk is, therefore, a central concern of the personal and occupational pension providers. By grouping scheme members in terms of age, gender, occupation and lifestyle behaviours it is possible to calculate the risk of them surviving or, if in a life insurance scheme, of dying. Thus, an unmarried male who is a heavy drinker, smokes, works in a dangerous occupation and rides a motorbike will find it expensive to get a good life insurance policy. On the one hand actuarial calculations like this might seem to benefit women, who are in general 'good' risks in the life assurance market. But actuarial calculations penalise them in terms of pensions because they are likely to claim their pension for longer. Thus the Association of British Insurers (ABI, 1995) discusses risk largely in terms of the problem that the pensioner poses: will they live to or beyond the projected life expectancy? In the US interactive websites have been offering potential customers an indication of their life expectancy for a several years now. The industry refers to this as 'longevity risk'. Whereas anyone contributing to a pension scheme hopes to live to a ripe old age collecting their pension for longer than the provider had anticipated, the industry relies on their customers dying. However, providers must also consider 'inflation risk' – the risk of the funds being incapable of matching inflation and not delivering the anticipated pension. Plus a great deal hinges on how funds perform in the finance and stock markets. If there is a lengthy period of slow growth it is plain that occupational and personal pension providers run the risk of over-committing themselves. While the long-term nature of the investment portfolios of the pension funds hedges their bets, they are, nevertheless, engaged in some very risky activities (Minns, 2001).

The case of one UK personal private pension provider, Equitable Life, illustrates this point. By promising a guaranteed annuity rate (GAR), guaranteeing a minimum return on fund investments, Equitable Life effectively spreads its liabilities between GAR policy holders and personal pension plan members who had policies that promised a 'with profits' dividend. The courts compelled Equitable Life to fulfil their commitments to their GAR members, even though it was apparent by the late 1990s that the stock market was no longer performing as well as had been anticipated when the policies were offered. The losers in this were the 'with profits' personal pension plan members who will, in effect, have to bail out the GAR members if, and when, the guarantees fail to materialise. In July 2001, Equitable Life informed members of 'with profits' schemes, who did not have a GAR, that their policies were worth 16% less than in the previous year. There was never any suggestion of wrong doing on the part of Equitable Life, it had simply taken a risk and failed.

Furthermore, Beck (1992, 2000) has drawn attention to the way that technical scientific measures of risk also tend to neglect social factors. Thus longevity risk, accumulation risk and inflation risk are essentially measures of average and general trends for particular social groups, and types of investment, under certain presumed circumstances. In reality these basic measurements cannot be accurately predicted; they are well-informed estimates. At a more sophisticated level the ability to assess risks becomes even more difficult and for the layperson, increasingly expected to reflect on the implications for their future well-being, baffling. Risk occurs at various points in the life of a pension, with the prospective retiree having to consider both how the fund operates during its accumulation/investment period and how to receive the pension (that is, as an annuity, an income stream or some combination of the two). In this context fiscal/tax liabilities and privileges become very important and the interaction between the tax and benefits systems will be vital for specific retirees.

Blake et al (1999, p 1) compared DC schemes, currently being promoted by companies and the government via stakeholders, with old style DB schemes, in respect of the options for the accumulation process, and concluded that: "[W]e find that defined contribution (DC) plans can be extremely risky relative to a defined benefit (DB) benchmark (far more so than most pension plan professionals would be likely to admit)". The following year they went on to consider the choices available to a personal (DC) pension scheme member on retirement for converting their fund into an income stream. They concluded:

The best programme is therefore an annuity programme rather than an income drawdown programme that leaves a bequest to the policy holder's survivors. The best programme also depends on the policy holder's attitude to risk: if he [sic] is highly risk averse, the appropriate programme is a conventional annuity; if he is more risk loving, the best programme involves a mixture of bonds and equities, with the optimal mix depending on the policy holder's degree of risk aversion. (2000, p 1)

It may be that these crucially important and, from the pension industry's perspective, critical comments will ultimately filter into the media and will in turn be translated, so that those of us who are risk loving can be assured we are not getting a pension product intended for someone who is averse to risk.

The most important point is that the more accurate and reliable the calculation of risk, the less likely it is that 'low risk' or low cost groups will be willing to effectively subsidise others. Individuals need to reflect on their behaviour and the risks they take and find the most suitable pension provider. The net result is that some groups will find it very difficult to gain access to a worthwhile life assurance policy or a meaningful pension. However, as Treasury officials Budd and Campbell point out, at least one insurance company already offers enhanced pensions to 'impaired lives'. "They intend to offer annuities which pay more to those with medical problems which are more likely to cause an early death" (1998, p 15). Good news for overweight smokers who enjoy being 'couch potatoes' perhaps, and it ought to reinforce Giddens' calls for individuals to be more reflexive regarding the risks they confront.

> Schemes of positive welfare, oriented to manufactured rather than external risk, would be directed to fostering the *autotelic self*. The autotelic self is one with an inner confidence which comes from self-respect, and one where a sense of ontological security, originating in basic trust, allows for the positive appreciation of difference. It refers to a person able to translate potential threats into rewarding challenges, someone who is able to turn entropy into a consistent flow of experience. The autotelic self does not seek to neutrallse risk or to suppose that 'someone else will take care of the problem'; risk is confronted as the active challenge which generates self-actualization. (Giddens, 1994, p 192, emphasis in original)

But as Adam and van Loon point out:

> [I]f reflexivity as self-confrontation is to mean anything in this context it is not a confrontation between two sets of calculations.... Instead, reflexivity requires us to be meditative, that is looking back upon that which allows us to reflect in the first place. (2000, p 7)

This leads neatly on to a discussion of identity, which has also been central to post-traditional accounts.

Identity and difference

Contemporary concerns with identity are seen by many scholars as indicative of post-modernity (Roseneil and Seymour, 1999). Questions of cultural identity (Hall and du Gay, 1996) also have a particular significance for pensioners, retirees and older people, illustrated by the fact that these three categories have to be distinguished from one another. Cultural and social identities, however, are invariably framed in relation to what they are not, to some 'other' identity. Thus, retirees are not unemployed and are not working; on the face of it an identity in limbo. Consequently closure and exclusion are key features of identity. By defining what *we* are, and what *we* are not, some people are embraced as like *us* and 'others' are excluded (Hall, 1996). Age can form a powerful barrier, both fixing *our* social identities in relation to specific cohorts and identifying *other* age cohorts, for example, the 'baby boomers' and 'Thatcher's children/generation'. This can make the experience of ageing and retirement quite traumatic. Older men are often seen as confronting particular difficulties once they become detached from paid work because their 'masculine identity' has been tied to being a 'breadwinner' and worker (Solomon and Szwabo, 1994; Thompson, 1994).

Phillipson has made a powerful case for researchers to focus on the social exclusion and marginalisation of older people. He suggests, "we have entered a period of crisis in respect of the identity of elderly people" (1998, p 2). In a world characterised by change and uncertainty older people may be excluded by ideas and debates that define them as an economic burden or even as 'useless'; by employer and trades union practices that want them to 'make way' during periods of restructuring and redundancy; by political processes and parties that relegate their needs and interests to those of other age groups; and by the neglect and undervaluing of their age-related social and physical needs. Alongside a focus on exclusion, he advocates a sociology of 'daily living' that is capable of exploring the points of engagement with various social, cultural and political institutions. This in turn would expose the isolation of some older people and the ways that they resist and reconstruct their 'selves' in circumstances that initially appear to offer little opportunity for resistance (Phillipson, 1998, pp 138-40; Thorpe, 1999).

By focusing on resistance, however, it should not be thought that this simply consists of pensioners 'storming the barricades' or occupying Post Offices. There are examples of such activities, but like most of us, older people resist in less obvious ways too. For example, 'dumb insolence' among residents of a residential care centre when urged to join in with the 'community singing', or teasing of staff by 'playing dead' when they bring in the morning tea (Hockey and James, 1993, p 182).

Williams (1996) points to three ways that identity, in terms of diversity and difference, have arisen in debates over social welfare since the 1980s. One strand has been a new 'managerialist' vocabulary that uses diversity and difference in the context of service provision. This has been most apparent in health and social care policies with the idea of purchasers and providers assessing the needs of the different and diverse users. Without making too much of this point, it is possible to see the British Labour government's 'modernisation' programme for welfare as profoundly managerialist. This should be no great surprise because, (a) it has often been pointed out that social democratic politics is centrally concerned with pragmatically managing (Clarke et al, 1994, p 5; Mann, 1984); and (b) for many Labour politicians their only political experience prior to 1997 was trying to manage local services within the constraints imposed by two decades of Conservative Party rule from Westminster. Thus the pragmatic managerialism of 'New' Labour looks much like the 'old' versions, but with a vocabulary drawn from populist politics, US communitarians and Giddens' (1994, 1998) 'third way' (Jordan, 1998; Deacon and Mann, 1999; Powell, 2000; Prideaux, 2001).

Second, notions of choice and individual preferences have elevated questions of cultural identity on the social and political agenda. In a large measure this has been driven by a market/consumerist welfare vocabulary. In Chapter Three it was suggested that the promotion of private/personal pensions has relied heavily on positive images of ageing, linked to consumer choice. The contrast is between dependency, usually discussed in terms of public welfare dependency, and independence, meaning reliance on private or occupational welfare. Dependency on informal welfare rarely features in these debates, but occupies a rather ambiguous position when it does. Moreover, and as noted earlier, the construction of 'risk' and the individual's responsibility for risk management hinges on their sense of 'self'; their identity. For Giddens, it is crucially important that retired people develop a strong sense of security, self-respect and self-actualisation, and in so doing confront their dependent status. They, and the rest of us, must come to see them as a resource, not a social problem. "The management of identity is the centre-point of how far a person's relation to the world [...] is experienced as incapacitating or generates opportunities for self-enhancement or self-renewal" (Giddens, 1994, p 187). Together with the consumer driven model this tends to promote an individualistic perspective on how identity and welfare interact. Individuals, either as consumers or as 'lifestyle managers', are reflecting on their needs, their behaviour and their 'selves'.

A third feature of Williams' account is how 'subject identities' have responded to change. Various welfare groups have "grasped the administrative categories (or subject positions) imposed upon them by policy makers, administrators and practitioners and translated these into political identities and new subjectivities" (1996, p 17). Williams' point is that despite the managerialist and individuating discourses, people are not empty vessels into which these ideas can be poured without some spillage. Active human subjects adopt and adapt the categories and labels applied to them. Many of the social movements that are cited as indicators of post-modernity and a post-traditional society (for example, ecological, anti-globalisation, feminist and disability politics, women's health and welfare groups, anti-racist campaigns, squatters and claimants groups) testify to the durability of active human subjects. Pensioners, retirees and older people have similarly asserted their social and political agendas. Grey panthers (and tigers) in the US, public pensioners picketing political conferences in the UK, lobby groups representing superannuants in Australia and a range of consumer and special interest groups across the developed economies testify to the possibilities (Wilson, 2000).

> Interestingly, the mobilisation of retirees and older people in the near future may be facilitated by information technology. Traditionally, politics has been conducted in public spaces, with marching, picketing and so on. However, e-mails and information via the World Wide Web, which both private and public pension providers increasingly expect retirees to use, may also enable older people to generate and communicate their concerns more widely.

However, to date these 'entrenched interests' (Giddens, 1998, p 115) look rather weak in comparison to the 'vested interests' that control the finance and pensions markets (Field, 1996, p 38).

The significance of subject identities is further highlighted by the language and categories they prefer. According to a review of existing research (Boaz et al, 1999), most older people in the UK prefer to be called 'senior citizens' and the identity label of 'retiree' is often preferred to pensioner. This may imply a more difficult time for pensioners relying on public welfare because their form of dependency is stigmatised, even by other retirees. Alternatively, however, the term 'senior citizen' asserts some traditional claims – age-based rights rather than tested needs or consumer redress. While Giddens may feel that Marshall's citizenship model "does not stand up to scrutiny" (1994, p 132), that need not prevent senior citizens mobilising successfully around the concept. Indeed, one way that subject identities may come to be more significant in the near future may be through a redefinition of citizenship rights. For example, a claim made throughout this book is that a definition of a working life that acknowledges the right to retire, alongside protection from age discrimination in paid work, would go some way towards alleviating the fear that exit from paid work will only be possible for people with a private or occupational pension.

The subject identities of older people may also assume more significance in the near future as the 'baby boom generation' of the late 1940s and early 1950s near retirement. This too is likely to polarise in terms of identity and experience. Anyone persuaded to take out a private pension by the positive images of what retirement can consist of (travel, consumption and so on), is unlikely to be reassured that their investment was worth making if they subsequently feel politically marginalised or socially excluded. Nor is it easy to imagine that a generation that grew up with the idea of a public welfare system from 'cradle to grave' will quietly accept that this must be scrapped.

In this context it is worth pausing to consider whether the activists of the 1960s and 1970s will quietly acquiesce, or be too tired to resist by 2010-30? It seems unlikely, and in Australia it was reported that most 51- to 65-year-old Australians were planning to 'SKIN their children' (Spend the Kids Inheritance Now), with 40% of this age cohort expecting to travel and a third of respondents anticipating "major changes to their lifestyle" once they had retired (*The Sydney Morning Herald*, 27 July 1998). In Britain too, the voice of the retiree is being raised. *The Guardian* (*Society*, 27 September 2000) had a special pull-out feature 'Older people speaking out', with a full page that reproduced Dylan Thomas' "Do not go gentle into that good night, rage, rage, against the dying of the light". The generation that made 'dope' a political and personal crusade, that used LSD to 'discover itself,' and more recently HRT and Viagra to sustain itself, may well pursue lifestyle politics beyond retirement age.

Giddens (1991) has suggested people in post-traditional societies reflect on and reconstruct their identities in the light of experience and the way in which they wish to sustain, or reframe, their sense of self. Viewed in this light, identities are not fixed but fluid, responding to events, ideas, and feelings. For example, how old we feel will reflect our self-perception, the way others behave, the social context (for example, a nightclub or a restaurant) and the relative ages of those around us. With consumers often targeted by age, and many social and cultural events geared to specific age cohorts, the boundaries can often feel quite rigid. Whether we feel ourselves to be included or excluded will also reflect the degree of recognition and respect that we achieve in specific social locations (Williams, 2000). However, feelings are highly subjective, with similar people capable of feeling very differently about a particular social event or location. Shared identities in retirement may promote an awareness of common interests, and social and political mobilisations, but then again, they may not. Divisions and distinctions within the retired population are likely to remain as significant as they are among the non-retired population.

Furthermore, as Phillipson argues, the rate and pace of change in contemporary societies, including the tremendous successes that have produced an ageing society, "seem to have undercut a language and moral space which can resonate with the rights and needs of older people as a group" (1998, p 49). We have today more diverse and different social identities. We are not as fixed by community, class or family as in the past and that adds both to the pleasures of contemporary social life and also to the anxieties. Post-modernity throws into doubt established identities, and for younger retired people this may be extremely attractive; no longer 'ghettoised' by age. Active and dynamic retirees provide a powerful challenge to negative stereotypes of frail and incompetent victims. But as Paul Hoggett (2001) reminds us, some people are frail, others are incompetent or incapable of making meaningful decisions and any welfare system that neglects this fact is in danger of evading responsibility for the weakest and least articulate groups in society. Turning 'experience' into a positive process of reflection and learning is all well and good, but physical and mental frailty will, in the final analysis, overwhelm even the most reflexive individual. Minds and bodies age and, as one of my favourite exam howlers put it, "we all tend to die". There are of course very big differences in how we experience both physical ageing and when we die. The trend is not uniform and gender, 'race', class and geography all provide very reliable data of differences that mirror socially structured inequalities, but to date no social group or individual has managed to buck the trend.

Death and identity

For most people approaching retirement today death will be perceived as still some way off. Traditionally, however, retirement, frailty and old age have been closely related. Poverty and the shadow of the Grim Reaper cast a gloom over retirement for much of the 20th century. This book is more concerned with how people approach retirement positively and how expectations have changed. Challenges to the marginalisation and exclusion of retired people are recurring themes. However, this can have the effect of reinforcing the isolation of those retired people who are frail and are approaching death. This will not be explored at length, but a brief discussion of death is important because it highlights some neglected themes pertinent to any discussion of identity, reflexivity and risk.

Hoggett's critical observations on Giddens' work (and of Deacon and Mann, 1999) stresses that, "... our capacity to be a reflexive agent is often constrained by the difficulties we have in facing our own fears and anxieties. Some ideas and experiences are just too painful to think about, even with the support and solidarity of others, and they therefore get split off" (2001, p 42). Death and dying is not something we care to ponder in a romanticised and youthful world. Like chameleons we can apparently change identities at will, but "we do have bodies which do cause us suffering (and some more than for others) and which do decay and die" (Hoggett, 2001, p 43). (Having watched my father die a slow, painful death shortly before he reached 65 years of age, Hoggett's point struck home.) Nature is often presented to us as furry, fluffy and cute, but it also rots, decomposes and can be ugly to observe. No amount of reflexivity can prevent the inevitable decline of the body, even if it is slowed, controlled or managed. Thus it is reasonable to ask at what point are we free of the need to "turn potential threats into rewarding challenges" (Giddens, 1994, p 192)? And when is it legitimate to be welfare dependent or to acknowledge ones own dependency? What if, having reflected on the likelihood of my dying within the next 15 years, I want to enjoy a period of retirement, spend some 'quality time' with my grandchildren, travel, feel the sun on my ageing skin and escape from the "bullshit" (Castles, 1997, p 99) at work? How much reflexivity does it take to know that death awaits us all?

These questions are crucial because Giddens proposes the scrapping of the retirement age and implies everyone should save for their retirement:

> The concept of a pension that begins at retirement age, and the label
> 'pensioner', were inventions of the welfare state. But not only do these
> not conform to the new realities of ageing, they are as clear a case of
> welfare dependency as one can find.... We should move towards
> abolishing the fixed age of retirement, and we should regard older people
> as a resource rather than a problem. (Giddens, 1998, pp 119-20)

This is a view echoed by government in a report (PIU, 2000) that
emphasised the belief that paid work was the benchmark of citizenship
rights and reiterated the myth of retirees as a potential burden. The
thrust of this report was that the economy needed older people to be in
paid work, that pension funds should not promote early exit and that
there was something deeply wrong with a culture that encouraged
retirement among people who could still be in paid work. Thus in the
Foreword, the Prime Minister Tony Blair wrote:

> I hope that our actions as Government will also promote a wider change
> in attitudes. This cultural change is a long-term project, with high
> stakes. In a century in which we can expect life expectancy to continue
> to increase, we will all suffer if we write people off on the grounds of
> age. (Foreword to PIU, 2000)

The carefully crafted tone of the report stresses the need for employers to
review their practices and calls on older people to consider the contribution
they can still make. This ties in with Giddens' broader view of welfare
reform in which the boundaries between work and non-work become
much more flexible. Whether this really marks a break with 'productivism'
(Giddens, 1994) is a debatable point (see Chapter Six). Clearly it would
mirror the demand for a more flexible labour market and it was perhaps
a coincidence that the report was issued at a time when unemployment
was at its lowest for 20 years and fears of labour shortages were being
voiced. For now it should simply be noted that scrapping the age of
retirement will probably impact on those who rely on public welfare by
extending their working life. Unless restrictions are also to be imposed
on members of occupational and private pension schemes, it will only be
the poorest who are affected. For those older workers without some
form of occupational or private pension – manual workers in the private
sector, women who have previously cared for relatives and children, people
who have been 'flexible' in terms of having only had part-time work or
interrupted periods of full-time work – the scrapping of the retirement

age could mean that they never fully retire, because they would never be able to generate an adequate retirement fund. Will some people be compelled to work until they are physically unable to do so?

It is against a backdrop of restraining the right to retire, and the rights of retired people, that questions of identity need to be located. Rose summarises the negative potential that exists: "The language of autonomy, identity, self-realization and the search for fulfilment forms a grid of regulatory ideals...." (1996, p 145). As consumers, savers and lifestyle managers, individual retirees (aka pensioners) are making "themselves 'interested' in their own government" (Rose, 1996, p 146). A dose of post-modern scepticism is appropriate in this context. For example, similarities between Giddens' (and Labour's) 'third way' and traditional, middle-class, Victorian efforts at promoting 'self-help' are remarkable. It is worth recalling the way that Smiles' (1860) ideological tract was used by the Charity Organisation Society, along with casework and counselling, to enforce respectability among the 'residuum' (Fido, 1977). Giddens' recent polemics promote a similarly individualistic approach to welfare in general, and retirement in particular. Moreover, his model of the reflexive, masculine 'self' operates with a chilling rationality and a high degree of autonomy in a world where opportunities are structured, but where he believes there are still lots of opportunities (Seidler, 1994; Hoggett, 2001; Taylor-Gooby, 2001). Those subject identities that struggle in circumstances where there are less opportunities and more risks, almost always the poorest in society, are portrayed as lesser identities. Thus choosing AVCs to top up an occupational pension is an indication of the (deserving) reflexive self. Passively relying on the public pension is 'welfare dependency' and therefore undeserving. Those in the 'retirement ghetto' (Giddens, 1998, p 120) must, by implication, be brought out (in some cases kicking and screaming no doubt) into the more worthwhile world of work, and "old age should not be a time of rights without responsibilities" (1998, p 121).

Summary and assessment

The approaches considered in this chapter are currently some of the most influential ideas in Britain. Within academic circles it can seem that everyone is now some sort of post-modernist or post-traditionalist, with the older Fabian, Marxist and Thatcherite troops in retreat or sheltering in the trenches (Clarke, 1998). After almost two decades in which social scientists were politically marginalised, there has been a rush of research (and some rebranding) that seeks to engage with social policy at a peak level. Moreover, it appears that in the area of retirement and pensions policy there has been a receptive audience at the highest level. It has also been suggested that concepts such as 'performativity' are distinctly different to traditional approaches and, with the presentation of policy assuming ever-greater significance, provide some illuminating insights. There is a clear challenge here to the SDW with its firm standpoint and unwavering commitment to welfare and social justice. A failure to acknowledge and take on board the qualitative changes that have occurred throughout the developed world looks like a form of dogma in the face of these new analyses. It has also been suggested that many of the ideas informing contemporary welfare debates have been drawn from social, political and cultural movements, and are therefore 'bottom up'. The work of Ulrich Beck and Anthony Giddens has been profoundly influential, and their approaches to risk and identity respectively cannot be ignored.

The risks associated with planning for retirement illustrate the more general problems confronting populations in the developed economies. Divorce, industrial change and globalisation are commonplace and illustrate how post-traditional societies impact on both the personal and macro level. Beck's account of risk, both the problems with scientific and technical measurements and how it is socially constructed, provides numerous invaluable insights for social policy. As we have seen, the insurance and pension industry operates with a model of risk that relies on and reinforces the existing patterns. This is highly regressive and socially divisive. It is at this point that we can see a link with the SDW rather than a conflict.

There is a hierarchy of risk that corresponds with some very traditional forms of social inequality and with the different elements of the SDW. These will be revisited in the final chapter, but it should be noted here that risks, rights and redress vary significantly within the SDW. Likewise, the ability of different subject identities to voice a challenge to their social or political exclusion is uneven. Again, much will depend on the form of welfare dependency. Occupational welfare has been earned and private/fiscal welfare paid for, but public welfare dependency is condemned by Giddens, among others, and informal welfare remains largely invisible. Giddens' approach initially looks to be the clearest example of a 'post-traditional' perspective on welfare and it has been very influential; it makes the grandest claims – going 'beyond Left and Right' to map out a 'third way'. It provides a robust critique of traditional approaches and draws on a variety of intellectual traditions to make a case for change. Moreover, he directly addresses welfare policy and uses retirement and pensions policy as one of his key examples of how the reflexive individual can cope in a post-traditional world. Giddens is undoubtedly promoting an ambitious and impressive agenda. It is also one that 'New' Labour appears to have embraced in Britain and this will prove an interesting test. The strengths and weaknesses of the approach considered in this chapter can be summarised as follows.

Main strengths of the approach

- Contemporary societies are profoundly different to those analysed by 'the founders' of social science in the late 19th and early 20th centuries.
- Complexity and confusion abound and confidence that the economy and society can be managed or engineered has evaporated.
- Presentation and performance elevates political style over content.
- Universalism lacks support and we need to address questions of difference and diversity.
- Today risks and desires arise from the successes of 20th century capitalism and coping with these requires a complete break with traditional social policy approaches; a 'third way'.
- Neither social policy nor politics can presume the traditional constituencies they previously had.
- Pensions and pensioners are labels for welfare dependency invented by a 'modern' welfare state and should be scrapped.
- Welfare has to be redefined and rethought.
- Concepts of the 'self' and social identity are important if we are to feel safe and secure in a rapidly changing world.

Weaknesses of the approach

- Some traditional forms of social division persist.
- It fails to appreciate the diversity of welfare provided by the SDW.
- Policy proposals are regressive and blinkered.
- It neglects interdependency and welfare dependency of everyone in a post-traditional society.
- It presumes everyone is competent and reneges on a commitment to welfare for those who fail, for various reasons.

- It undervalues the structured hierarchy of risks and identities.
- There is a danger of imposing conditional rights and onerous responsibilities on social groups with the least resources for addressing these.

SIX

Looking (or put out) for greener grass? Some comparative measures of 'success'

Introduction

This chapter explores some of the attractions and difficulties associated with comparative approaches to social policy. By exploring the question of whether early retirement/early exit is a 'good' thing or not, and comparing trends and policies in a number of OECD countries, the chapter highlights some recurring difficulties for comparative approaches.

- The first of these is the problem of having an appropriate theoretical model that will allow meaningful comparisons. The work of Esping-Andersen (1990) is used as the template here because it marked a shift in comparative approaches to social policy that took a more critical, less evolutionary, approach.
- A second problem for comparative approaches is ensuring that the definitions and meanings of specific policies are consistent between countries and that these policies are measured in the same way. In the case of retirement pensions it is plain that definitions of both 'retirement' and 'pensions' can vary significantly between countries (apRoberts, 1994).
- Perhaps the most difficult issue is selecting an appropriate measurement of comparison. Esping-Andersen measures the degree to which benefits either reinforce labour market discipline or are provided on the basis of need. It is in this context that the data on early exit/early retirement is explored.

From this discussion three further points emerge:

- First, it is possible to invert his welfare regime model by pointing out that workers in Australia and the UK exit paid work at an earlier age than Swedish workers. It may be a little mischievous to present the data in this way, but it serves to show how difficult it is to find a measure that is truly independent of the observers' own values.
- Second, and more seriously, feminist critics of his work have shown how Esping-Andersen's measure is limited by its focus on paid labour and neglects the significance of unpaid work and informal welfare (Lewis, 1992).
- Third, Esping-Andersen's account overlooks the different means by which welfare may be realised. Thus Castles (1997) points out that the decision to exit paid work can be influenced by a number of variables, housing costs for example, and that there is a need to consider how welfare is addressed by various and different means.

Although this chapter has a more critical edge, it should not be read as a rejection of comparative approaches in favour of some narrow and nationally chauvinistic view of social policy. On the contrary, Esping-Andersen has opened up comparative studies enabling observers to consider how specific nation states promote different forms of welfare. This is extremely important at a time when politicians claim to be powerless in the face of the economic restraints of globalisation. As Esping-Andersen makes plain, politics matters when it comes to social policy and the fact that similar needs are addressed differently focuses our attention on how things might be changed. This in turn poses questions that involve not only the distribution of resources by the state, but also the distribution and meaning of care, work, opportunities and leisure.

Welfare regimes

Esping-Andersen asserts that politics matters in shaping welfare policy. With politicians in many countries abdicating responsibility by claiming that globalisation and/or economic forces dictate social policy, this assertion makes a refreshing change. By suggesting that politics matters, Esping-Andersen's work contrasts with 'convergence' approaches that identify the similarities between the most developed countries (Wilensky, 1975; Overbye, 1996; Sykes and Alcock, 1998; Bonoli, 2000). For Esping-Andersen the making of social policy in the 20th century was marked by a series of class contests and alliances. He stresses the different ways policy is 'made' and how nation states can respond to the needs of their citizens. One of the most important variables he identifies is the form and direction of class-based political movements. Solidarity within the trades union movement, a robust social democratic political party and cross-class coalitions will be more successful in promoting generous, universal, public welfare reforms. Conversely, divisions within the labour movement and the pursuit of sectional interests will be more likely to promote means testing, divisive types of welfare and reinforce patterns of social exclusion. Esping-Andersen's approach is developed from Korpi's work (1978, 1983) and is heavily influenced by the radical political economy tradition (see Chapter Two). It draws on Therborn's (1983) idea that homogeneity is a key variable influencing the successful outcome of class struggles, dips into Titmuss's concept of the SDW and relates the development of state welfare to the extension of citizenship rights. Thus: "Few can disagree with TH Marshall's (1950) proposition that social citizenship constitutes the core idea of the welfare state" (Esping-Andersen, 1990, p 21). Like Marshall and Titmuss he stresses the role of public welfare in promoting social solidarity and reconciling nominally antagonistic class forces within a social democratic framework. In so doing, "social rights push back the frontiers of capitalist power" (1990, p 16). His model of welfare regimes also offers an empirically verifiable measure of how successful welfare regime types have been. The benchmark of success is the degree to which labour is 'de-commodified' by welfare services. "De-commodification occurs when a service is rendered as a matter of right, and when a person can maintain a livelihood without reliance on the market" (1990, pp 21-2).

Using the idea of de-commodification enables Esping-Andersen to cluster various countries into what he calls "welfare regimes", based on the degree to which their provisions reinforce capitalist labour market relations. The defining characteristics being: how far de-commodification has gone, how it is manifest and how it is 'won'. So, for example, it may be that means-tested benefits provide a measure of de-commodification, a simple safety net for the poorest, but this is a meagre success for labour. The welfare recipient is subject to enquiries and conditions, while the benefits do not, as a rule, permit full and active engagement in 'normal' social activities. Esping-Andersen identifies three types of welfare regime: liberal, corporatist and social democratic. He states that there is no 'pure' example of each type of welfare regime and they are best thought of as 'clustered', rather than graduated in a line. "In one cluster we find the 'liberal' welfare state, in which means tested assistance, modest universal transfers, or modest social insurance plans predominate. Benefits cater mainly to a clientele of low income, usually working class, state dependants ...." (1990, p 26).

In liberal welfare regimes the market is seen as the most appropriate provider of welfare and the state usually encourages private provisions. Indeed, by being "reserved for the poor" (Deacon and Bradshaw, 1983), this type of welfare regime stigmatises public welfare and simultaneously enhances the services provided by the market. Moreover, "... this type of regime minimises de-commodification effects" (Esping-Andersen, 1990, p 27) and tends to provide minimal safety-net benefits for public welfare recipients, while the majority population can access a range of market-based welfare services, with a 'class–political dualism' between the two types of welfare. The "archetypical examples of this model are the United States, Canada and Australia" (1990, p 27).

His second cluster includes Austria, France, Germany and Italy and he describes these as 'corporatist'. The preservation of status differentials was the dominant issue in these countries and, along with the Church, these have influenced the development of welfare. Traditionally, corporatist welfare regimes have tried to promote particular visions of the family and have largely accepted the central role of the state in establishing welfare. Because policy reinforces status this type of welfare regime is socially conservative and does not involve any significant redistributive features. However, "market efficiency and commodification was never pre-eminent and, as such, the granting of social rights was hardly ever a seriously contested issue" (1990, p 27). In these welfare regimes occupationally related benefits and the private market as welfare providers are "truly marginal" (1990, p 27).

The smallest welfare cluster (which only consists of Scandinavia) has seen the greatest advances in de-commodification and universal welfare rights. The sustained successes of social democracy in the Scandinavian countries have been possible because of the labour movement's political alliances with significant sections of the middle classes and agriculture. These he calls "de-commodifying welfare states" and they are typically associated with strong social democratic political parties and high levels of labour movement mobilisation. He claims that: "Decommodifying welfare states are, in practice, of very recent date. A minimal definition must entail that citizens can freely, and without potential loss of job, income or general welfare, opt out of work when they themselves consider it necessary" (1990, p 23).

The crucial measures of de-commodification would therefore be:

- access to paid employment for all who desire it;
- an income maintenance scheme that protects the individual's general welfare;
- a 'choice' for individuals to opt out of paid work if, and when, they wish to.

In terms of retirement provisions this definition would appear to enable anyone to decide to retire at any time with an income close to their former earnings, or if they had not been in the paid labour market, to attain a pension close to AWE. Social divisions and exclusion are less likely in the social democratic welfare model because high quality services are designed for all, to be paid for by all. By British or US standards this would be considered a very generous pension system indeed. However, Esping-Andersen acknowledges that his social democratic welfare regime is an ideal type that only Sweden comes close to matching.

All three criteria pose tremendous difficulties in reality. Knowing whether someone really wants to work cannot be assessed by what they say. Benefit systems often distort the picture by requiring the claimant to register for work or to show signs that they are seeking it. How keen the individual claimant is to find work can also vary enormously. On the other hand, some benefit systems favour claimants who switch from long-term unemployment benefit to some form of disability benefit. Older men who are defined as long-term unemployed may feel disability benefits are less stigmatising, others may switch simply because the benefits are more generous.

For example, there have been some phenomenal increases (as much as 300% between 1973-1995) in the numbers of men claiming disability benefits in some countries. Likewise, the numbers claiming long-term sickness benefits have also increased in many countries at record rates during periods of industrial restructuring. However, this data does not correspond with other aggregate health trends for the groups most affected (Unikowski, 1996, p 133). Similarly, older women may want paid work but describe themselves as a 'housewife' or, if their spouse has retired, as retired themselves.

Trying to assess whether income maintenance schemes protect the general welfare of individuals is also fraught with difficulties. Needs too often blur into wants and desires when discussing the appropriate level of income required to ensure that there is no loss of 'general welfare'. Even a system that guaranteed a 100% replacement rate – that is, a benefit level equivalent to former earnings – would still reproduce income inequalities derived from the paid labour market. But anything less than a 100% replacement rate for some of the lowest paid workers would undoubtedly impact on their general welfare.

Consequently early exit is a far from reliable guide to de-commodification and it cannot be assumed that individuals have 'choice' over when to 'opt out' of paid work simply because they are defined, or define themselves, as 'retired'. Esping-Andersen is alert to how misleading the data on early exit is (1990, pp 148-53), but less willing to consider the idea that it might, for some people, represent a meaningful choice. In so doing he neglects one of his own key variables in the formation of welfare regimes, namely that organised labour may have influenced welfare provisions. In this case the provision of occupational pensions, demanded by trades union activists in many countries, appears to have facilitated early exit (Mann, 1991; Unikowski, 1996; Sass, 1997; Walker with Howard, 2000).

Looking for exits and being shown the door

There are a number of reasons for examining early exit/early retirement as a potential measure of de-commodification in more detail, of which the most important are:

- It is discussed (but implicitly dismissed) in Esping-Andersen's account.
- The 'right to retire' can be seen as one of the earliest welfare rights that citizens were able to gain.
- There are pressures to restrain the 'right to retire' in the near future – and thus the ability to resist is significant.
- The data poses some interesting questions and problems for comparative accounts more generally.
- Key social divisions, most notably gender divisions, become much more visible when the decision to 'retire' is explored.
- Some of the more sophisticated ways in which people respond to welfare regimes become apparent in looking at how the retirement 'choice' is constructed.

However, before these points can be addressed, it is necessary to qualify the meaning of early exit and to stress the fact that the decision is taken in a context of socially constructed restraints and opportunities. One of the difficulties in suggesting that retirement, including early retirement, should be viewed as a 'right', is that for many retired citizens there has been very little meaningful choice in whether they retired or not (Laczko and Phillipson, 1991). Clearly many of those who exit early do so under tremendous pressure and even those who wanted to escape early may subsequently regret their decision (Jacobs et al, 1991).

Early exit may be a consequence of a range of factors acting independently or in combination (Guillemard and van Gunsteren, 1991). Some of these will feature in the subsequent discussion, but there is not space here to explore all of them and for the sake of brevity some of the more important ones can be catalogued in the following manner:

- Employer labour market strategies: for example, changes in labour process and costs of retraining, ageist assumptions about abilities of older workers to adapt, early exit packages (enhanced pension/lump sums).
- Trades union strategies: for example, calls for enhanced pension rights and voluntary redundancy packages, last in and first out policies.
- The matrix of state policies and welfare measures: for example, disability schemes; tax privileges for occupational and private pensions, certain types of assets and savings; level of unemployment benefits; level of basic tax rates; allowances for carers; public pension provisions.
- Social and cultural factors that influence expectations: for example, the idea that older workers should 'make way' for younger ones (a view that may be shared by employers, trades unions, governments and widely held throughout society), rates of home and share ownership, propensity to save, the strength of the work ethic versus a consumption or care ethic, gender-specific ideas and attitudes (male 'breadwinner', female 'carer' expectations), community and friendship networks, ideas about the 'lifecourse' (for example, "I have done my bit"), ideas of what constitutes a 'working life', recreational facilities and services such as local bowls clubs, and so on.
- Economic conditions generally: for example, unemployment and vacancy rates, wage and salary rates, inflation, likelihood of redundancy within specific industry types, opportunities for self-employment, changes in the housing or property markets.
- The desire to exit, albeit influenced by the push and pull factors above, but also by: declining attachment to full-time paid employment, disinclination to

change/retrain, sickness and disability of self or spouse, feelings of stress at work, aspirations and plans of spouse, desire to pursue hobbies, leisure and pleasure, sense of material well-being (no need to work), opportunities for other paid work/part-time work, possibility of inheriting money or property from parents, individual and household assessments of the risks and benefits.

Individuals will be confronted by a range of these factors and others that will be specific to them. People from ethnic minority groups may be subjected to additional pushes and pulls; for example, racism at work or, for those who migrated, a desire to visit or spend some time with friends and family 'back home' (Dwyer, 2000; Ackers and Dwyer, 2002). For married women the decision to retire may be heavily influenced by the expectations of their husband and his retirement intentions, by the restricted labour market opportunities available to older women, and especially care responsibilities for relatives and grandchildren (Arber and Ginn, 1995b). It also needs to be considered that, along with a clear trend towards early retirement in all developed economies, since the 1970s the proportion of women in the paid labour force over the age of 50 has simultaneously increased, although a high proportion are working part time (Walby, 1997). However, this too may reflect constrained choices and a widespread desire for more flexibility in the relationship between work, care and leisure (Jarvis, 1999; Walsh, 1999).

The definition of early retirement must also be heavily qualified, along with the recognition that there are different definitions between countries (Kohli and Rein, 1991). But once all the necessary caveats have been made, it is also vital to acknowledge the very real choices that some people feel they are making. Huhtaniemi (1995) found that among Finns a key factor in thinking about early retirement was the sense of 'life control' that individuals felt they had. Similarly, Thompson and Shaver (1998) reported that many Australians were looking forward to retirement very positively. In the UK, over a third of early retirees report that they chose to retire and give reasons such as a desire to enjoy life "while young and fit" (Tanner, 1997, p 25). However, the decision to exit is not made in a vacuum. Resources, stress at work, ill health, care commitments and many of the other variables noted earlier were cited by Finns, Britons and Australians. Furthermore, not everyone is hoping to exit early and many people express a preference for paid work, although early retirement is an option that many people say they desire. Whether their desires and expectations can be met, or are realistic, is of course a different matter.

Figure 7: Average retirement ages and labour force participation rates of older workers in selected countries

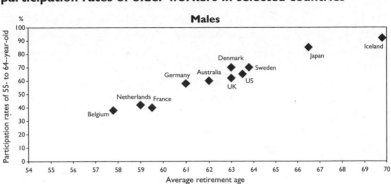

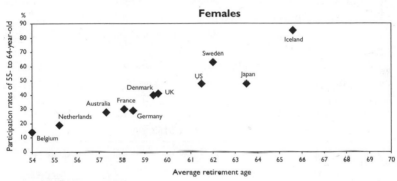

Source: OECD (1998b, p 82)

Figure 7 provides 'at a glance' details of the average age of retirement and the overall labour force participation rates of men and women between 55 and 64 years of age within the OECD in 1995. What is noticeable is the tremendous difference between countries. Compare, for example, the average retirement age in Japan (over 66 for men and close to 64 for women) with their Belgian counterparts (close to 58 for men and 54 for women). The labour force participation rate for the Japanese is also much higher, for men it is over 86%, for Japanese women roughly 50%, while Belgian rates are 38% for men and 14% for women. There is a gender gap in every country, with women exiting paid work earlier and having lower participation rates than men, but this tells us little about the unpaid work activities associated with caring and informal welfare. Nevertheless, it is plain that in some countries more older people are in paid work, and for some years longer, than in others.

Table 2 focuses on five countries selected on the basis that they represent various types of welfare regime outlined by Esping-Andersen (1990). It needs to be repeated that early exit is not necessarily an appropriate measure of de-commodification, merely that it provides an indicator of aspirations.

Table 2 clearly shows that early exit is occurring in every type of welfare regime. The trend towards early exit is detectable for the whole of the second half of the 20th century and could be seen as an indicator of a declining attachment to the work ethic. Anti-age discrimination legislation appears to have little or no effect, as the trend in the UK is roughly in line with those countries (Australia, Sweden and the US) that do have such legislation. It should be noted that Sweden (the country that is closest to Esping-Andersen's social democratic welfare regime) does not buck the trend, it merely lags behind. Ironically, the data for the US and Sweden puts them much closer than might have been expected. This is reinforced by the data on labour force participation rates and changes since 1971.

Figure 8 only covers males aged between 55-64, in part because women's retirement ages are often still set at 60, but also to highlight the trend to

Table 2: Estimates of the average age of transition to Inactivity among older workers in selected countries

Males						Change
	1960	1970	1980	1990	1995	1960-95
Australia	66.1	65.0	62.7	62.4	61.8	−4.3
France	64.5	63.5	61.3	59.6	59.2	−5.3
Sweden	66.0	65.3	64.6	63.9	63.3	−2.7
UK	66.2	65.4	64.6	63.2	62.7	−3.5
US	66.5	65.4	64.2	64.1	63.6	−2.9
Females						Change
	1960	1970	1980	1990	1995	1960-95
Australia	62.4	60.3	58.2	57.6	57.2	−5.2
France	65.8	64.0	60.9	59.0	58.3	−7.5
Sweden	63.4	62.5	62.0	62.4	62.1	−1.3
UK	62.7	62.4	62.0	60.5	59.7	−3.0
US	65.1	64.8	62.8	62.2	61.6	−3.5

Source: OECD (1998b, p 53)

Figure 8: Male labour force participation rates and trends of 55- to 64-year-olds in selected countries (1971-95)

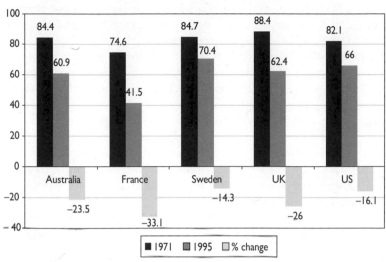

Source: OECD (1998b)

early exit among men – a trend that may reflect a slight fracturing of the male 'breadwinner' myth, particularly in older age. Although we must bear in mind that part-time employment may play a crucial part in the move to retirement, with many early retirees anticipating this, it should not be thought that the differences between countries can be accounted for so easily. There is little correspondence between part-time rates of employment in different countries and early exit rates, but this could still be significant within a particular country (OECD, 1998b, p 91; Unikowski, 1996, pp 10-12). The links between benefit rules, the age restrictions on certain statutory rights, and qualifying ages for complimentary pensions would also require some clarification before any firm conclusions can be made. Nevertheless, it is clear that how people pick their way through the benefit systems is as important as the formal entitlements.

What stands out is that in France, between 1971-95, a further 33.1% of men in the 55-64 age range left paid work. Thus in 1995 only 41.5% of French men in this cohort, compared to 70.4% of their Swedish counterparts, were in the paid labour force. This decline was lowest in Sweden (14.3%), with again the US (16.1% of cohort) statistically much closer to the social democratic model than any of the other countries.

If the data is presented in terms of inactivity rates among 55- to 64-year-olds (see Table 3), Belgium appears at the top (76.9% inactivity rate) and Sweden (31.9%) at the bottom. For anyone aged over 55 who wants to remain in the paid labour force, Sweden appears to offer the most opportunities, although one in three Swedes in this age group are inactive. Again, the countries with data closest to Sweden are not noted for their social democratic welfare regime status. On the contrary the US, Japan and New Zealand are often portrayed as highly commodified, market oriented anti-welfare nation states. It is tempting to suggest that the key variable may simply be Weber's (1976) 'Protestant ethic' and that social and cultural values associated with paid work are stronger in some countries than in others. Interestingly, when I presented this data to a group of Swedish civil servants they initially expressed surprise, then one of them asserted, without dissent from the others, "The Government will not let us leave work".

Table 3: Unemployment and inactivity rates of 55- to 64-year-olds, by country (%)

Country	Unemployment rate	Inactivity rate
Belgium	4.7	76.9
Austria	4.5	71.4
Netherlands	2.5	67.5
France	8.5	63.3
Spain	11.3	62.2
Italy	4.8	61.3
Finland	15.0	58.8
Greece	3.2	57.9
Ireland	6.0	57.4
Germany	14.5	56.3
Australia	7.2	54.1
Canada	7.6	51.6
Portugal	4.7	51.5
United Kingdom	6.3	48.3
Denmark	5.1	45.9
New Zealand	4.0	43.2
United States	2.9	41.1
Japan	3.9	33.1
Sweden	8.0	31.9

Source: taken from PIU (2000) based on OECD (1998b)

Trying to explain the trend towards early exit in terms familiar to a traditional citizenship perspective is not easy. On the one hand it might be argued that Swedish workers are not being pushed out of the labour market, although they are much more likely to be in part-time work than elsewhere (almost four times more likely than their Australian counterparts). This line of argument would also mean that the US appears to be very similar to the Swedish model in terms of attachment and access to full-time paid work. Alternatively, if Esping-Andersen's claim that being able to 'opt out of work' represents an extension of social rights is accepted, it is possible to query whether the social democratic model has gone furthest in extending social rights. A linear view of rights, that sees the state meeting the needs of citizens, is hard to sustain in either case. For women early exit is most likely to mean relying on their spouse's income. For men disability or sickness benefits, some form of transitional benefit, or a complimentary pension will often underpin early exit. With 65 being the qualifying age for the state pension in most countries, it is plain that the state is not underwriting early exit for all.

If, however, the right to retire is underpinned by the private pensions market, former employer pension schemes or the retiree's spouse, Marshall's citizenship model seems rather unhelpful. Likewise, Esping-Andersen's attempt to take de-commodification as the benchmark for measuring the success of welfare regimes in extending social rights must deny that early exit represents a 'right' and any sort of meaningful choice. This in turn would mean denying that trades union struggles to extend occupational pension rights were an improvement for their members. There is also the nonsensical prospect that those countries that have the highest retirement age, even perhaps compelling older people to work until they collapse, could be considered more successful. Consequently the points made by some feminist scholars, that the traditional model of citizenship has less value for an explanation of women's welfare rights — because it locates paid work at its core — may be equally valid, albeit for different reasons, in respect of the trend towards early exit for both men and women (Lewis, 1992, 1997; Lister, 1997).

Controlling desires

To explain the trend towards early exit we have to acknowledge a sea change in people's expectations, aspirations and desires. On the one hand governments want to promote and engage with these ideas in order to encourage retirement planning and saving. As we have seen, stimulating these aspirations has been a feature of the private pensions industry. Diversity among, and 'choice' for, prospective retirees poses a major challenge for traditional models of citizenship and welfare that need to convince a sceptical public that the state is the only guarantor of social rights. In a world where consumer rights often appear to override citizenship rights that may be a difficult task (Dwyer, 1998). Pre-retirement planning and the desires stimulated by this reflexive exercise emphasise identity, options and choices (Featherstone, 1987; Giddens, 1991; Rose, 1996). On the other hand, the growing numbers and proportions of populations that are either thrown out of, or planning to escape from, full-time paid work is clearly a trend that has economic as well as social implications.

There is a very real tension between the social and economic dynamics of the market. Consumption and lifestyle expectations generated in part by pension providers, come up against labour market and economic demands. How governments attempt to reconcile these will be one of the major issues of the 21st century. These tensions between, and within, economic and social policy objectives are not a new development and there have been numerous claims of an impending crisis in the past (Walker, 1996, p 2). During the 1990s, however, these were taken more seriously by national governments as economists urged them to reform their public pension systems. Budd and Campbell (1998) reviewed the data and cited estimates for 2030 that indicated liabilities attributable to future pension commitments amounted to 100% or more of GDP in the US, Germany, France and Italy. In Japan, where early exit is hardly commonplace (see Table 3 and Figure 7), they claimed that liabilities for pensions will be 300% of GDP! Demographic factors play a major part in precisely when particular countries will reach crisis point, but there are dire predictions for any generous public pension scheme (Budd and Campbell, 1998, p 1). It seems that the ghost of Thomas Malthus (see Chapter Two of this book) haunts the data and retirement prospects of future retirees. Basic needs may still be met, but for more than this 'citizens' are increasingly expected to make their own provisions in the market. Of course, sellers in the private pensions market are unlikely to refrain from actively stimulating the aspirations of potential buyers and nor are they expected to do so.

The OECD (1998a, 1998b; Visco, 2001) has been to the fore in calling for reforms to public welfare provisions that promote early exit. Although it is claimed that there is no need to compel people to work longer, it is suggested that this would be good for the well-being of older people themselves, as well as the economy in general of course. The vocabulary is significant because it identifies the negative effects for future retirees. The older worker is described as a 'resource' wastefully discarded by employers, forced out of the labour market by ageist stereotypes or a lack of training programmes, and so on. That is certainly the experience of many in declining industries, particularly the unskilled and those whose skills are surplus to requirements. Lifelong learning, retraining programmes and imploring employers to reconsider their attitudes is, however, simply the soft sell. Beneath this benign concern lies a claw that threatens to snatch away the plans many people have made for an early escape from paid labour. Economic and labour market considerations are to the fore, not lifestyles or choice:

> Population ageing in OECD countries over the coming decades could threaten future growth in prosperity. Governments should take action now across a broad range of economic, financial and social policies to ensure the foundations for maintaining prosperity in an ageing society. While reforms are already underway, much deeper reforms will be needed to meet the challenges of population ageing. (OECD, 1998a, p 1)

Cutting the value of public pensions, reducing entitlements and increasing contributions are all options, but restraining early exit is clearly the goal:

> Taxes to support the retired will be easier to bear, when the working-age population can look forward to rising prosperity. Encouraging people to work longer would raise economic growth, increase the tax base, and reduce the numbers of dependent older persons, a triple gain. The higher national saving, if used productively, will result in higher capital stock and thus more output over the long term. (OECD, 1998a, p 4)

> [But] current public pension systems, tax systems and social programmes interact to provide a strong disincentive for workers to remain in the labour force after a certain age. Removing these disincentives, perhaps even providing positive incentives to work longer, coupled with effective steps to enhance the employability of older workers, could make an important contribution to sustaining the growth of living standards. (OECD, 1998a, p 3)

Responses and reforms

Following the OECD's (1998a, 1998b) edicts and Giddens' (1998) 'third way' treatise, the British government issued a Cabinet report that should alarm anyone who hopes to retire:

> The very concept of 'retirement' needs to be challenged. Retirement fits well with a situation where leaving one's lifelong job is associated with the end of one's working life. This is an increasingly inaccurate description of what happens. It would be useful in the short term to blur, and in the long term to abolish, the concept of retirement. (PIU, 2000, p 47)

And yet in Britain leading figures in the Treasury reported the good news that the economic costs of the public welfare system of supporting retirees are entirely manageable (Budd and Campbell, 1998). The bad news being that this is largely a consequence of the pitifully low value of public pensions. Changes to SERPS and in the value of the basic NI pension introduced in the 1980s are calculated to have reduced the value, and future costs, of both schemes. Further savings will be made from 2010 as women's public pension age is increased in phases to 65. These changes in the value of benefits and entitlement conditions "helps to explain, in large part, why the UK avoids the longer-term fiscal crises forecast (on current policies) elsewhere" (Budd and Campbell, 1998, p 1). The effect has been to cut the basic NI pension in relation to average earnings by roughly 30% between 1978 and 1998. Stakeholder reforms introduced by Labour in 2001 claim to be targeted at low earners, and to address the needs of people with discontinuous employment histories. Apart from the government, however, few observers feel that the scheme will be sufficiently attractive and compulsory saving is likely to follow (Walker, 1999). As the previous quote suggests, the next major reform will probably be to graduate the exit age in a similar fashion to the US and Sweden. The idea of raising the retirement age, compulsory saving for the poorest, creating obstacles to early exit and compelling older workers to accept their responsibility to retrain, is even being promoted by 'radicals' who ought to be aware of the regressive impact of such reforms (Pensions Reform Group, 2001).

Britain is not alone in tinkering with the state pensions system and virtually every OECD country has tried to adjust their pension commitments in the past decade (Bonoli, 2000; OECD, 1998b). These adjustments seek to curtail entitlement or the value of the benefits, or both. Restrictions have been imposed on the age of retirement, the tax system has been adjusted to the disadvantage of early leavers and pensioners who have saved, the value of benefits has been allowed to slide downwards, universal schemes have become means tested, and governments around the world could be seen as having reneged on their predecessors''pensions promises' (Bonoli, 2000; Goode, 1993).

In the US the age at which full social security benefits are payable has been raised to 67 from 65, with a sliding scale of benefit reductions based on age cohorts. For many African and Hispanic Americans this could have the effect of ending their right to retire. The main factors affecting access to a retirement income are similar to those in the UK, but the pattern is clearer, the social divisions deeper and the implications greater. A combination of lower labour force participation rates, lower incomes, labour market discrimination, economic restructuring in the 1980s, lower educational qualifications, more childcare responsibilities and shorter life expectancy will reinforce racial and gender divisions in retirement. Hispanic American women look likely to have the lowest retirement incomes from 2010-30, while African American men can expect the least amount of time in retirement (Dailey, 1998; Elo, 2001). Moreover, "the overwhelming majority of baby boom women will not have earned the right to retire in spite of spending almost thirty years in the paid labor force" (Dailey, 1998, p 1). Unsurprisingly, childcare, interrupted periods of full-time work, limited access to the better (DB) pension schemes and lower earnings that make contributing difficult (especially when young children take precedence over saving for oneself in 30-40 years time), are some of the obstacles for US baby boom women that will be familiar to their British and Australian counterparts, although there are also some interesting variations between these countries (Bryson et al, 1994; Morris, 1990).

Using a sliding scale of entitlement based on age cohorts is a particularly clever, if insidious, reform. By delaying the implementation for 10-30 years, younger people often realise that their rights have been undermined when it is too late to protest. By graduating entitlements, the impact of the changes only affects a limited proportion of the population each year and could be seen as a cynical manipulation of public opinion and younger people's understandable, but misplaced, complacency regarding future retirement rights. In this way, the right to a retirement income is increasingly blurred, a strategy that can conveniently conceal government intentions. The rationale used points to increased life expectancy among age cohorts, and thus demographic data and actuarial assumptions appear to justify reform. But this is very misleading and highly regressive in its effects. Life expectancy varies enormously within age cohorts according to social class, gender, race, region and former occupation (Payne and Payne, 2000). Moreover, the need for a public pension is inversely related to life expectancy. Put bluntly, poorer people die younger. The use of aggregate data for age cohorts conceals this fact and distorts the picture of who benefits from the matrix of policies that underwrite the different elements of the SDW.

Any reliable economic and actuarial audit for the US would have to calculate life expectancy according to social class, gender, ethnicity and lifestyle, not simply crude dependency ratios. Among other factors this would include the cost of fiscal measures that underwrite private and company pensions, the cost to general taxpayers of generous pensions for public employees (costs that rise substantially with income and professional status) and the lost tax revenues that result from early exit by high earners who do not have to rely on public welfare.

> Estimates in 1996 suggested that 6.6 million retired people in the US had annual incomes of over US$50,000 and relatively few of these would be affected by the age restrictions imposed by the social security system (Kollmann, 1996, p 2).

In the US, as elsewhere, it is the poorest, those who have had the least opportunities with the lowest rewards over their working life, who will be expected to delay their retirement. Given the demographics, economics and social composition of the US, the prospect of white, retired, fortress America, being catered for by a largely female, black and Hispanic service class, older than themselves, is not unlikely.

As Einer Overbye (1996) points out, expectations and aspirations regarding the balance between work and retirement have been major issues in Sweden as well. The Swedes have not been immune to the sirens of the market and reforms have been similar in principle, if not in practice. He suggests that the social pressures and processes associated with increasing affluence and greater expectations about the quality of life in retirement are occurring across all OECD states. Bonoli (2000) also sees a common political agenda promoting welfare convergence by putting pressure on political parties to meet the desires of their electorate while restraining expenditure. This in turn promotes a two-tier pension system with a safety net underpinning 'complimentary' schemes common across Europe, the US and Australia (Bonoli, 2000; apRoberts, 1994). These two-tier schemes provide a pension that allows for more flexibility in the meeting of aspirations, or at least the aspirations of those that can access them (Overbye, 1996). This can be seen in the reforms to the Swedish pension system that were introduced in the 1990s and came into effect in 2001. These witnessed a shift from DBs to DCs, increased employee contributions, the introduction of a funded element to the state scheme and a graduated income, very similar to that in the US, based on the age of retirement from 61 to 67, with penalties being applied to younger retirees. Although remarkably generous by British standards the Swedish system had, from the mid-1980s, increasingly struggled to retain the support of higher earners and those who wanted to exit early. Whereas in 1984 less than 5% of Swedish adults had a private pension there was a five-fold increase in just over a decade to 25% by 1996 (DN 10/8/95 and 28/12/96, cited in Gould, 2001). In part this may have reflected understandable concerns about the future of the state schemes during the reform period. It should also be noted that, like elsewhere, private provisions were facilitated by fiscal support from the government. Whatever the causes, the increase in private provisions fractures the image of a universal system that retains the support of all. A key test of the recent pension reforms will, therefore, be whether they meet the aspirations of those Swedes who did not turn to private pensions. If significant disparities emerge between the exit ages of different social classes, with higher earners who took out private plans having more flexibility and choice, it remains to be seen whether Sweden will be able to sustain its enviable record of popular support for public welfare.

So far the question of early exit has been discussed in the context of paid work. It has been suggested that if early exit represents a measure of de-commodification then, with a slightly mischievous twist of the data, it is a measure that would see Esping-Andersen's welfare regimes model being inverted. Moreover, it has been pointed out that the right to retirement appears to be in a rather fragile condition in many countries, with some powerful economic arguments being made to abolish the concept entirely. However, it is important to emphasise that the meaning of 'early exit' and of retirement itself is not, and never has been, universal. Esping-Andersen's account focuses primarily on the ability of public welfare systems to address class interests and to resolve class antagonisms. The rest of this chapter will be concerned with informal welfare and other welfare means and mechanisms that have to be borne in mind when making comparisons.

Informal welfare and early exit

The neglect of informal welfare by Titmuss was discussed in Chapter One, but the implications of that neglect become starkly apparent in the context of welfare regimes, de-commodification and choices about early exit. First, for many women their relationship to, and experience of, paid labour will differ significantly to that of many men. The establishment of a sexual division of labour, with women as 'carers' and men as 'breadwinners', went hand in glove with working-class strategies that resisted the establishment of a capitalist social division of labour (Seccomb, 1986). Although Esping-Andersen pays scant attention to exclusion and intra-class contests it is, ironically, an example that supports his claim that politics matters. The ways in which 'dependency' and 'independence' have historically been constructed in relation to paid labour, the neglect of informal care arrangements and the failure to acknowledge interdependence, are made visible by an approach informed by the SDW (Mann, 1992; Rose, 1981).

Second, women's traditional caring responsibilities make it harder to distinguish an exit point from work, and thus any definition of de-commodification that is premised on paid labour alone has to be queried. Likewise, assumptions regarding future care needs, or changes in caring practices that may be negotiated informally within households as a result of retirement, need to be considered. This in turn suggests that we need a more sensitive approach to the way 'choices' about retirement may be presented to, and made by, women and men.

Esping-Andersen's neglect of informal welfare in the making of the SDW derives, in part, from his view of how class forces have mobilised. He observes various class alliances, and even acknowledges fractures within dominant classes, but fails to see that divisions and distinctions within 'the' working class can be crucially important. Thus, Esping-Andersen is correct to look at how respective trades unions, labour organisations and political parties provided a voice that governments listened to. Although he fails to notice that in most countries it has been the voice of the male, skilled, white, able-bodied, full-time worker that has been listened to the most carefully. Nor is this point confined to gender since the 'making' of social policy reflected the interests of those whose voices could be heard. 'Other' voices – the unskilled, the disabled, the migrant and the female – existed, but were only rarely listened to. The sexual and social divisions of labour have been crucial sites for excluding 'others', which has in turn resulted in exclusion from the relatively privileged aspects of the SDW

(Castles, 1985; Mann, 1992; Sass, 1997). This has been re-emphasised of late by Selma Sevenhuijsen who, drawing on Tronto's (1993) idea of 'privileged irresponsibility', states:

> ... it still seems necessary to deconstruct the normative image of the independent wage earning citizen that is still at the heart of contemporary notions of social participation and citizenship and to acknowledge the fact that everybody is dependent on care.... Stating this in terms of inclusion and exclusion, there is a need to analyse the gendered dynamics of access to and exit from caring arrangements and the corresponding patterns of access and exit in the spheres of paid labour and political decision making. (2000, p 24)

Indeed, and we might add that the patterns of informal decision making influencing access and exclusion are less visible than those that take place on the larger political stage.

Consequently the meaning of retirement and the decision to retire have to be explored with care and caring responsibilities to the fore. For many women the decision to exit the paid labour market, the resources they will rely on when they do so, and the meaning of 'exit' will differ significantly to that of many men. The point was made in Chapter One, but it is worth repeating, that as both providers of, and dependants upon informal welfare, women are frequently disadvantaged. As providers of care women are excluded from the full benefits of occupational pensions, find their public pension rights diminished and are rarely able to access private (with fiscal support) welfare benefits of any value. This in turn often means a process of informal negotiation within households over access to resources in which claims have very little correspondence with enforceable rights. Women are therefore usually in a weaker economic position than their male partners when reflecting on or making retirement plans (Arber and Ginn, 1995b).

Among the range of 'push and pull' factors that confront individuals close to retirement, some are more clearly gendered than others. The following summary draws heavily on examples from the UK to illustrate some of the most significant factors. It is a rather lengthy list, but it is important to provide it because so many of the points are often overlooked.

- Age-related sex discrimination in the labour market, underpinned by the state pension age for women. Most countries are standardising the age of retirement, but it will be another 20 years or so before this is realised. The effect is to reduce the time women can contribute to a pension, thereby reducing their pension rights, and it can also mean employers are reluctant to train or employ older women.

- State-defined exit ages can also be significant within specific households. Within heterosexual relationships men tend to be older than their partners by a couple of years. It might be thought that this would promote a joint exit age, thus the aggregate data shows women across the OECD exiting 3-4 years earlier than men. However, Arber and Ginn found that "only a small minority of British couples left their last jobs at about the same time" and they concluded that "cultural norms which militate against women being in paid employment when their husbands are not working are much weaker among older couples than they are at earlier stages of the life-course" (1995b, p 85). This might suggest that informal negotiations within households become more democratic as we approach retirement (Giddens, 1991).
- The value of many women's future pension, and ability to sustain contributions, is most clearly affected by their prior caring commitments and lower incomes. As a result many women may feel that they cannot afford to exit when they would like to (Arber and Ginn, 1995b).
- Unfulfilled ambitions and career goals may also influence the decision to exit. For women whose career trajectory has been delayed or interrupted by prior caring commitments this may mean they are reluctant to exit.
- The glass ceiling of age (Bernard et al, 1995), whereby ambitions can be frustrated by employers who look to promote younger workers premised on ageist assumptions, may also encourage women to exit earlier than men. (For example, a woman aged 56 and a man aged 61 are both four years from the state pension age in the UK, but the woman hits the glass ceiling of age five years earlier.)
- Traditional gender inequalities in domestic labour and care responsibilities may promote a concern among many women that retirement will simply mean that their male partner is free to pursue his leisure activities, leaving them more isolated.
- Loss of economic independence on leaving paid work may also restrain many women's retirement options.
- Divorce has a negative impact on the retirement incomes of many women and will continue to do so for many years to come, despite recent changes in UK law. The decision to exit for divorced women may well be influenced by a lack of resources.
- Knowledge of pension rights and accrued assets is a key factor in making the decision to retire, but many people are poorly informed. Women in particular appear to over-estimate their likely pension entitlements and to have few

reliable sources of information on which to base their retirement decision (Goode, 1993). Without access to reliable information women may simply accept their spouse's retirement decisions (Bernard et al, 1995).

- Care for others in the paid labour market also influences the experience and meaning of early exit in numerous ways. In the paid labour market women are closely associated with care, for example, as nurses, cleaners, health visitors and care assistants. Many of these jobs are relatively poorly paid, and although public sector workers can usually access an occupational pension scheme, the value of the pension will reflect the individual's previous earnings. Often these caring tasks rely on women's part-time working patterns. The growth of privately provided care, for example residential homes, home care and home helps, will exacerbate the problem for paid carers because there are rarely any occupational pension provisions. Delaying exit may boost any pension rights that exist (Ungerson, 2000).

- A desire to care may mean the opportunity of exiting early is taken as soon as possible. For example, grandparents may want to spend more time with their grandchildren. Again, traditional gender expectations may mean women are quicker to take on these responsibilities than men.

- On the other hand there may be unwelcome expectations and pressures placed on prospective retirees to provide care for grandchildren or relatives. This too may be felt more keenly by women than men.

- Likewise, caring for infirm parents and partners is more likely to fall to women, in part because of social norms but also because of the demographics of ageing. Thus it is more likely to be a female relative who is in need of care, because women outlive men, but they will often be cared for by daughters and daughters-in-law. However, there is some evidence that the balance of caring responsibilities is shifting, particularly among older couples (Ungerson, 2000).

- A host of practices within the paid labour market creates a complex pattern interwoven with gender expectations. A few examples should suffice. Calls for 'voluntary redundancy' and early retirement packages may place particular and different pressures on men and women to leave. The cost to an employer of shedding part-time workers is usually much lower than full time, and women are more likely to be working part time. Likewise, trades union agreements with employers can contain a 'last in first out' clause if there are to be redundancies. Again, because women are more likely to have interrupted employment histories they are also more likely to be the most recent recruits – that is, the last in and therefore the first out.

- The idea of the 'male breadwinner' is so deeply embedded in the popular consciousness that this can effectively legitimate discriminatory practices.

> More insidiously, such concepts may influence the way both men and women consider the question of who ought to leave, with older women feeling they should make way for younger men.

The above list is by no means comprehensive but it serves to emphasise the fact that even the decision over when to retire, and what this might then mean, is likely to be different for men and women. Most obviously care responsibilities are not shared, either within households, or society. As Lewis (1992, 1997) has made plain, the construction of welfare regimes that are incapable of reflecting the gendered dynamics of welfare are inadequate and potentially misleading. Thus for men too it is important to recognise the ways in which both the experience of retirement and routes to it may be gendered (Gradman, 1994).

Simultaneously we should be careful not to see gender as a determinant and the evidence of gender differences is not straightforward. Social class retains a sharp edge capable of cutting across gender inequalities. While economic dependency may be a common experience for women in retirement, this will be mediated by social class and the resources that go with it. For example, higher income non-manual worker males tend to exit through early retirement, while lower income manual worker males often exit due to redundancy or ill health. Social class differences between men can be more striking than generic gender differences (Laczko and Phillipson, 1991; Tanner, 1997). However, this ignores the impact of gender within particular social settings. Clearly for those women whose husbands were formerly manual workers, and in the absence of any meaningful pension rights of their own, the result is dependency on someone who is themselves relatively poor.

In the US, similar concerns have been raised regarding the trend towards social divisions within the retired population and the implications this has for any meaningful retirement 'choice'. Dailey (1998) has made a strong case for treating the question of choice in retirement as an issue that has specific implications for 'baby boom women'. She emphasises the demographic and political themes that will play a part. Her concern is that: "Marital instability, single parenting, and new family structures have served to cement the care giving role of women in our society.... Baby boom women will shift their caregiving from children to the frail elderly as they move towards old age" (1998, p 125). Only a minority of women in the US – she estimates about 20% – will have the financial means to avoid care giving and enjoy their retirement. For many women the challenge is likely to be even greater. As Dailey (1998) makes plain, without adequate financial security, which she equates with private and occupational provisions, women are likely to find themselves undertaking a 'caring' role for older relatives during their own early retirement. If they reject this traditional responsibility it is not clear that anyone else, male relatives or the state being the obvious alternatives, will step into the breach. Consequently, older relatives, mainly the mothers and sisters of the baby boom women, will have an even worse experience of older age.

The breaking up of the 'breadwinner' ethos may not, in this scenario, have many positive effects, but may leave older women even more exposed and more individuated at a time in their lives when they will be least able to articulate their needs. For those baby boom women who can make provisions for themselves, following a path that is geared towards paid employment, the ability to access the good jobs will often have involved a rejection of providing informal welfare, or at least paying someone else to do so, at crucial times in their careers. Making a second decision to reject the calls for them to provide informal welfare/care as their own retirement looms will require additional resolve and resources. Those resources will not be available to most women. Moreover, because women tend to outlive men, and men are more likely to have a more generous pension, women who divorce or stay single may be paying a "pension penalty" (Ginn and Arber, 1993). Dailey concluded that: "Finally, as difficult as it may be for women to believe, the best insurance policy for baby boom women is to stay married" (1998, p 127).

Interestingly both Esping-Andersen and feminist scholars, some of whom are critical of his account (for example, Lewis, 1992), often use a measure of welfare success that identifies 'choice', measured in terms of independence and reflected in citizenship rights, as central (Ginn and Arber, 1992b). For the former it is independence from wage slavery and for the latter independence from men and domestic slavery that usually provides the test. The consensus extends to the conclusion that the Scandinavian countries have gone furthest towards extending citizenship rights. Similarly, Ginn and Arber (1992b) compared provisions in Germany, Denmark and the UK, and explored the penalties pension systems imposed on women in relation to their caring responsibilities. They concluded that the UK and German pension systems were predicated on the idea that women would depend on their husband's/spouse's pension rights. Part-time workers and women with discontinuous employment histories were effectively excluded from occupational welfare in both the UK and

Germany. However, the German system is more generous towards dependants and favours the informal welfare arrangements made within traditional households. The Danish pension system was seen by Ginn and Arber as preferable because it made allowances for interrupted employment, part-time work and was underpinned by a generous universal pension. The Danish system was also 'better' because it offered most choice, draws on all forms of welfare and was more flexible, reflecting different types of dependency in different circumstances. A flexibility that will be more important for all, if changes in working practices are sustained in the future. Ginn and Arber also concluded that further moves to increase women's economic independence in retirement, combined with labour market changes across Europe, were likely to make this a priority issue for the EU in the future. In which case nation states may no longer be the guarantors of citizenship rights and comparative accounts of social policy might have to explain processes of convergence rather than difference. It should be recalled, however, that the Danish system is also supported with some generous fiscal welfare measures (Kvist and Sinfield, 1996). This in turn should remind us that welfare can be provided by various and different means.

Other means and different meanings

An approach based on the SDW inevitably draws attention to the different ways in which welfare can be provided, delivered and funded. Thus it is necessary to consider some of the less visible costs and resources that can influence decisions. Kvist and Sinfield (1996) have made a powerful case for comparative work to consider, and governments to make accessible, the complex ways that tax and welfare systems interact. Furthermore, some essential forms of expenditure, for example housing costs, will have a profound impact on the lifestyle of retirees (Castles, 1997). By explicitly comparing Swedish and Australian patterns of early exit from paid employment, in relation to the resources and costs this involves, the picture of Scandinavian success looks less clear.

Esping-Andersen states that in Sweden the "social democrats have pursued a welfare state that would promote an equality of the highest standards" (1990, p 27).

Compared to the UK, the Swedish system looks remarkably attractive with a minimum pension worth 40% of AWE, compared to 15% in the UK and 25% in Australia, but there are some hidden 'costs' and potential drawbacks. The so-called transition to retirement for many Swedes in the 1990s involved part-time work, with 34% of men and 60.5% of women aged between 60 and 65 working part time, compared with 16.2% and 70.6% in the UK, and a lowly 9% of men and 10% of women in Australia (Unikowski, 1996, pp 11-12; OECD, 1998b, p 91).

On the face of it, for anyone seeking to fully retire, or retire early, the Swedish system looks much less attractive than the Australian, and vice versa of course. However, and apart from being more 'generous', the Swedish system demonstrates more similarities than differences with other OECD countries. Of course a great many British pensioners would welcome such generosity from their government and it seems churlish to query the Swedish success story. But this 'generosity' has to be set in context. It tends to be forgotten that the cost of paying for more generous benefits has to be met by someone. Employee contributions to public pension schemes can vary significantly.

For example, the Swedish government deducts nearly 20% of the average wage earners income to pay for the public pension. The UK takes roughly 14%, while the Australian public pension is paid for from general taxation and employees do not have a specified contribution rate. Nor are Australians required by the state to contribute to the compulsory occupational pension, the SGC, although most employers require this as a condition of employment. The SGC requires all employers to pay, not employees (much to the chagrin of the Confederation of Australian Industry when the SGC was proposed). In theory, if not in practice, there are no compulsory employee contributions for either the Age Pension, or the basic occupational (SGC) pensions (Mann, 1993; Olsberg, 1997; OECD, 1998b, p 100).

Whereas the insurance principle for funding public welfare was adopted in many European countries, this was, and still is, fiercely resisted as a form of regressive taxation by the Australian labour movement. It should be stressed that in practice most Australian employees make substantial contributions to their occupational pension, because they and their employers pay more than the minimum contributions. The retirement benefits that most Australians can anticipate are largely an outcome of trades union/employer negotiations set within the context of the Wage Award system. Like the Swedish system of negotiation and consultation, and in line with Esping-Andersen's model, it is clear that organised labour in Australia has asserted itself in the interests of its core membership. This means that, like any earnings-related scheme, you need to be earning before you begin to benefit, and the more you earn, the more you are likely to benefit (Mann, 1993; Olsberg, 1997; Thompson and Shaver, 1998).

Given the value of the pension, it might be thought that the Swedish system would encourage earlier retirement and lower labour force participation rates than in Australia or the UK, but as we have seen this is not so. Bearing in mind Esping-Andersen's definition of de-commodification – the ability to exit paid labour when it suits the needs of the individual – the data is initially rather perplexing.

Castles (1997) has considered male early retirement (ages 55-64) rates in a number of countries and reflected on the apparent anomalies. Despite the fact that Australia has a relatively low level of state expenditure on public welfare, and that the Age Pension is not available before the age of 65, early exit is quite high. Between 1980 and 1992, 37.4% of Australian males between the ages of 55 and 65 had left the paid labour force, compared with 24.2% in Sweden (Castles, 1997, p 100). The average Australian male is likely to exit more than two years earlier than their Swedish counterpart. The data for women provides an even starker contrast, with the average retirement age in 1995 being nearly five years older in Sweden and with more than twice as many women over 54 participating in the paid labour market, than in Australia (See Figure 7; OECD, 1998b, p 82).

The question of why so many more Australians exit the labour force early is an interesting one. There are a number of complex reasons cited by Castles (1997), of which the salient ones are: the extensive occupational and private pension funds; public welfare schemes that permit earlier exit or support for older unemployed workers; disability/sickness pensions, and, importantly, homeownership rates. Castles (1997) shows that the extraordinarily high level of home ownership in Australia – at over 73% ownership for all income deciles over 55 years of age and 81% on average – serves as a form of welfare. It may enable some to escape from paid labour and for others it provides a buttress against poverty once they have done so. Without paying rent, the effective disposable income of retirees is higher and the decision to retire may be influenced by the date at which the mortgage is finally paid off. It should be stressed that Esping-Andersen (1990, p 102) acknowledges this and calculates it amounts to a 15-20% income supplement for retirees in countries like Australia and the US. However, homeownership can also often be translated into equity by 'trading down' in the housing market. This will only be a realistic option for those in urban areas where property prices have been quite high, for example Sydney and Melbourne in Australia, and may involve moving away from the city centres to retirement enclaves on the coast. There may be some negative effects from such a process, with former friends, family and neighbourhood networks being less able (always assuming that they were previously willing) to provide informal care in later life. That said, trading down in the value of the property, and thereby realising some of the equity, appears to be an option for some who want to exit early and does not necessarily equate with poor housing. Getting out of the city and down to the beach may even be preferable for many retirees (Castles, 1997; Unikowski, 1996; Olsberg, 1997).

Castles is keen to emphasise the fact that the 'retirement decision' is not always one that necessarily conforms to the idea of 'lifestyle planning' and reflexivity (Giddens, 1991, 1994; see Chapter Five of this book).

> Castles uses the example of 'Joe', who makes it clear that his decision to retire was made with an idea of what sort of lifestyle he wanted, but that the "bullshit" at work and the disposable income he would have, meant he was prepared to adapt his lifestyle accordingly (1997, p 99). Joe was more fortunate than some of his friends because he had been able to stay with the same employer for a long time, generating a reasonable superannuation pension.

Labour mobility, a key feature of contemporary labour markets, may result in less flexibility in the future for individuals when they approach retirement age. Thus decisions and choices are made, but the consequences of these are difficult to predict. Whether people approaching retirement in the 21st century will have correctly anticipated changes in house prices, in the cost of living and their expected pension rights is doubtful. In Britain, even people close to retirement often miscalculate their likely pension benefits (Goode, 1993; Tanner, 1997). Thus it would be a big gamble to predicate any future retirement plans on the way markets, families, work, care needs and society might change during a lifetime.

The point is, to paraphrase Marx, 'choices' are being made, but not under conditions of our own choosing. Hindsight and post hoc rationalisations often impose a logic to decisions made when we were younger. In Castles' example, Joe did not realise that property prices for the eastern inner city suburbs of Sydney would soar. Some pensioners may have made calculated decisions and planned for their retirement, but others will simply find that options present themselves. The informal, fiscal and occupational systems of welfare may, therefore, facilitate possibilities, but these are not predictable.

A further difficulty that social democratic welfare regimes confront is in funding their more generous welfare system. Esping-Andersen acknowledges that there is a need for such welfare regimes to maximise revenue income and to minimise social problems if they are to be viable. The Swedish electorate has thus far been prepared to return governments to power that in Britain would be described as 'tax and spend'. Both direct taxation on income and indirect consumption taxes are relatively high in Sweden. Even so, the demands on welfare have to be restrained. Ironically Esping-Andersen accepts that: "This is obviously best done with most people working, and the fewest possible living off social transfers" (1990, p 28). Consequently, the Swedish system tries to discourage early exit; whereas the trades union movement in Australia has, in effect if not intention, promoted a welfare system that enables early retirement. The irony is that Esping-Andersen's measure of welfare success is 'de-commodification' – defined as the ability to exit when it suits the individual.

The crucial point is that early exit from paid work appears to be an option for more Australians than it is for older workers in many other OECD countries. This does not mean that the Australian system is 'better' than the Swedish system, in many respects it is not (Scheiwe, 1999; Thompson and Shaver, 1998). However, if the measure of welfare success is the ability to exit the paid labour market when it suits the individual, then it appears that de-commodification, as Esping-Andersen defines it, has gone further in Australia than in Sweden. Against this rather mischievous conclusion we have to add that this is a measure of de-commodification that applies to the paid labour force only, and therefore may be more appropriate for men than women (Lewis, 1992, 1997). Alternatively, it may be that the search for an appropriate comparative measure is the Holy Grail of social policy.

Summary and assessment

Too often comparative accounts of social policy create the impression of a nosy neighbour peering over the fence – the grass is always greener on the other side. Many people approaching retirement are likely to feel much the same. Getting out looks very attractive, but once out the reality can be different and some will return to the paid labour market.

What stands out most clearly from this chapter is that a focus on public welfare can obscure some of the other significant means by which needs, desires and expectations are addressed. In contrast to Walker (1996, p 16), it has been argued here that market-oriented welfare states such as Australia and the US are not predictable, and are interesting. It is the unpredictability and uncertainty of informal, fiscal and occupational welfare in the market-oriented welfare states that is noteworthy. For people with resources who can access more than public welfare there are also more options and choices. However, for those who are excluded from the more privileged features of the SDW in the UK, US and Australia, the reliability and predictability of the Swedish system is its greatest asset.

Esping-Andersen uses the idea of a social division of welfare, but not always as explicitly as he might, and he acknowledges Titmuss's influence on his work. However, he overlooks the parallels with Durkheim's (1933) functionalist analysis that run through Titmuss's account. Consequently, it might be appropriate to refer to the 'social democratic welfare regime cluster' as 'the functionalist welfare state' instead; societies in which social solidarity is premised on shared norms and values, promoted by universal provisions mediated by the state, and with a fairly homogenous population and culture. Like Titmuss, Esping-Andersen is concerned with the role of welfare as a stabilising force on society as a whole: "Many countries became self-proclaimed welfare states, not so much to give a label to their social policies as to foster national social integration" (1996, p 2). Certainly the vocabulary of social integration echoes Durkheim's and Titmuss's (1958, pp 53-5) thinking about social solidarity (Levitas, 1996). Plus, both Titmuss and Esping-Andersen believe public welfare, via generous universal services, is most able to retain widespread support, and thereby serves to enhance the 'conscience collective'.

However, Esping-Andersen is content to use a number of other sociological traditions and is, quite rightly, unafraid of eclecticism. He draws on at least four other political and sociological approaches in constructing his analysis:

- radical political economy;
- the Marxist social historian's tradition;
- Weberian 'ideal types';
- and positivism.

First, a concern with class interests and the balance of class forces within the overall political economy of nation states underpins his analysis. But he breaks with radical political economy in pointing to class alliances that mean it is possible, within a social democratic framework, to overcome irreconcilable class interests. This leads him on to his second theoretical tool because these class alliances have to be 'made'. At this point Esping-Andersen seems closer to the sort of analyses provided by Marxist social historians (Kaye, 1984). Assessing the relative success of class mobilisations and alliances is facilitated by the third distinctive feature in his approach; the construction of his various 'welfare regimes', which look similar to Weberian ideal types. The fourth strand is Esping-Andersen's positivism. As Watts has observed:

> From the older liberal-functionalism represented by Wilensky (1975) to the more sophisticated neo-Marxist analyses associated with Korpi and Esping-Andersen ... there is no doubting the seductive pull of the persistent belief shared among comparative policy analysts that measurement will somehow lead to theoretical generalisations possessing the predictive and explanatory capacity that a real 'science' ought to possess. (1997, p 5)

The point is not that Esping-Andersen is eclectically picking only the best cherries but, on the contrary, he appears to have selected some bruised fruit. The assumption of opposing class interests that is central to radical political economy, whether these can be reconciled or not, pays inadequate attention to interests that might not appreciate the smothering embrace of class. This in turn may neglect the part that intra-class divisions have played in the making of the SDW (Mann, 1986, 1992). The resultant political alliances and the 'universal' measures enacted may, therefore, have the effect of promoting social solidarity, but this might be experienced as a stifling conformity, or inappropriate homogeneity (Williams, 1989, 1996). Moreover, the 'ideal type' method is inclined to promote a tautology that reinforces the assumptions of the observer. Thus, the definition of a social democratic welfare regime identifies features of that 'type', and simultaneously defines 'types' of welfare regimes in terms of the features they have that correspond. Different typologies will generate different regime clusters, but may simply promote taxonomic invention or interminable semantic squabbles (Lewis, 1997, pp 165-6). The charge of positivism reflects the criticisms made here of Esping-Andersen's 'measure' – de-commodification. However, it is a charge that can easily be bandied around and those that do so tend to err towards some fairly rarefied and relativist theories. Nevertheless, the point Watts (1997) makes is valid, and Esping-Andersen is certainly keen to measure 'success' using some predetermined, but rather clumsy and contestable, calibrations.

Nevertheless, and despite the above, there can be little dispute over Esping-Andersen's contribution to comparative analyses. While commentators are rarely prepared to unequivocally endorse his account it has provided the basis for an extensive debate and has, albeit unintentionally, highlighted the central problems any comparative approach must try to tackle. Most countries appear to be promoting a longer working life for economic reasons, irrespective of whether this is socially desirable. Abolishing retirement would, among other advantages for employers and governments, increase competition in the labour market, reduce public welfare expenditure and generate tax revenue. It would also reinforce existing disparities in the 'working life', generate further social and income inequalities, make private and occupational pensions even more attractive, bolster the work ethic and impinge on the retirement plans many people made that were premised on the commitments governments gave 20-40 years ago. In effect, abolishing the right to retire would represent a degree of re-commodification.

Politics matters in this context, and the fact that there are tremendous differences between countries in the way the SDW enables, or restrains such options, confirms Esping-Andersen's claim. The need to ensure that older people are not discriminated against, or pressed into servicing the economy and/or their families, or treated as some sort of reserve army, is vital. Simultaneously, there is a need to consider what a 'working life' might look like, and how long this should be. Particular countries, and more recently the EU, have established norms for a working day, a working week and even a working year, but as yet there is no agreement on what a 'working life' might consist of. Any attempt to do so would, however, have to recognise the fact that work need not be paid, and need not be formally structured. Informal welfare providers and dependants clearly require their work and their needs to be acknowledged. However, the academic point that emerges most strongly from this chapter is that the search for an appropriate 'measure' of comparison is rather pointless, unless and until we have a more sensitive theoretical model. Once again we can summarise the strengths and weaknesses of the approach considered in this chapter as follows.

Main strengths of the approach

- Acknowledges the SDW and the different forms that welfare can take.
- Locates the SDW within specific socio-political and economic contexts.
- Provides comparative social policy with a theoretically informed template.
- Explicitly considers social exclusion and social divisions in relation to welfare.
- Takes retirement choice as one of the benchmarks of welfare success.
- Highlights the way that politics matters, for example, even relatively small nations like Sweden and Australia differ.
- Sets an engaging agenda that identifies some of the vital issues.
- Takes a standpoint and holds out the prospect of change.

Weaknesses of the approach

- Overlooks Titmuss's functionalism.
- Neglects informal welfare and care.
- Under-estimates the impact of intra-class divisions in the making of the SDW.
- Consumption trends, preferences and aspirations are under-valued.
- The typology privileges universal public welfare and downgrades welfare by other means.

SEVEN

Prophets, profits and uncertain conclusions

The final task of this book is to draw together the key features of the approaches set out in the preceding chapters and to show how these can be reconciled with a revised version of the SDW. Hopefully, this will both guide the reader as they rethink retirement, and highlight the social, ethical and political questions that need to be considered.

Before a reconstructed account of the SDW is attempted, it is important to acknowledge the continuing significance of the key points Titmuss made in the 1950s:

- public welfare is not the only form that welfare takes and those that assume it is are either mischievous, or naive;
- welfare dependency affects everyone and is a feature of all developed societies;
- interdependency is unavoidable;
- social divisions in retirement are directly related to the SDW and to the forms of welfare social groups can access;
- trying to ensure social justice and equity between the different forms of welfare that exist is a legitimate goal.

Although the SDW remains an adaptable mid-range theory, Titmuss's version, however, has to be heavily revised along the lines set out in Chapter One (Sinfield, 1978; Rose, 1981). Titmuss's functionalist perspective simply fails to explain the development of dependency and interdependency, but that has been addressed earlier and at length elsewhere (Mann, 1992). Above all else, the SDW has to take on board feminist critiques and locate informal welfare alongside occupational, fiscal and public provisions. That does not mean that informal welfare accounts for all the blatant and persistent gender divisions among the retired population. On the contrary, there are profound gender divisions in respect of each aspect of the SDW. Informal welfare also plays a major part in the pattern of inequality within the other elements of the SDW. But informal welfare is distinctive because there are very few formal mechanisms that can compensate providers for the loss of retirement and pensions rights. Nor is the law necessarily the solution. For example, splitting pensions on divorce is likely to generate nightmares for actuaries, with minor improvements for some women, but substantial legal fees for lawyers (*Pensions World*, April 2001). Moreover, lone mothers and working-class women whose spouses do not have occupational or private pensions, will still have to rely on means-tested, increasingly residualised, public welfare when they retire. Without some mechanism to promote equity between the different elements of the SDW, women, especially working-class women, will continue to be punished for caring. Consequently, the distribution of caring responsibilities has to be shared more equitably, and not just between men and women, but across society. This needs to be underpinned by a generous system of retirement pension credits/transfers that recognise and value care. These are mutually compatible and, in tandem, might go some way to promoting an 'ethic of care'.

Sevenhuijsen (1998, 2000) has explored the question of care and its relationship to welfare in some depth. Drawing on examples that the Dutch government has introduced, she proposes a mixture of measures that would permit, and encourage, a more equitable balance between care and work. Existing features of the SDW could be enhanced and the more privileged elements extended. For example, care can be part of the occupational welfare package (for example, nurseries, elder care leave and extended care leave). Sevenhuijsen also makes the point that trying to manage time is one of the recurring problems for carers. Trades unions and employers in the Netherlands have negotiated greater flexibility over working hours to enable carers to balance their commitments. In the context of retirement saving this could go further and we could think of flexibility in terms of years. A recurring theme in this book has been the need to define a working life, and in a way that fully acknowledges the value of care. Such a definition is needed because the statutory retirement age is likely to be, or has been, scrapped in many countries. Alongside resource transfers towards future pension rights, a definition of a working life that included time spent caring would go some way to reassuring carers and the poorest that they retain a right to retire.

Equity between the different forms of welfare is, however, not simple. Even an accurate audit of the different elements of the SDW is virtually impossible (Kvist and Sinfield, 1996). For example, how should we cost informal welfare and the time spent caring? Should fiscal welfare include all forms of tax relief and expenditure? What about social and environmental costs – firms laying off older workers and providing company cars for example? And given the discrepancies and variations in the time committed, or taken, to care, the impact on one person's career rather than another, and the various informal arrangements people make, any idea that a uniform system, let alone a couple of policy proposals sketched out here, can resolve the inequalities is clearly misplaced. There are, however, some principles that might guide policy.

A situated ethic of care

It needs to be recalled (Chapter One) that for Titmuss, public welfare served as the moral 'glue' of society. In many respects, his fears about the expansion of the SDW and its impact on social divisions and social solidarity have been borne out. Society may not have imploded with anomic energy, but there has been a sectional scramble for a more privileged place within the SDW that has seen social divisions widen. Interestingly, Sevenhuijsen could be seen as replacing Titmuss's commitment to welfare, his moral glue, with an ethic of care manifest in social institutions.

> Taking care as a point of entry could also lead to enriched ideas about inclusive democracy..., When we take care as a lens to evaluate different social practices, it can have extensive consequences for better integrating the values of care in a variety of social institutions.... When a norm of equality of access to the giving and receiving of care in both public and private contexts is combined with democratic notions of voice ..., we can imagine that these institutions would have the capacity of generating loyalty and commitment on the part of those who participate in them and thus could work as vessels for solidarity and social cohesion. (Sevenhuijsen, 2000, p 29)

A less optimistic analysis might point to ways that competing voices and existing interests are currently recognised and mirrored in the SDW. In the UK, working-class women in particular seem to have found it harder to get their voice heard and their particular needs recognised. Sinfield (1978) was surely right to highlight the greater ability of some social groups and classes to influence policy than others. Sevenhuijsen is clearly sensitive to this and in her discussion of citizenship, 'race', political decision making and social inequalities, emphasises the disparities of power and voice. However, establishing an ethic of care might involve considerable conflict and dispute before we witness any solidarity and cohesion. Thus, while accepting that an ethic of care has to inform retirement and pensions policies, it is not clear how this can be achieved without some attempt at distributive justice. The pension penalties incurred by women who care for children are imposed 30-50 years later. Without mechanisms for redistributing income and care these will continue to be experienced, primarily, but not exclusively, by working-class women and women from ethnic minority groups. Simultaneously, the mechanisms have to discriminate between claims if they are not to be counterproductive. Taking an extreme example, will the voice of middle-class women who claim to care for their executive husbands be on a par with those of working-class lone mothers? Moreover, while caring for children or elderly parents might not be contentious, is cooking the dinner, as Rose (1981) implies, always a form of care?

Clearly some sticky questions remain whether we rely on the moral glue of Titmuss's 'commitment to welfare' or replace it with an ethic of care. Nevertheless, and here I think I am closer to Sevenhuijsen, it is possible to address questions of distributive justice if they are situated and contextualised. A situated ethic of care would attempt to engage with the particular and diverse needs of different constituencies. Situation ethics involves a break with the smothering embrace of universalism, while clinging to a commitment to social justice premised on care (Fletcher, 1966). Consequently, ensuring that care providers can approach retirement with security and confidence is an important social policy objective. To facilitate this will require adequate resources to be set aside for the future. By considering the situations and contexts that care occurs in, however, it is possible to distinguish and differentiate between claims.

Markets and crisis

In Chapter Two the challenge to Titmuss's account of the SDW came from the twin, but opposing, traditions of political economy: on the one hand the achievements of capitalism and on the other, the power of vested interests and the potential for crisis. Markets, including the finance markets, have been far more innovative and flexible than the state in responding to social change. With an increase in life expectancy, more people who are healthy and fit retiring, huge sums of capital intended for retirement incomes, and with a more consumerist culture, the prospects for retirement look quite rosy. However, it has not been the private pensions market or Titmuss's beloved public welfare system that has facilitated the transformation of retirement for most people in the UK and Australia, but occupational pensions. Paternalistic employers, astute trades unionists and favourable labour market conditions have done far more to improve the quality of life for many retirees than public welfare (Walker with Howard, 2000). Private pensions still only cater for a minority in the UK. Orthodox political economists, obsessed with individuating welfare through the insurance market, would do well to pay more attention to Adam Smith's moral economy in which employers have welfare responsibilities towards former employees. Private insurance companies have recently recognised market opportunities by catering for same sex relationships, professional single women and, under the repulsive rubric of 'impaired lives', enhanced annuity policies for disabled people. In comparison, the public welfare system has been normalising, minimal, inflexible and looks increasingly inappropriate for the needs of many people (Williams, 1992; Thompson and Hoggett, 1996; Waters, 1996). Part of the responsibility for that lies with politicians who paid too much attention to orthodox political economists in the 1980s. Indeed, tax handouts, a naive belief in the market's ability to regulate itself, and an underlying ethos that seemed to suggest 'greed is good', combined to produce an environment in which both the Maxwell and misselling scandals could occur.

Capitalism has certainly succeeded in raising the living standards, life expectancy and desires of most people in the Western economies. But the success of capitalism hinges on the discipline and competition of the market, and this requires failure as well as success. Uncompetitive companies, declining industries and economic downturns are, as radical political economists assert, the other side of success. Unemployment and redundancy are necessary to ensure the continuing success of the economic system. Individuals are buffeted by these economic forces with very little chance of anticipating, let alone controlling, events. Retirement in these circumstances can look like a convenient mechanism for employers wishing to close down or restructure their organisation. Older workers often find that they are expected to adapt to the new economic realities. When unemployment rates are high, they can expect to be 'retired' early. When the labour market is buoyant, however, they can expect retirement ages to be raised, penalties for exiting early and demands that they undertake training opportunities. Social divisions in retirement are, therefore, reproduced and generated by an economy that is structured by access to property, income and opportunity. Individuals have little control over these structural inequalities, and even those who are lucky enough to access the better paying and (apparently) secure jobs, may suddenly be 'spat out' by the forces of global economic competition.

What is more, even the best laid retirement plans can come undone. If, as Deaton (1989) suggests, the pension fund industry is as vulnerable to the vagaries of the market as any other, then this too means we should all approach retirement with considerable trepidation. The phenomenal capital assets of the pension funds that are expected to provide a retirement income for many people in the developed economies are, as we saw in Chapter Two, premised on some big assumptions. A prolonged economic recession sparked perhaps by oil price rises or, less dramatically, a levelling off of economic growth, could have profound implications for the ability of pension funds to meet their welfare commitments (Minns, 2001). Misplaced investment strategies, such as the fashion for dotcom industries in the 1990s, could affect some funds and others may be plunged into crisis by unforeseen environmental or political events. There is also the possibility that any minor tremors in fund performance will promote further calls for more accountability and control by members. Political interference might, in turn, provoke the finance markets into a period of recession, or contest, with national governments. Indeed, the possibilities for some sort of crisis, albeit relatively short term, seem so likely in the next 10 to 30 years – precisely the time when many funds will be expected to deliver so much on their promises – that only the most optimistic economic forecasts will witness the necessary results.

Even if they succeed in fulfilling their promises, the pension funds will reinforce exclusion and social divisions as the gap widens between those who can access meaningful membership of a reliable occupational or private pension fund and those who will have to rely on public/state provision.

The Titmuss paradigm has clearly under-estimated the political as well as the economic power that vested interests have. The strengths of both versions of political economy can, however, be acknowledged and reconciled with the SDW. Capitalist markets provide a structural context within which social divisions arise. Competition between capitalist enterprises, not a functionalist version of the division of labour, ensures that the labour process is in constant flux and the labour market a crucial site of closure and competition (Mann, 1992). Occupational welfare has been promoted in this context by employer labour market strategies and trades union demands. Retirement has been used as a socially legitimate means of shedding labour when it has suited employers. The prospect of a more politicised debate over pension funds and their activities is also very real.

However, while the diagnosis provided by political economists may be broadly correct, it fails to identify some of the key features of those who are affected and the prescribed 'medicine' is potentially poisonous. Thus, neither version of political economy looks very attractive in practice, although ironically, both approaches to political economy claim their ideas have never been properly applied. More medicine is needed! Orthodox versions dismiss the idea that Britain from 1979 to 1997 provides a valid test for their ideas. Radical accounts say much the same about the former Soviet Russia. In both cases, the state distorted or half-heartedly applied the respective doctrines. Moreover, orthodox accounts dismiss social divisions and the exclusion of pensioners as a necessary spur to individual effort. Radical accounts conveniently overlook the fact that the poorest pensioners are overwhelmingly women, and that people from ethnic minority groups have frequently been excluded from the jobs that provided occupational pensions by sections of the labour movement (Mann, 1992).

Consumption cleavages

Approaching retirement as a time for consumption, and welfare provisions as a form of consumption, was explored in Chapter Three. The positive images and the diverse products offered by the private pensions market provide a challenge to universal public welfare provisions. Retaining a commitment to a public welfare system that is 'basic', minimal and unable to respond to consumption trends, probably spells the end of universal public welfare provisions. Advertisements for pensions have hardly been dynamic propaganda exercises in support of retirees and older people, but they have drawn on, and tried to engage with, a more diverse constituency than government campaigns of the past. Presenting diverse identities and positive images may be more inclusive and may, unintentionally perhaps, give some retirees more of a voice. People in retirement retain identities that are as varied, diverse and hybrid – drawing on and melding different identities – as non-retired people. Positive images of older people enjoying themselves in retirement may help to undermine ageist stereotypes of infant-like welfare dependency (Hockey and James, 1993; Wilson, 2000). Similarly, Laslett's (1989) idea of a 'third age' stresses the dynamic aspects of retirement. A time to realise ambitions and pursue interests that have been unfulfilled or subdued is often how private pensions are sold, and Laslett provides an attractive text to their images. Throughout this book it has been suggested that the expectations and aspirations of people approaching retirement need to be recognised. Laslett's normative model is easy to subscribe to, with some minor qualifications. Unfortunately, in reality there are some familiar social divisions revealed by consumption patterns within the retired population.

In Britain, gender and class are the most apparent and recurring consumption cleavages among the retired population. Car and home ownership, holidays abroad and virtually every other indicator of consumption reflect inequalities generated by the paid labour market and care responsibilities. 'Race' and ethnicity are likely to become much more significant in the next 10 to 20 years, as those who migrated in the second half of the 20th century begin to retire in greater numbers (Blakemore and Boneham, 1994; Nesbitt and Neary, 2001). The roots of consumption theory can be traced to Weberian sociology in the 1960s and 1970s when 'racial' discrimination in housing policies was most blatant. Subsequently, the focus shifted to social divisions and the residualisation of public welfare (Dunleavy, 1986; Forrest and Murie, 1983). As the value and attractiveness of public welfare declines, those that can afford to do so buy into private provisions. The trend has been accelerated by fiscal handouts as governments realised they could offer access to more privileged forms of welfare, thereby engaging with many people's aspirations. Consequently, with a declining proportion of the population relying on public welfare, the political constituency promoting it also declines. In this context images of a more dynamic retiree, often in some exotic location, may have an ideological effect, promoting economic individualism that in time undermines social solidarity, much as Titmuss feared (1958). Of course the advertisements simply reinforced a multitude of similar messages proclaiming the legitimacy of our desires and expectations (Bauman, 1998). However, any ideological effect was to reinforce, rather than create, widely held views that occupational and private pensions were 'better'. Even research that was intended to promote improvements in public pensions often confirmed what many people already knew; that those who could access an occupational pension or afford a private scheme, were indeed better off (Townsend, 1979). Cuts to SERPS, the declining value of the public pension and increasing the use of means testing, were the sticks prodding people towards private provision. The images and tax breaks added to the temptations, but, and this is crucial, the desire was already there.

As we saw, many who were tempted to take out private pensions were misled about the prospects and costs. Personal private pensions attracted many low paid women with their promises of flexibility, portability and, of course, images aimed at women. The fact that so many working–class women saw private pensions as meeting their needs says a great deal about their perceptions of the state schemes (Ginn and Arber, 2000). Much was made of the pensions misselling scandal by Labour politicians and national newspapers, but in some respects this too reinforced ideas of consumer power. Insurance companies and mutual societies were pilloried, sales staff sacked and compensation demanded. The 'victims' of the personal pensions fiasco found it relatively easy to voice their grievances regarding the way that they had been misled. In contrast, those who joined and remained in SERPS and the NI scheme have seen the state renege on its pensions promises time and again, and with little or no redress. Ironically, the scandal may have even bolstered the idea that the market is more responsive than the state – consumer rights appeared to be more easily enforced than citizenship rights (Dwyer, 1998). Subsequently, Labour politicians have endorsed and reinforced this view. The voice of the aggrieved heroic consumer is listened to intently, but the aggrieved citizen is told they cannot expect the state to meet its previous commitments.

> Thus, Alistair Darling, Labour's Social Security Minister, made it brutally clear to the House of Commons on 15 December 1998, "... once stakeholder pensions are established, it is my intention to ensure that we amend the system further so that, if people stay in the state system, they will lose money" (Hansard, 1999, vol 337, col 771).

Consumption-based approaches complement the SDW and are entirely compatible with it (Harrison, 1986). Indeed, using the SDW as a way of collating consumption patterns makes visible the way social divisions are reinforced by different, but often overlapping, social processes. Consumption accounts have a further attraction because they generally see social divisions arising from widely held social values and aspirations. Social exclusion is therefore apparent from the lack of choices, poorer services and weaker voice of excluded people. In this light the state rarely constructs social divisions, but it can reinforce them by adjusting fiscal and public welfare provisions.

Expert advice

In Chapter Four we saw that post-structuralists provide an alternative approach to retirement and pensions policy by turning our gaze away from the pensioner and towards the pensions experts. Approaching retirement and pensions policy from this perspective highlighted some less tangible, but vitally important, features of exclusion. Power, knowledge and the mapping of discursive boundaries were the crucial factors. The insidious 'taken for granted' parameters within which fund managers manage, actuaries calculate and trustees decide, can frustrate any alternative debates. Government, big business and the labour movement increasingly rely on the advice of the pensions expert when proposing changes. Reforms, like the introduction of compulsory superannuation in Australia, are tailored so that they do not disrupt or disturb the pensions industry. Any questioning, or proposal for change, has to be framed in a manner that accepts the icy logic, the language and science that informs the experts' *modus operandi*. Fund managers, for example, tend to err in favour of established companies, follow investment market trends and, more surprisingly, appear to have a short-term view of their investment strategy. Their activities tend to be conservative, cautious and, until quite recently, cloaked in secrecy (Myners, 2001). They rarely reflect on their role as welfare service providers, and unlike other welfare experts, are not treated as such. With the control of so much investment capital and the well-being of so many people depending on the success of pension funds, politicians are nervous of pressing for changes that might be seen as disruptive. Consequently, while the funding of public pensions is subject to scrutiny and a recurring political theme, private and occupational pension funds and the details of their activities, remain largely invisible. And, as Sinfield (1978) observed, the invisibility of some elements of the SDW ensures that they are less accountable. Many of the principles that govern the pensions experts are highly regressive, ensuring that the lowest paid and least secure members often feel penalised by the rules and regulations. What is more, the very means of calculating and measuring risk, life expectancy, investment returns and administrative charges serves to exclude, disenfranchise and penalise those whose needs are the greatest but whose resources are most constrained. There is nothing in this that is intentional or conspiratorial, it simply reflects the limited horizons of the pensions world.

Approaching retirement from a post-structuralist perspective highlights three key features of exclusion, but there are others. First, the way that an exclusive focus on public welfare recipients as a subject identity generates a vocabulary and discourse that serves to suppress their voice (Dean and Taylor-Gooby, 1992). Second, there is a stark contrast between 'them' and 'us' that reproduces an older discourse of deserving and undeserving that has long been associated with the different elements of the SDW. In the 20th century, NI and occupational pension schemes catered for the deserving. The undeserving had to rely on means-tested benefits or informal welfare provisions (Mann, 1992). Currently the vocabulary is shifting from distinctions made within broad social classes – as in Booth's and Beveridge's accounts – to a more individuating discourse. 'They' impose costs, 'we' save for the future. 'We' are active lifestyle managers planning for our retirement in a responsible manner. As Jordan (1998) suggests, the new welfare orthodoxy being propagated stresses that the individual must accept responsibility for their own welfare needs, despite the authoritarian demands of the global economy. Thus, it is worth recalling Rose's points regarding the way that the language of politicians and the new vocabulary of social reform, with its emphasis on responsibility, planning for the future, consumption identities and reflexivity, "forms a grid of regulatory ideals" (1996, p 145). Third, post-structuralism has the potential for illuminating the power of the expert to frustrate change. Knowledge, credentialism and professional power are the veils concealing a pernicious form of exclusionary social closure. The objective and scientific methods of the pensions experts, ensuring that the operation and provision of the most privileged forms of welfare, remain concealed.

Post traditional welfare

Retirement may have emerged alongside modernity, but it also typifies some major features of a post-modern society. In Chapter Five it was argued that observers of post-modernity, but especially scholars described as post-traditionalists, provided a major challenge to the SDW. It was accepted that traditional approaches to welfare are difficult to sustain. The social and political constituencies they appealed to have shrunk, along with the type of risks public welfare has traditionally addressed. Although such changes should not be exaggerated, a failure to acknowledge them looks rather dogmatic. Despite the critical stance taken, particularly of Giddens' (1998) 'third way', most of this book could be read as an engagement with his ideas. That was not the intention, but some of the major items on his agenda seem to have slipped (unreflexively?) into most of the chapters. The focus of Chapter Five was on Beck's and

Giddens' accounts of risk and identity and these were seen to offer a number of insights on how we might all approach retirement. Giddens' positive model of welfare offers the possibility of a more balanced view of work, care, leisure and retirement, one in which difficult but important choices have to be made. In seeing welfare as more than simply resource transfers, Giddens reminds us of the various social and political movements since the 1960s that have raised these issues (for example, feminist campaigns and Claimants Unions). Likewise, Beck's account of risk, the problems he sees with scientific and technical measurements, the way it is socially manifest and the global implications, were all seen as relevant to retirement policies. As we saw, the insurance and pension industry operates with a model of risk that relies on and reinforces the existing patterns of privilege, and neglects the global and ethical issues involved in fund management.

On closer inspection, however, Giddens' approach looks rather familiar. The 'third way' returns us along a very traditional road paved with Victorian ideas of self-help and largely inhabited by the aspirational (male) working classes and the 'reflexive' professional middle classes (Mann, 1998; Walker, 1999). Despite the discussion of globalisation, which often looks remarkably like Titmuss's deterministic view of industrialisation, there is no consideration of the huge resources invested by pension funds or of the tax privileges for private pensions. Consequently, the dismissal of public pensioners as embedded in a culture of welfare dependency is offensive and, given his neglect of occupational, fiscal and informal welfare, is either mischievous or naive. The hierarchy of risk that corresponds with the different elements of the SDW is completely overlooked. His exclusive focus on public welfare simply neglects the fact that everyone is welfare dependent in a post-traditional society. Rather than focus on extending the privileges of the rich and the middle classes to all (something that would break with traditional approaches), he promotes an individualistic agenda that blames the poorest for not being more like the middle classes. As Peter Taylor-Gooby has tactfully pointed out:

> It would be unfortunate if the risk society approach served to justify policies which support the interests of groups most able to deal with the contingencies of a more flexible society and oppose the interests of those groups least able to meet the needs they experience – in short, if the Third Way became an ideology serving the interests of the more privileged classes by denying the continuing importance of class divisions in vulnerability. (2001, p 210)

The final paradox is that, like the Fabians he is so critical of, Giddens' political strategy is to engage directly with Labour politicians, civil servants and intellectuals. Thus, the post-traditional approach is flawed, from a perspective that takes the SDW as given, largely because it is not very far past the post. That is, Giddens is far more traditional and far less radical, than he, or 'New' Labour proclaim.

Different worlds

Comparative approaches to social policy have been heavily influenced by Esping-Andersen's welfare regime model. In Chapter Six, we saw that a consideration of why people retire early, a trend that crosses the different types of welfare regime he identified, poses some interesting questions. Although Esping-Andersen's approach is informed by the SDW, his attachment to the Scandinavian model and his uncritical adoption of Titmuss's version is frustrating. Taking early exit as an example, one that may need to be more qualified than it is in Chapter Six, suggests that Sweden may be less attractive for anyone wanting to retire early than countries that are supposedly more commodified. Furthermore, his failure to acknowledge informal welfare not only overlooks a key element in the SDW, it makes his measure of success – de-commodification in the paid labour market – look even more limited.

However, Esping-Andersen's argument that politics matters, that governments are not all the same and that globalisation need not produce convergence, is not contested. Indeed, throughout this book it has been shown that politics matters a great deal. But politics matters in framing informal, occupational and fiscal welfare, as well as public welfare. In Britain, Australia and the US, the trades union and labour movements have not always pursued public welfare objectives, but have often sought access to the more privileged elements of the SDW. Esping-Andersen (1990, 1996) has acknowledged the strategy, but is reluctant to concede that it may have benefited significant sections of the population, thereby enabling many to exercise choices apparently denied to their Swedish counterparts. However, it has also, as Esping-Andersen notes, generated wider social divisions than in Sweden. Thus, if you are poor, Sweden looks far more attractive than if you are part of the apparently contented majority in the US, UK and Australia. Although Sweden has been peculiar in its commitment to a generous universal system, there are indications, not least in the numbers opting for private pensions, that consumer-led expectations and desires will pose a stern test in the near future. There are also a number of trends that could be taken as indicators of convergence (Overbye, 1996; Bonoli, 2000). In this context the following tendencies are most significant: DC rather than DB schemes, a sliding scale of age-related conditions of entitlement, the closing of some early exit routes, greater reliance on the private life insurance and annuities markets, more fiscal supports to promote private provision, reduced benefits for those with the weakest labour market links and compulsory retirement saving. The combined effect of many of these policies will be to reinforce social class divisions, with working-class women and people from certain ethnic minority groups being penalised most. But similar trends do not mean politics is irrelevant and that convergence is inevitable. The differences between the US, Australia and Britain are much more significant than the similarities and, despite the recent reforms, Sweden has retained a much firmer commitment to income redistribution and public welfare than elsewhere. There is clearly plenty of scope for social and political movements to influence the SDW. Politics not only matters, it is crucially significant. But which voices are heard, who shouts the loudest and what principles will inform the debate, may not conform to the traditional ones that Esping-Andersen identifies.

Prospects

A reconstructed version of the SDW, as proposed here, involves a recognition of the innovative potential and considerable power of market capitalism. The structural constraints this imposes on retirement policies cannot be overlooked, but nor can the tensions within the market and the potential dangers of literally investing our retirement futures in it. Pension funds are increasingly being queried and questioned regarding their activities.

On the one hand, they are criticised for being too careful and conservative, with even Prime Minister Tony Blair asking them "to examine whether they and other institutional investors are being too cautious when it comes to venture capital and investing in early stage companies" (*Financial Times*, 7 July 1999). On the other hand, they are being asked to address ethical investment issues and to intervene when companies are not 'performing'. This is the type of political interference and intervention that Deaton (1989) pointed towards and his analysis suggested a crisis would ensue. The requirement in the UK that trustees produce a SIP will increase the potential for social and political movements to apply pressure on institutional investors. With occupational pension funds feeling aggrieved at the intrusions into their world, there is the real possibility of pension funds becoming much more politicised. Tensions are already apparent, and calls for more information and accountability have increased in the last 10 years. The cold, calculating body of knowledge formed by actuarial principles, fund management techniques, demographic modelling, auditing processes and trust law, is increasingly being scrutinised. The pensions experts behind the veils of knowledge and information, who are so used to gazing at their subject populations, are now being gazed at. Like other professionals and experts, their exclusive discourse is increasingly being interrupted by dissonant voices calling for the removal of every veil. But once exposed, all we are likely to see is an increasingly nervous set of individuals concerned that cherished traditions are being changed and uncertain how they should respond. Their sciences and expertise allow little room for ethical considerations and the more questions that are asked of them about their social responsibilities, the clearer it is that they have few answers. Reconciling people's expectations and aspirations for the future, bearing in mind these are likely to be even higher in 30-40 years time, with ethical considerations will be a major task. An ethic of care would certainly serve as a useful principle and it could ensure a more equitable distribution of responsibilities and resources within developed economies. It might also inform the investment behaviour of fund managers and minimise resource transfers from the developing economies to the developed (Minns, 2001). However, whether ethics and profits can be reconciled to enable everyone to approach retirement with confidence seems unlikely.

The prospects for the poorest, once again, look poor. If public welfare fails to engage with the aspirations of most people, remaining a minimal safety net, it soon becomes reserved for the poorest. The political constituency for public welfare will then diminish and it will be a residual system. In the UK, the stakeholder scheme will probably fail to attract sufficient numbers of the poorest because they need money now and do not have any 'spare cash' to save. Despite the rhetoric of diversity and choice, the temptation will be to make the scheme compulsory, imposing responsibilities, but with few rights or benefits. It would become a regressive tax on the poor that is morally reprehensible and socially unjust. The middle classes will undoubtedly maximise the tax advantages and loopholes while working-class households, particularly lone mothers and low-paid women, will be penalised. If annuity providers are also forced to equalise their payments (a further intrusion into the finance markets), it will mean resource transfers from low-paid working-class men and women, who die younger, to middle-class women who live longest. Similarly, scrapping the age of retirement may be appreciated by some older workers, but the implications for carers and manual workers are deeply disturbing. Will women (and hopefully men) who care for children or relatives be compelled to return to paid work until their stakeholder pension has 'earned' them enough to retire on? Will we see 80-year-old cleaners in schools or 75-year-old scaffolders and hod-carriers clambering around on building sites? In this context, where the middle classes have pension schemes that provide generous tax free lump sums, exit ages that are more flexible, careers that start 4-6 years later and finish 5-10 years earlier, inequalities of income and time are both resources that have to be addressed. Of course, a more flexible retirement age that allows those that want to continue working is a worthy goal. If this was underpinned by anti-age discrimination legislation and a public welfare system that made the choice meaningful, it would be an achievement. Simply scrapping the age of retirement with the possibility of a sliding scale of age-related benefits, as in the US, would effectively kill off the right to retire. Young people should pay especially close attention to what happens to the public pension because governments will be tempted to delay the implementation of these types of policy for 20-30 years. This is a timeframe that politicians will sell on the basis that it gives people time to plan and prepare.

As we have seen, governments, the OECD and the private pensions industry are urging us, in different ways, to rethink and reconceptualise retirement. However, concepts that promote ideas of the heroic consumer, in which reflexive individuals plan for their retirement, reiterate a very traditional individualistic mantra. Reflexivity presumes certain intellectual, cultural and material resources, along with sufficient space and time in people's lives. It is too easy for those with resources to presume that they have attained these as a consequence of wise decisions, hard work and individual effort. Too often it can seem that excluded people are responsible for their situation: "It is the fault of the excluded that they did nothing, or not enough, to escape exclusion; perhaps they even invited their fate, making the exclusion into a foregone conclusion" (Bauman, 1998, p 85).

As Titmuss made plain, the effects of the SDW are likely to be felt strongest by pensioners:

> The outlines of a dangerous social schism are clear, and they are enlarging. The direction in which the forces of social and fiscal policy are moving raises fundamental issues of justice and equality: not just issues of justice

> between taxpayers as a separate class, or between contributors as a separate class, but between all citizens. Already it is possible to see two nations in old age: greater inequalities in living standards after work than in work: two contrasting social services for distinct groups based on different principles, and operating in isolation of each other as separate, autonomous, social instruments of change. (Titmuss, 1958, pp 73-4)

Nevertheless, many of Giddens' central concerns do have to be addressed. Appeals to traditional political constituencies, interests and identities are unlikely to succeed. It might be argued that any appeals will fail in a global economy and that politics no longer matters. However, abandoning politics and refusing to take a standpoint on social justice, social divisions and exclusion means we lose sight of what it is to be human. As Hoggett (2001) reminds us, that means considering every aspect of human potential, failure and inadequacy. Giddens is therefore right to stress potential and to argue that not only material well-being, but also self-respect and security are fundamental. Potential is not, however, evenly distributed and opportunities for realising it are unevenly restrained. Indeed, in some cases one person's achievement necessarily means another person's failure. The successes of welfare capitalism do need to be applauded, and relying on sociological models that have hardly changed since the 19th century is clearly inappropriate. In a post-traditional society, the fate of everyone is inextricably tied to taking risks – it provides one of the most important motivating factors for individuals and society. But that has to occur in a context of knowing that failure will not be condemned. Consequently, knowing that someone will care, that if you take risks and fail or if you are simply incapable, that care will be provided, underpins a risk society (Sevenhuijsen, 2000; Williams, 2000). Ontological and social security are therefore vital and intertwined.

It is also likely that excluded groups will themselves organise around issues of consumption, or define themselves in relation to welfare and consumption cleavages (for example, the disability rights and pensioner movements). Even consumption images may be used and re-presented by social and political movements. Calls for early retirement to be restrained may be frustrated by expectations raised by the private pensions industry. Personal private pensions have been sold on the basis that they will enable people to exit early. There could be considerable political fallout if those ambitions are subsequently frustrated. And if private pensioners are allowed to exit early, occupational pensioners, and their employers, might call for similar flexibility. This raises the possibility that it will only be the rights of public pensioners that are restrained or made conditional. Again, the prospect of some sort of consumer citizenship, predicated on rights that have been purchased, overwhelming the traditional model of 'worker citizenship' where rights were earned, is very real (Dwyer, 1998). In some respects this may be preferable, since concepts of rights predicated on labour market activity are themselves often exclusive (Lister, 1997; Mann, 1992). Traditional models of public welfare rights reproduced a deserving/undeserving distinction predicated on the contributory insurance principle and the Poor Law. There would be a perverse irony, however, if in breaking with a male wage earner/ breadwinner model, the effect was to enable the salaried middle classes rights and options, while reinforcing wage slavery for the poorest. Without a right to retire, or at least some concept of a working and caring life, and some recognition that consumer choices are severely constrained for many people, the poorest could be compelled to work until they drop. The pessimistic scenario assumes consumption cleavages will increase and that sectional self-interests will fragment broader social movements. Optimism hinges on the possibilities for the traditional call for solidarity and social justice to combine with ideas of shared identities, a respect and recognition of difference (Williams, 2000), and the collective experience of uncertainty.

Bibliography

Abel-Smith, B. and Townsend, P. (1965) *The poor and the poorest*, London: Bell and Sons.

ABI (Association of British Insurers) (1995) *Risk, insurance and welfare: The changing balance between private and public protection*, London: ABI.

ABS (Australian Bureau of Statistics) (1995) *The labour force Australia*, Catalogue No 62030, Canberra: Australian Government Publishing Service, April.

Ackers, L. and Dwyer, P. (2002: forthcoming) *Senior citizenship? Retirement, mobility and welfare in the EU*, Bristol: The Policy Press.

ACTU (Australian Council of Trade Unions) (1991) *Congress resolutions*, Melbourne: ACTU.

ACTU (1992) *Superannuation directed investment in development capital*, Melbourne: ACTU.

ACTU/TDC (1987) *Australia reconstructed: Report of the 1986 ACTU/TDC mission to Western Europe*, Canberra: AGPS.

Adam, B. and van Loon, J (2000) 'Introduction: repositioning risk: the challenge for social theory', in B. Adam, U. Beck and J. van Loon (eds) *The risk society and beyond: Critical issues for social theory*, London: Sage Publications, pp 1-46.

Adam, B., Beck, U. and van Loon, J. (eds) (2000) *The risk society and beyond: Critical issues for social theory*, London: Sage Publications.

Aldridge, A. (1997) 'Engaging with promotional culture', *Sociology*, vol 31, no 3, pp 389-408, August.

apRoberts, L. (1994) 'Complimentary retirement pensions: towards a definition of terms', in ISSA, *Complimentary pensions: European perspectives*, European Series No 21, Geneva: ISSA, pp 1-18.

Arber, S. and Ginn, J. (eds) (1995a) *Connecting gender and ageing*, Buckingham: Open University Press.

Arber, S. and Ginn, J. (1995b) 'Choice and constraint in the retirement of older women', in S. Arber and J. Ginn (eds) (1995) *Connecting gender and ageing*, Buckingham: Open University Press, pp 69-86.

Bagguley, P. and Mann, K. (1992) 'Idle thieving bastards: scholarly representations of the underclass', *Work, Employment & Society*, vol 6, no 1, pp 113-26, March.

Ball, S. (1998) 'Performativity and fragmentation in "postmodern" schooling', in J. Carter (ed) *Postmodernity and the fragmentation of welfare*, London: Routledge, pp 187-203.

Barr, N. (1999) *A public-private partnership in pensions: Getting the balance right*, CASE Paper 24, London: Centre for Analysis of Social Exclusion, London School of Economics, pp 30-46.

Baudrillard, J. (1975) *The mirror of production*, St Louis, MO: Telos Press.

Baudrillard, J. (1987) *Forget Foucault*, New York, NY: Semiotext.

Bauman, Z. (1972) *Between class and elite*, Manchester: Manchester University Press.

Bauman, Z. (1992) *Intimations of postmodernity*, London: Routledge.

Bauman, Z. (1993) *Postmodern ethics*, Oxford: Blackwell.

Bauman, Z. (1995) *Life in fragments: Essays in postmodern morality*, Oxford: Blackwell.

Bauman, Z. (1997) *Postmodernity and its discontents*, New York, NY: New York University Press.

Bauman, Z. (1998) *Work, consumerism and the new poor*, Buckingham: Open University Press.

Beck, U. (1992) *Risk society: Towards a new modernity*, London, *Theory, Culture and Society* series in association with Sage Publications.

Beck, U. (2000) 'Risk society revisited: theory, politics and research programmes'. in B. Adam, U. Beck and J. van Loon (eds) *The risk society and beyond: Critical issues for social theory*, London: Sage Publications, pp 211-29.

Beresford, P., Green, D., Lister, R. and Woodard, K. (1999) *Poverty first hand: Poor people speak for themselves*, London: Child Poverty Action Group.

Berkery, P.M. Jr (1996) *Personal financial planning for gays and lesbians*, San Francisco, CA: Human Rights Campaign Foundation.

Berkery, P.M. Jr and Diggins, G.A. (1998) *Gay finances in a straight world*, New York, NY: John Wiley.

Berkowitz, S.A., Finney, L.D. and Logue, D.E. (1988) *The investment performance of corporate pension plans; why they do not beat the market regularly?*, New York, NY and London: Quorum Books.

Bernard, M., Itzin, C., Phillipson, C. and Skucha, J. (1995) 'Gendered work, gendered retirement', in S. Arber and J. Ginn (eds) *Connecting gender and ageing*, Buckingham: Open University Press, pp 56-68.

Berthoud, R. (1998) *The incomes of ethnic minorities*, Report 98-1, Colchester: Institute for Social and Economic Research, University of Essex.

Best, G.F.A. (1972) *Mid-Victorian Britain 1851-1875*, New York, NY: Shoken.

Beveridge, W. (1942) *Social insurance and allied services*, Report by Sir William Beveridge, London: HMSO.

Blake, D. (1992a) *Modelling pension fund investment behaviour*, London: Routledge.

Blake, D. (1992b) *Issues in pension funding*, London and New York, NY: Routledge.

Blake, D., Cairns, A.J.G. and Dowd, K. (1999) 'PensionMetrics I: Stochastic pension plan design and value-at-risk during the accumulation phase', ASI-Gamma Foundation, Working Paper, Collection No 19, presented at the 3rd annual BSI-Gamma Foundation Conference on Global Asset Management, Lugano, November.

Blake, D., Cairns, A.J.G. and Dowd, K. (2000) 'PensionMetrics II: Stochastic pension plan design during the distribution phase', ASI-Gamma foundation, Working Paper, Collection No 20, presented at the 4th annual BSI Gamma Foundation Conference on Global Asset Management, Rome, October.

Blakemore, K. (1985) 'Ethnic inequalities in old age: some comparisons between Britain and the United States', *Journal of Applied Gerontology*, vol 4, no 1, pp 86-101.

Blakemore, K. and Boneham, M. (1994) *Age, race and ethnicity*, Buckingham: Open University Press.

Boaz, A., Hayden, C. and Bernard, M. (1999) *Attitudes and aspirations of older people: A review of the literature*, Report No 101, Department of Social Security Research, London: The Stationery Office.

Boden, D. (2000) 'Worlds in action: information, instantaneity and global futures trading', in B. Adam, U. Beck and J. van Loon (eds) *The risk society and beyond: Critical issues for social theory*, London: Sage Publications. pp 183-97.

Boneham, M. (1989) 'Ageing and ethnicity in Britian: the case study of elderly Sikh women in a Midlands town', *New Community*, vol 15, no 3, pp 47-59.

Bonoli, G. (2000) *The politics of pension reform institutions and policy change in Western Europe*, Cambridge: Cambridge University Press.

Booth, C. (1892) *Pauperism and the endowment of old age*, London: Macmillan.

Borchorst, A. (1994) 'Welfare state regimes, women's interests and the EC', in D. Sainsbury (ed) *Gendering welfare states*, London: Sage Publications, pp 26-44.

Braverman, H. (1974) *Labor and monopoly capital*, New York, NY: Monthly Review Press.

Bryson, L., Bittman, M. and Donath, S. (1994) 'Men's welfare state, women's welfare state: tendencies to convergence in practice and theory?' in D. Sainsbury (ed) *Gendering welfare states*, London: Sage Publications, pp 118-31.

Budd, A. and Campbell, N. (1998) *The roles of the public and private sectors in the UK pension system*, London: HM Treasury (www.hm-treasury.gov.uk/pub).

Bury, M. (1995) 'Ageing, gender and sociological theory', in S. Arber and J. Ginn (eds) *Connecting gender and ageing*, Buckingham: Open University Press, pp 15-29.

Bussemaker, J. and van Kersbergen, K. (1994) *Gender and welfare states: some theoretical reflections*, in D. Sainsbury (ed) *Gendering welfare states*, London: Sage Publications, pp 8-25.

Byrne, D. (1994) 'Planning for and against the divided city: a case study of the North East of England', in R. Burrows and B. Loader (eds) *Towards a post-Fordist welfare state?*, London: Routledge, pp 136-53.

Byrne, D. (1995) 'De-industrialisation and dispossession: an examination of social division in the industrial city', *Sociology*, vol 29, no 1, pp 95-115, February.

Byrne, D. (1999) *Social exclusion*, Buckingham: Open University Press.

Cabinet Office (2000) *Winning the generation game*, London: The Stationery Office.

Carter, J. (ed) (1998) *Postmodernity and the fragmentation of welfare*, London: Routledge.

Castles, F.G. (1985) *The working class and welfare*, Hemel Hempstead: Allen & Unwin.

Castles, F.G. (1997) 'Leaving the Australian labour force: an extended encounter with the state', *Governance*, vol 10, no 2, pp 97-121.

Clarke, J. (1998) 'Thriving on chaos? Manageralisation and social welfare', in J. Carter (ed) *Postmodernity and the fragmentation of welfare*, London: Routledge, pp 171-87.

Clarke, J., Cochrane, A. and McLaughlin, E. (eds) (1994) *Managing social policy*, London: Sage Publications.

Coates, D. (1980) *Labour in power 1974-9*, London: Longman.

Colwill, J. (1994) 'Beveridge, women and the welfare state', *Critical Social Policy*, vol 14, no 2, pp 53-78, Autumn.

Connell, R. (1995) *Masculinities*, Cambridge: Polity Press.

Cook, D. (1989) *Rich law, poor law: Differential responses to tax and supplementary benefit fraud*, Milton Keynes: Open University Press.

Cooke, T.E., Matatko, J. and Stafford, D.C. (eds) (1992) *Risk, portfolio management and capital markets*, Basingstoke: Macmillan.

Cousins, C., Leigh, S. and Younger, T. (eds) (2000) *Pensioners incomes series 1999/00*, London: Analytical Services Division, The Stationery Office.

Crossick, G. (1978) *An artisan elite in Victorian society*, London: Croom Helm.

Culpitt, I. (1999) *Social policy and risk*, London: Sage Publications.

Cunningham, M. (1981) *Non-wage benefits*, London: Pluto Press.

Curtis, Z. (1993) 'On being a woman in the pensioners movement', in J. Johnson and R. Slater (eds) *Ageing and later life*, London: Sage Publications in association with the Open University, pp 193-99.

Dailey, N. (1998) *When baby boom women retire*, Westport, CT: Praeger.

Damant, D. (1992) 'The revolution in investment management', in T.E. Cooke, *Risk, portfolio management and capital markets*, Basingstoke: Macmillan, pp 7-18.

Daniel, W.W. (1968) *Racial discrimination in England*, Hamondsworth: Penguin.

Davies, B. (1992) *Locking the stable door: The ownership and control of occupational pensions*, London: Institute for Public Policy Research.

Davies, B. and Ward, S. (1992) *Women and personal pensions*, London: Equal Opportunities Commission/HMSO.

Davis, K. (1988) *Power under the microscope*, Dordrecht: Foris Publishing.

de Swaan, A. (1988) *In care of the state, health care, education and welfare in Europe and the USA in the modern era*, Cambridge: Polity Press.

Deacon, A. (1993) 'Richard Titmuss twenty years on', *Journal of Social Policy*, vol 22, no 2, pp 235-42.

Deacon, A. (1997) 'The case for compulsion', *Poverty*, London: Child Poverty Action Group, no 98, Autumn, pp 8-10.

Deacon, A. and Bradshaw, J. (1983) *Reserved for the poor*, London: Blackwell.

Deacon, A. and Mann, K. (1997) 'Moralism and modernity: the paradox of New Labour thinking on welfare', *Benefits*, vol 20, pp 2-6.

Deacon, A. and Mann, K. (1999) 'Agency, modernity and social policy', *Journal of Social Policy*, vol 28, no 3, pp 413-35.

Dean, H. (1992) 'Poverty discourse and the disempowerment of the poor', *Critical Social Policy*, vol 12, no 2, pp 79-88.

Dean, H. and Taylor-Gooby, P. (1992) *Dependency culture*, Hemel Hempstead: Harvester Wheatsheaf.

Deaton, R.L. (1989) *The political economy of pensions politics and social change in Canada, Britain and the United States*,Vancouver, Canada: University of British Columbia Press.

Defert, D. (1991) 'Popular life and insurance technology', in G. Burchell, C. Gordon and P. Miller (eds) *The Foucault effect: Studies in govermentality*, Chicago, IL/Hemel Hemstead: Chicago University Press/Harvester Wheatsheaf, pp 211-28.

Dilnot, A., Disney, R., Johnson, P. and Whitehouse, E. (1994) *Pensions policy in the UK*, London: Institute for Fiscal Studies.

Disney, R. and Whitehouse, E. (1992) *The personal pensions stampede*, London: Institute for Fiscal Studies.

Disney, R., Grundy, E. and Johnson, P. (eds) (1997) *The dynamics of retirement: Analyses of the retirement surveys*, London: DSS/The Stationery Office.

Dobbin, F. (1992) 'The origins of private social insurance: public policy and fringe benefits in America, 1920-1950', *American Journal of Sociology*, vol 97, no 5, pp 1416-50, March.

Dobbin, F. and Boychuk, T. (1996) 'Public policy and the rise of private pensions: the US experience since 1930', in M. Shalev (ed) *The privatization of social policy? Occupational welfare and the welfare state in America, Scandinavia and Japan*, Basingstoke: Macmillan Press, pp 104-35.

Donzelot, J. (1979) *The policing of families: Welfare versus the state*, London: Hutchinson.

Drucker, P.F. (1993) *Post-capitalist society*, Oxford: Heinemann.

DSS (Department of Social Security) (1998a) *Partnership in 'pensions'*, Cm 4179, London: The Stationery Office.

DSS (1998b) *New ambitions for our country: A new contract for welfare*, Cm 3805, London: The Stationery Office.

Dunleavy, P. (1986) 'Sectoral cleavages and the stabilization of state expenditures', *Environment and planning D: Society and Space*, vol 4, pp 128-44.

Durkheim, E. (1933) *The division of labour in society*, New York, NY: Free Press.

Dwyer, P. (1998) 'Conditional citizens? Welfare rights and responsibilities in the late 1990s', *Critical Social Policy*, vol 18, no 4, pp 493-517.

Dwyer, P. (2000) 'Movements to some purpose? An exploration of international retirement migration in the European Union', *Education and ageing*, vol 15, no 3, pp 353-77.

Dyson, S. (1999) 'Genetic screening and ethnic minorities', *Critical Social Policy*, vol 19, no 2, pp 195-215, May.

Edgell, S., Hetherington, K. and Warde, A. (eds) (1996) *Consumption matters*, Oxford: Blackwell.

Edwards, R. (1979) *Contested terrain: The transformation of work in the twentieth century*, London: Heinemann.

Elias, N. (1982) *The civilizing process, Vol 1: The history of manners; Vol 2: Power and civility*, New York, NY: Pantheon.

Elo, I.T. (2001) 'New African American life tables from 1935-1990', *Demography*, vol 38, no 1, pp 97-114, February.

Esping-Andersen, G. (1990) *The three worlds of welfare capitalism*, Cambridge: Polity Press.

Esping-Andersen, G. (1996) 'Occupational welfare in the social policy nexus', in M. Shalev (ed) *The privatization of social policy? Occupational welfare and the welfare state in America, Scandinavia and Japan*, Basingstoke: Macmillan.

Esping-Andersen, G. (ed) (1997) *The welfare state in transition*, London: Routledge.

Ewald, F. (1991) 'Insurance and risk', in G. Burchell, C. Gordon, and P. Miller (eds) *The Foucault effect: Studies in govermentality*, Chicago, IL/Hemel Hemstead: Chicago University Press/ Harvester Wheatsheaf, pp 197-210.

Featherstone, M. (1987) 'Leisure, symbolic power and the life course', in D. Jary, S. Home and A. Tomlinson (eds) *Sport, leisure and social relations*, London: Routledge, pp 113-38.

Featherstone, M. (1991) *Consumer culture and postmodernism*, London: Sage Publications.

Featherstone, M. and Hepworth, M. (1989) 'Ageing and old age: reflections on the postmodern lifecourse', in B. Bytheway, T. Keil, P. Allat and A. Bryman (eds) *Becoming and being old*, London: Sage Publications, pp 143-57.

Featherstone, M. and Hepworth, M. (1995) 'Images of positive ageing: a case study of *Retirement Choice* Magazine', in M. Featherstone and A. Wernick (eds) *Images of ageing: Cultural representations of later life*, London: Routledge, pp 29-47.

Featherstone, M. and Wernick, A. (eds) (1995) *Images of ageing: Cultural representations of later life*, London: Routledge.

Fennel, G., Phillipson, C. and Evers, H. (1988) *The sociology of old age*, Milton Keynes: Open University Press.

Fido, J. (1977) 'The COS and social casework in London 1869-1900', in A. Donadgrodzki, *Social control in nineteenth century Britain*, London: Croom Helm.

Field, F. (1996) *Stakeholder welfare*, Choice in Welfare Series, No 32, London: IEA.

Field, F. and Owen, M. (1993) *Private pensions for all: Squaring the circle*, Fabian Society Discussion Paper No 16, London: Fabian Society.

Fitzgerald, R. (1988) *British labour management and industrial welfare 1864-1939*, London: Croom Helm.

Fletcher, J. (1966) *Situation ethics: The new morality*, Philadelphia, PA: Westminster Press.

Forrest, R. and Murie, A. (1983) 'Residualisation and council housing: aspects of the changing social relations of housing tenure', *Journal of Social Policy*, vol 12, no 4, pp 453-68.

Forrest, R. and Murie, A. (1986) 'Marginalization and subsidized individualism: the sale of council houses in the restructuring of the British Welfare State', *International Journal of Urban and Regional Research*, vol 10, no 1, pp 46-66.

Forrest, R. and Murie, A. (1989) 'Fiscal reorientation, centralization and the privatization of council housing', in L. McDowell, P. Sarre and C. Hamnett (eds) *Divided nation: Social and cultural change in Britain*, London: Hodder and Stoughton, pp 235-50.

Forrest, R., Murie, A. and Williams, P. (1990) *Home ownership: Difference and fragmentation*, London: Unwin Hyman.

Foucault, M. (1976) 'Politics; the study of discourse', *Ideology and Consciousness*, vol 3, pp 7-26.

Foucault, M. (1977) *Discipline and punish: The birth of the prison*, Harmondsworth: Penguin.

Fraser, D. (1984) *The evolution of the British welfare state* (2nd edn), London: Macmillan.

Friedman, M. and Friedman, R. (1980) *Free to choose*, London: Secker and Warburg.

Fry, V.C., Hammond, E.M. and Kay, J.A. (1985) *Taxing pensions: The taxation of occupational pension schemes in the UK*, London: Institute of Fiscal Studies.

Giddens, A. (1990) *The consequences of modernity*, Cambridge: Polity Press.

Giddens, A. (1991) *Modernity and self identity*, Cambridge: Polity Press.

Giddens, A. (1994) *Beyond Left and Right*, Cambridge: Polity Press.

Giddens, A. (1998) *The Third Way: The renewal of social democracy*, Cambridge: Polity Press.

Gilbert, B.B. (1966) *The evolution of National Insurance in Great Britain: The origins of the welfare state*, London: Michael Joseph.

Ginn, J. (2001) 'Pensions for women of all ages', in *All our tomorrows* (report of a conference organised by Southwark Pensioners Action Group), London: Eunomia Publications, pp 6-18.

Ginn, J. and Arber, S. (1992a) 'The transmission of income inequality: gender and non state pensions', in K. Morgan (ed) *Gerontology: Responding to an ageing society*, London: Jessica Kingsley Publications, pp 63-83.

Ginn, J. and Arber, S. (1992b) 'Towards women's independence: pension systems in three contrasting European welfare states', *Journal of European Social Policy*, vol 2, no 4, pp 255-77.

Ginn, J. and Arber, S. (1993) 'Pension penalties: the gendered division of occupational welfare', *Work, Employment & Society*, vol 7, no 1, pp 47-70.

Ginn, J. and Arber, S. (1996) 'Patterns of employment, gender and pensions: the effect of work history on older women's non-state pensions', *Work, Employment & Society*, vol 10, no 3, pp 469-90, September.

Ginn, J. and Arber, S. (1999) 'Changing patterns of pension inequality: the impact of privatisation', *Ageing and Society*, vol 19, pp 319-42.

Ginn, J. and Arber, S. (2000) 'Personal pension take up in the 1990s in relation to position in the paid labour market', *Journal of Social Policy*, vol 29, no 2, pp 205-28.

Glennerster, H. (1991) 'The radical right and the welfare state in Britain: pensions and health care', in H. Glennerster and J. Midgley (eds) *The radical right and the welfare state: An international assessment*, Hemel Hemsptead: Harvester Wheatsheaf, pp 45-62.

Golding, P. and Middleton, S. (1982) *Images of welfare*, Oxford: Martin Robertson.

Goldthorpe, D., Lockwood, J., Bechhoffer, F. and Platt, J. (1968) *The affluent worker: Industrial attitudes and behaviour*, Cambridge: Cambridge University Press.

Goode, R. (1993) *Pension law reform: The report of the Pension Law Review Committee* (Chaired by Sir Roy Goode), vols I, II Cm 2342-1, London: HMSO.

Goodin, R.E. and Le Grand, J. with Dryzek, J., Gibson, D.M., Hanson, R.L., Haveman, R.H. and Winter, D. (1987) *Not only the poor: The middle classes and the welfare state*, London: Allen & Unwin.

Gosden, P.H.J.H. (1973) *Self-help voluntary associations in the 19th century*, London: Batsford.

Gough, I. (1979) *The political economy of the welfare state*, London and Basingstoke: Macmillan.

Gould, A. (2001) *Developments in Swedish social policy*, London: Palgrave.

Government Actuary Report (1991) *Occupational pension schemes 1987*, Eighth Survey by the Government Actuary, London: HMSO.

Government Actuary (1999) *National Insurance Fund: Long term financial estimates*, Cm 4406, London: The Stationery Office.

Gradman, T.J. (1994) 'Masculine identity from work to retirement', in E.H. Thompson (ed) *Older men's lives*, London: Sage Publications, pp 104-21.

Green, D.G. (1996) 'Welfare and civil society', in F. Field (edited by A. Deacon) *Stakeholder welfare*, Choice in Welfare Series, no 32, London: Institute of Economic Affairs, pp 75-96.

Green, F., Hadjimatheou, G. and Smail, R. (1984) *Unequal fringes: Fringe benefits in the United Kingdom*, London: Low Pay Unit.

Groves, D. (1987) 'Occupational pension provision and women's poverty in old age', in H. Glendinning and J. Millar, *Women and poverty in Britain*, Brighton: Wheatsheaf, pp 199-217.

Guillemard, A.-M. and van Gunsteren, H. (1991) 'Pathways and their prospects: a comparative interpretation of the meaning of early exit', in M. Kohli, M. Rein, A.M. Guillemard and H. van Gunsteren, *Time for retirement: Comparative studies of early exit from the labour force*, Cambridge: Cambridge University Press, pp 362-87.

Hakim, C. (1996) *Key issues in women's work: Female heterogeneity and the polarization of women's employment*, London: Athlone Press.

Hall, S. (1996) 'Introduction: Who needs "identity"?', in S. Hall and P. du Gay (eds) *Questions of cultural identity*, London: Sage Publications, pp 1-17.

Hall, S. and du Gay, P. (eds) (1996) *Questions of cultural identity*, London: Sage Publications.

Hamill, J. (2002: forthcoming Phd) 'The development of the UK pension structure and the making of pensions policy', Leeds: Leeds University.

Hannah, L. (1986) *Inventing retirement: The development of occupational pensions in Britain*, Cambridge: Cambridge University Press.

Hansard (1999) *Parliamentary Questions*, House of Commons, vol 337, London: HMSO.

Harrison, M.L. (ed) (1984) *Corporatism and the welfare state*, Aldershot: Gower.

Harrison, M.L. (1986) 'Consumption and urban theory: an alternative approach based on the social division of welfare', *International Journal of Urban and Regional Research*, vol 10, no 2, pp 232-42.

Harrison, M.L. (1990) 'Tensions in the management of consumption: property struggles in housing and planning', in J. Simmie and R. King (eds) *The state in action*, London: Pinter Press, pp 119-33.

Harvey, D. (1994) 'Flexible accumulation through urbanisation: reflections on "post-modernism" in the American city', in A.M. Amin (ed) *Post-Fordism: A reader*, Oxford: Blackwell, pp 361-86.

Hay, J.R. (1975) *Origins of the liberal welfare reforms 1906-1914*, London: Macmillan.

Hearn, J. and Roseneil, S. (1999) *Consuming cultures: Power and resistance*, Basingstoke: Macmillan.

Henry, S. (1978) *The hidden economy: The context and control of borderline crime*, London: Martin Robertson.

Hills, J. (1996) 'Does Britain have a welfare generation?', in A. Walker (ed) *The new generational contract: Intergenerational relations, old age and welfare*, London: UCL Press, pp 56-80.

Hillyard, P. and Watson, S. (1996) 'Postmodern social policy: a contradiction in terms?', *Journal of Social Policy*, vol 25, no 3, pp 321-46.

Himmelfarb, G. (1984) *The idea of poverty*, London: Faber and Faber.

Hockey, J. and James, A. (1993) *Growing up and growing old: Ageing and dependency in the life course*, London: Sage Publications in association with *Theory, Culture and Society*.

Hoggett, P. (2001) 'Agency, rationality and social policy', *Journal of Social Policy*, vol 30, no 1, pp 37-56, January.

Holden, C. (1999) 'Globalization, social exclusion and labour's new work ethic', *Critical Social Policy*, vol 19, no 4, pp 529-38.

Huhtaniemi, P. (1995) *The sense of life control and thoughts of early retirement*, Finland: University of Turku.

ISSA (International Social Security Association) (1994) *Complementary pensions: European perspectives*, Social Security Documentation no 21, Geneva: ISSA.

IDS (Incomes Data Services) (1999) *Pensions in practice 1999/2000: From primary legislation to practical implementation*, London: IDS.

IDS (2000) *Pensions in practice 2000/01: From primary legislation to practical implementation*, London: IDS.

Inland Revenue (1998) *Inland Revenue statistics 1998*, London: The Stationery Office.

IPPR/Report of the Commission on Social Justice (1994) *Social justice: Strategies for national renewal*, London: Vintage.

Jacobs, K., Kohli, M. and Rein, M. (1991) 'The evolution of early exit: a compararative analysis of labour force participation patterns', in M. Kohli, M. Rein, A.M. Guillemard and H. van Gunsteren, *Time for retirement: Comparative studies of early exit from the labour force*, Cambridge: Cambridge University Press, pp 36-67.

Jacoby, A.M. (1996) 'From welfare capitalism to the welfare state: Marion B. Folsom and the Social Security Act of 1935', in M. Shalev (ed) *The privatization of social policy? Occupational welfare and the welfare state in America, Scandinavia and Japan*, Basingstoke: Macmillan, pp 44-72.

Jarvis, H. (1999) 'The tangled webs we weave: household strategies to co-ordinate home and work', *Work, Employment & Society*, vol 13, no 2, pp 225-47.

Johnson, N. (1987) *The welfare state in transition: The theory and practice of welfare pluralism*, Brighton: Wheatsheaf.

Johnson, P. (1994) *The pensions dilemma*, London: IPPR.

Johnson, P. and Falkingham, J. (1992) *Ageing and economic welfare*, London: Sage Publications.

Johnson, J. and Slater, R. (eds) (1993) *Ageing and later life*, London: Sage Publications in association with the Open University.

Johnson, P., Conrad, C. and Thomson, D. (eds) (1989) *Workers versus pensioners: Intergenerational justice in an ageing world*, Manchester: Manchester University Press.

Jordan, B. (1998) *The new politics of welfare*, London: Sage Publications.

Joshi, H. and Davies, H. (1992) 'Pensions, divorce and wives' double burden', *International Journal of Law and the Family*, vol 6, no 2, pp 289-320, August.

Kangas, O. and Palme, J. (1996) 'The development of occupational pensions in Finland and Sweden: class politics and institutional feedbacks', in M. Shalev (ed) *The privatization of social policy? Occupational welfare and the welfare state in America, Scandinavia and Japan*, Basingstoke: Macmillan, pp 211-40.

Katz, S. (1996) *Disciplining old age: The formation of gerontological knowledge*, Charlottesville, VA: University Press of Virginia.

Kaye, H.J. (1984) *The British Marxist historians: An introductory analysis*, Cambridge: Polity Press.

Kaye, H.J. and McClelland, K. (1990) *E.P. Thompson: Critical perspectives*, Cambridge: Polity Press.

Kincaid, J. (1984) 'Richard Titmuss', in P. Barker. (ed) *Founders of the welfare state*, London: Heinemann, pp 114-20.

Kingson, E.R. and Williamson, J.B. (1993) 'The generational equity debate: a progressive framing of a conservative issue', *Journal of Aging and Social Policy*, vol 5, no 3, pp 31-53.

Kingston, G. (1997) 'Efficient timing of retirement', School of Economics Discussion Paper 97/1, Sydney: University of New South Wales.

Knights, D. and Wilmott, D. (eds) (1986) *Managing the labour process*, Aldershot: Gower.

Kohli, M. and Rein, M. (1991) 'The changing balance of work and retirement', in M. Kohli, M. Rein, A.M. Guillemard and H. van Gunsteren, *Time for retirement: Comparative studies of early exit from the labour force*, Cambridge: Cambridge University Press.

Kohli, M., Rein, M., Guillemard, A.M. and van Gunsteren, H. (1991) *Time for retirement: Comparative studies of early exit from the labour force*, Cambridge: Cambridge University Press.

Kollmann, G. (1996) 'Means testing social security benefits: an issue summary', CRS Report for Congress, Congress Research Service, 94-791 EPW, 23 August, Washington: Library of Congress.

Korpi, W. (1978) *The working class in welfare capitalism: Work unions and politics in Sweden*, London: Routledge.

Korpi, W. (1983) *The democratic class struggle*, London: Routledge.

Kvist, J. and Sinfield, A. (1996) *Comparing tax routes to welfare in Denmark and the United Kingdom*, Copenhagen: Danish National Institute of Social Research.

Larson, P. (1997) *Gay money: Your personal guide to same sex strategies for financial security, strength and success*, San Francisco, CA: The Advocate Press.

Laczko, F. and Phillipson, C. (1991) *Changing work and retirement*, Milton Keynes: Open University Press.

Laslett, P. (1989) *A fresh map of life: The emergence of the Third Age*, London: Weidenfeld and Nicolson,.

Lee, P. and Raban, C. (1988) *Welfare theory and social policy: Reform or revolution?*, London: Sage Publications.

Levitas, R. (1996) 'The concept of social exclusion and the new Durkheimian hegemony', *Critical Social Policy*, vol 16, no 1, pp 5-20, February.

Levitas, R. (2000) 'Discourses of risk and utopia', in B. Adam, U. Beck and J. van Loon (eds) *The risk society and beyond: Critical issues for social theory*, London: Sage Publications, pp 198-210.

Lewis, G., Gewirtz, S. and Clarke, J. (2000) (eds) *Rethinking social policy*, London, Sage Publications in association with the Open University.

Lewis, J. (ed) (1986) *Labour and love: Women's experience of home and family 1850-1940*, London: Basil Blackwell.

Lewis, J. (1992) 'Gender and the development of welfare regimes', *Journal of European Social Policy*, vol 2, no 3, pp 159-73.

Lewis, J. (1997) 'Gender and welfare regimes: further thoughts', *Social Politics*, pp 160-77, Summer.

Lewis, J. (2000) 'Gender and welfare regimes', in G. Lewis, S. Gewirtz and J. Clarke (eds) *Rethinking social policy*, London: Sage Publications in association with the Open University, pp 37-51.

Lewis, J. and Piachaud, D. (1987) 'Women and poverty in the twentieth century', in C. Glendinning and J. Millar, *Women and poverty in Britain*, Brighton: Wheatsheaf, pp 28-53.

Lister, R. (1997) *Citizenship: Feminist perspectives*, Basingstoke: Macmillan.

Littlewood, M. (1998) *How to create a competitive market in pensions: The international lessons*, Choice in Welfare Series, no 45, London: IEA.

Loader, B. (1998) 'Welfare direct: informatics and the emergence of self-service welfare?', in J. Carter (ed) *Postmodernity and the fragmentation of welfare*, London: Routledge, pp 220-36.

Lowe, R. (1993) *The welfare state in Britain since 1945*, Basingstoke: Macmillan.

Lucas, H. (1977) *Pensions and industrial relations*, London: Pergamon Press.

Lyotard, J.F. (1984) *The postmodern condition: A report on knowledge*, Manchester: Manchester University Press.

McCloughlin, I. and Clark, J. (1988) *Technological change at work*, Milton Keynes: Open University Press.

McGoldrick, A. (1984) *Equal treatment in occupational pension schemes*, London: Equal Opportunities Commission.

Macnicol, J. (1994) 'Beveridge and old age', in J. Hills., J. Ditch and H. Glennerster (eds) *Beveridge and social security: An international retrospective*, Oxford: Clarendon Press, pp 73-96.

Macnicol, J. (1998) *The politics of retirement in Britain 1878-1948*, Cambridge: Cambridge University Press.

Macnicol, J. and Blaikie, A. (1989) 'The politics of retirement, 1908-1948', in M. Jeffreys (ed) *Growing old in the twentieth century*, London: Routledge, pp 21-42.

Maltby, T. (1994) *Women and pensions in Britain and Hungary*, Avebury: Aldershot.

Mann, K. (1984) 'Incorporation, exclusion, underclasses and the unemployed', in M.L. Harrison (ed) *Corporatism and the welfare state*, Aldershot: Gower, pp 41-60.

Mann, K. (1986) 'The making of a claiming class – the neglect of agency in analyses of the welfare state', *Critical Social Policy*, vol 5, no 3, pp 62-74.

Mann, K. (1991) 'The social division of welfare: a class struggle perspective', in N. Manning (ed) *Social Policy Review, 1990-91*, Harlow: Longman in collaboration with the Social Policy Association, pp 243-61.

Mann, K. (1992) *The making of an English 'underclass'?*, Milton Keynes: Open University Press.

Mann, K. (1993) 'Supermen, women and pensioners: the politics of superannuation reform', *International Journal of Sociology and Social Policy*, vol 13, no 7, pp 29-62.

Mann, K. (1998) 'Lamppost-modernism: traditional and critical social policy', *Critical Social Policy*, vol 18, no 1, pp 77-102, 18 February.

Mann, K. and Anstee, J. (1989) *Growing fringes: Hypothesis on the development of occupational welfare*, Leeds: Armley Publications.

Marshall, T.H. (1950) *Citizenship and social class*, Cambridge: Cambridge University Press.

Midwinter, E. (1985) *The wage of retirement*, London: Centre for Policy on Ageing.

Midwinter, E. (1991) *Out of focus, old age, the press and broadcasting*, London: Centre for Policy on Ageing.

Midwinter, E. (1997) *Pensioned off: Retirement and income examined*, Buckingham: Open University Press.

Miliband, R. (1973) *The state in capitalist society*, London: Quartet.

Mine, K. (1994) 'Glad to be grey', *New Statesman and Society*, vol 7, no 316, pp 16-17, August.

Minns, R. (1980) *Pension funds and British capitalism*, London: Heinemann.

Minns, R. (2001) *The cold war in welfare: Stock markets versus pensions*, London: Verso.

Modood, T., Berthoud, R., Lakey, J., Nazroo, J., Smith, P., Virdee, S. and Beishon, P. (eds) (1997) *Ethnic minorities in Britain*, London: Policy Studies Institute.

Morris, J. (1993) *Independent lives: Community care and disabled people*, Basingstoke: Macmillan.

Morris, L. (1990) *The workings of the household: A US–UK comparison*, Cambridge: Polity Press.

Murphy, R. (1988) *Social closure: The theory of monopolization and exclusion*, Oxford: Clarendon Press.

Myners, P. (2001) *Myners review of institutional investment: Final report*, London: HM Treasury (www.hm-treasury.gov.uk/docs/2001_report0602,htm).

Nesbitt S. (1995) *British pensions policy making in the 1980's*, Aldershot: Avebury.

Nesbitt, S. and Neary, D. (2001) *Ethnic minorities and their pensions decisions: A study of Pakistani, Bangladeshi and white men in Oldham*, York: Joseph Rowntree Foundation.

Oakley, A. (1974) *The sociology of housework*, London: Robertson.

Occupational Pensions Board (1997) *1973-1997 Final report*, London: HMSO.

O'Connor, J. (1973) *The fiscal crisis of the state*, New York, NY: St Martins Press.

OECD (Organisation for Economic Co-operation and Development) (1988) *Reforming public pensions*, Paris: OECD.

OECD (1998a) *Maintaining prosperity in an ageing society*, Policy Brief No 5, Paris: OECD.

OECD (1998b) 'The retirement decision in OECD countries, ageing working papers' (AWP1.4Eng) in S. Blondal and S. Scarpetta, *Maintaining prosperity in an ageing society: The OECD study on the policy implications of ageing*, Paris: Economics Department, OECD.

Oliver, M. (1990) *The politics of disablement*, Basingstoke: Macmillan.

Olsberg, D. (1997) *Ageing and money*, St Leonards: Allen & Unwin.

O'Neill, J. (1995) *The poverty of postmodernism*, London: Routledge.

Orloff, A.S. (1993) 'Gender and the social rights of citizenship: the comparative analysis of gender relations and welfare states', *American Sociological Review*, vol 58, no 3, pp 303-28, June.

Orloff, J. (1997) 'Comment on Jane Lewis's "Gender and welfare regimes: Further thoughts"', *Social Politics*, pp 188-202, Fall.

Overbye, E. (1996) 'Public and occupational pensions in the Nordic countries', in M. Shalev (ed) *The privatization of social policy? Occupational welfare and the welfare state in America, Scandinavia and Japan*, Basingstoke: MacMillan, pp 159-86.

Owen, M. (1993) *Making sense of pensions*, London: Fabian Society.

Oyen, E. (ed) (1986) *Comparing welfare states and their futures*, Aldershot: Gower.

Pahl, J. (2000) 'Theories about money – implications for policy', Paper presented at 'Futures of Social Policy and Practice?', Social Policy Association Annual Conference, 18-20 July, Roehampton: University of Surrey.

Pampel, F. and Williamson, J. (1992) *Age, class politics and the welfare state*, Cambridge: Cambridge University Press.

Papadakis, E. and Taylor-Gooby, P. (1987) *The private provision of public welfare: State, market and community*, Brighton: Wheatsheaf.

Parkin, F. (1979) *Marxism and class theory: A bourgeois critique*, London: Tavistock.

Payne, J. and Payne, G. (2000) 'Health', in G. Payne (ed) *Social divisions*, Basingstoke: Macmillan.

Pensions Reform Group (2001: forthcoming) *Pensions for all: Modernising pensions for the millennium*, 11 January, Draft paper from the Office of Frank Field, MP.

Phillips, T.P. (1954) *Committee on the economic and financial problems of the provision for old age* (Chaired by Sir Thomas Phillips), Cmnd 9333, London: HMSO.

Phillipson, C. (1993) 'Poverty and affluence in old age: resolving issues of economic and social justice', in A. Sinfield (ed) *Poverty, inequality and justice*, New Waverly Papers, Social Policy Series No 6, Edinburgh: University of Edinburgh, pp 63-78.

Phillipson, C. (1998) *Reconstructing old age*, London: Sage Publications.

Phillipson, C. and Walker, A. (eds) (1986) *Ageing and society: A critical assessment*, Aldershot: Gower.

Piachaud, D. (1987) 'Problems in the definition and measurement of poverty', *Journal of Social Policy*, vol 16, no 2, pp 147-64.

PIU (Performance and Innovation Unit) (2000) *Winning the generation game*, Cabinet Office Report, London: The Stationery Office.

Plant, R. (1988) *Citizenship, rights and socialism*, London: Fabian Society.

Plowman, D. and Weaven, G. (1988) *Superannuation: A union perspective*, Sydney: University of New South Wales.

Poster, M. (1984) *Foucault, Marxism and history: Mode of production vs mode of information*, Cambridge: Polity Press.

Powell, M. (2000) 'New Labour and the Third Way in the British welfare state: a new and distinctive approach?', *Critical Social Policy*, vol 20, no 1, pp 39-60.

Preteceille, E. (1986) 'Collective consumption, urban segregation and social classes', *Environment and planning D: Society and Space*, vol 4, pp 145-54.

Prideaux, S. (2001) 'New Labour, old functionalism: the underlying contradictions of welfare reform in the US and the UK', *Social Policy and Administration*, vol 35, no 1, pp 85-115.

Prior, G. and Field, J. (1996) *Pensions and divorce*, Research report no 50, DHSS, London: HMSO.

Pusey, M. (1991) *Economic rationalism in Canberra*, Cambridge: Cambridge University Press.

Raphael, M. (1964) *Pensions and public servants*, Paris: Mouton.

Rattansi, A. (1994) '"Western" racisms, ethnicities and identities in a "postmodern" frame', in A. Rattansi and S. Westwood (eds) *Racism, modernity and identity*, Cambridge: Polity Press, pp 15-86.

Rattansi, A. (1995) 'Review essay: forget postmodernism? Notes from De Bunker', *Sociology*, vol 29, no 2, pp 339-49.

Regional Trends (2001) *Age specific death rates: By gender, 1998*, Regional Trends Dataset from www.statistics.gov.uk/statbase/xsdataset.asp?vlnk=302, Source ONS adapted from *Regional Trends 35*, 2000, updated 19 March 2001.

Rein, M. (1996) 'Is America exceptional?', in M. Shalev (ed) *The privatization of social policy? Occupational welfare and the welfare state in America, Scandinavia and Japan*, Basingstoke: Macmillan, pp 27-43.

Rex, J. (1971) 'The concept of housing classes and the sociology of race relations', *Race*, vol 12, pp 293-301.

Rex, J. (1973) *Race, colonialism and the city*, London: Routledge and Kegan Paul.

Rex, J. and Moore, J. (1967) *Race, community and conflict*, London: Oxford University Press.

Rodger, J. (1992) 'The welfare state and social closure: social division and the "underclass"', *Critical Social Policy*, vol 12, no 2, pp 45-63, Autumn.

Rojek, C. and Turner, B. (eds) (1993) *Forget Baudrillard?*, London: Routledge.

Rose, H. (1981) 'Rereading Titmuss: the sexual division of welfare', *Journal of Social Policy*, vol 10, no 4, pp 477-502.

Rose, N. (1994) 'Government, authority and expertise under advanced liberalism', *Economy and Society*, vol 22, no 3, pp 273-99.

Rose, N. (1996) 'Identity, genealogy, history', in S. Hall and P. du Gay (eds) *Questions of cultural identity*, London: Sage Publications, pp 128-50.

Roseneil, S. and Seymour, J. (eds) (1999) *Practising identities: Power and resistance*, Basingstoke: Macmillan Press.

Rubner, A. (1962) *Fringe benefits: The golden chains*, London: Putnam.

Sainsbury, D. (ed) (1994) *Gendering welfare states*, London: Sage Publications.

Sass, S.A. (1997) *The promise of private pensions: The first hundred years*, Cambridge, MA: Harvard University Press.

Saunders, P. (1986) 'Comment on Dunleavy and Preteceille', *Environment and Planning D: Society and Space*, vol 4, pp 155-63.

Saunders, P. and Harris, C. (1990) 'Privatisation and the consumer', *Sociology*, vol 24, no 1, pp 57-74.

Sawchuk, K.A. (1995) 'From gloom to boom: age identity and target marketing', in M. Featherstone and A. Wernick (eds) *Images of ageing: Cultural representations of later life*, London: Routledge, pp 173-87.

Scheiwe, D. (1999) *Why Australia's pension system is not a good international model*, Discussion Paper PI-9912, London: Birkbeck College, Pensions Institute.

Scheiwe, D. with Katter, N. (2000) 'Superannuation: negligence and the labour union', Unpublished paper, School of Accountancy, Queensland University of Technology.

Scheiwe, K. (1994) 'German pension insurance: gendered times and stratification', in D. Sainsbury (ed) *Gendering welfare states*, London: Sage Publications.

Schieber, S.J. and Shoven, B. (eds) (1997) *Public policy toward pensions*, Cambridge, MA: The Twentieth Century Fund, Massachusets Institute of Technology.

Schuller, T. (1986) *Age, capital and democracy*, Aldershot: Gower.

Schuller, T. and Hyman, J. (1983) 'Trust law and trustees: employee representation in pension schemes', *Industrial Law Journal*, pp 84-98, June.

Schuller, T. and Hyman, J. (1984) 'Forms of ownership and control: decision making within a financial institution', *Sociology*, vol 18, no 1, pp 51-70, February.

Seccombe, W. (1986) 'Patriarchy stabilized: the construction of the male breadwinner wage in 19th century Britain', *Social History*, vol ll, no 1, pp 53-80.

Seidler, V.J. (1994) *Unreasonable men: Masculinity and social theory*, Routledge: London.

Seldon, A. (1996) 'Pensions without the state', in A. Seldon (ed) *Re-privatising welfare: After the lost century*, IEA Readings 45, London, pp 63-70.

Sevenhuijsen, S. (1998) *Citizenship and the ethics of care: Feminist considerations on justice, morality and politics*, London: Routledge.

Sevenhuijsen, S. (2000) 'Caring in the Third Way, the relation between obligation, responsibility and care in Third Way discourse', *Critical Social Policy*, vol 20, no 1, pp 5-38, February.

Shakespeare, T. (2000) 'The social relations of care', in G. Lewis, S. Gewitz and J. Clarke, *Rethinking social policy*, London: Sage Publications, pp 52-65.

Shalev, M. (ed) (1996) *The privatization of social policy? Occupational welfare and the welfare state in America, Scandinavia and Japan*, Basingstoke: Macmillan.

Shragge, E. (1984) *Pensions policy in Britain: A socialist analysis*, London: Routledge.

Sim. J. (1990) *Medical power in prisons: The prison medical service in England 1774-1989*, Milton Keynes: Open University Press.

Simpson, D. (1996) *Regulating pensions: Too many rules too little competition*, Hobart Paper 131, London: IEA.

Sinfield, A. (1978) 'Analyses in the social division of welfare', *Journal of Social policy*, vol 7, no 2, pp 129-56.

Sinfield, A. (1986) 'Poverty, privilege and welfare', in P. Bean and D. Whynes, *Barbara Wooton: Essays in her honour*, London: Tavistock, pp 108-23.

Smart, B. (1992) *Modern conditions, postmodern controversies*, London: Routledge.

Smart, C. (1993) 'Proscription, prescription and the desire for certainty?', *Studies in Law and Society*, vol 13, pp 37-54.

Smart, C. (1995) *Law, crime and sexuality: Essays in feminism*, London: Sage Publications.

Smith, A. (1976, 3rd edn, first published 1784) *The wealth of nations*, Oxford: Clarendon Press.

Smiles, S. (1860) *Self-help: With illustration of character and conduct*, London: J. Murray.

Solomon, K. and Szwabo, P.A. (1994) 'The work oriented culture – success and power in elderly men', in E.H. Thompson (ed) *Older men's lives*, London: Sage Publications, pp 42-64.

Soper, K. (1993) 'Postmodern subjectivity and the question of value', J. Squires (ed) *Prinicipled positions; postmodernism and the rediscovery of values*, London: Wishart.

SSCS (Senate Select Committee on Superannuation) (1992) *Safeguarding super: The regulation of superannuation*, First report of the SSCS, Commonwealth of Australia, Canberrra, June.

Standard Life (1998) *Life times*, Issue 11, no 2, Edinburgh: Balfour Publishing.

Stegman, T., Schott, K., Robson, P. and Scott, G. (1987) 'The future of income policies in Australia', Conference Proceedings Papers, Centre for Applied Economic Research, University of New South Wales.

Stevens, B. (1996) 'Labor unions and the privatization of welfare: the turning point in the 1940s', in M. Shalev (ed) *The privatization of social policy? Occupational welfare and the welfare state in America, Scandinavia and Japan*, Basingstoke: Macmillan.

Sykes, R. and Alcock, P. (eds) (1998) *Developments in European social policy: Convergence or diversity?*, Bristol: The Policy Press.

Tanner, S. (1997) 'The dynamics of retirement behaviour', in R. Disney, E. Grundy and P. Johnson (eds) *The dynamics of retirement: Analyses of the retirement surveys*, London: DSS, The Stationery Office, pp 25-73.

Taylor-Gooby, P. (1981) 'The empiricist tradition in social adminstration', *Critical Social Policy*, vol 1, no 2, pp 6-21.

Taylor-Gooby, P. (1994) 'Postmodernism and social policy: a great leap backwards', *Journal of Social Policy*, vol 23, no 3, pp 385-404.

Taylor-Gooby, P. (2001) 'Risk, contingency and the Third Way: evidence from the BHPS and qualitative studies', *Social Policy and Administration*, vol 35, no 3, pp 195-211.

Therborn, G. (1983) 'Why some classes are more successful than others', *New Left Review*, no 138, pp 37-56.

Thomas, J.L. (1994) 'Older men as fathers and grandfathers', in E.H. Thompson (ed) *Older men's lives*, London: Sage Publications, pp 197-217.

Thompson, E.H. (ed) (1994) *Older men's lives*, London: Sage Publications.

Thompson, E.P. (1968 edn) *The making of the English working class*, Harmondsworth: Penguin.

Thompson, M. and Shaver, S. (1998) *Citizenship, social rights and income in retirement: First report to participants*, Sydney: Social Policy Research Centre, University of New South Wales.

Thompson, S. and Hoggett, P. (1996) 'Universalism, selectivism and particularism: towards a postmodern social policy', *Critical Social Policy*, vol 16, no 1, pp 21-43, February.

Thorpe, M. (1999) 'Marginalisation and resistance through the prism of retirement', in J. Hearn and S. Roseneil (eds) *Consuming cultures: Power and resistance*, Basingstoke: Macmillan, pp 109-30.

Tinker, A. (1997, revised edn) *Older people in modern* society, Harlow: Longman.

Titmuss, R. (1958) *Essays on 'The welfare state'*, London: Allen & Unwin.

Titmuss, R. (1962) *Income distribution and social change*, London: Allen & Unwin.

Titmuss, R. (1968) *Commitment to welfare*, London: Allen & Unwin.

Titmuss, R. (1970) *The gift relationship: From human blood to social policy*, London: Allen & Unwin.

Tomlinson, A. (ed) (1990) *Consumption, identity, style*, London: Routledge.

Townsend, P. (1979) *Poverty in the United Kingdom*, Harmondsworth: Penguin.

Townsend, P. (1981) 'The structured dependency of the elderly', *Ageing and Society*, vol 1, no 2, pp 5-28.

Tronto, J. (1993) *Moral boundaries: A political argument for an ethic of care*, New York, NY: Routledge.

Troyansky, D. (1996) 'Progress report: the history of old age in the western world', *Ageing and Society*, vol 16, no 2, pp 233-43.

Twine, F. (1992) 'Citizenship: opportunities, rights and routes to welfare in old age', *Journal of Social Policy*, vol 21, no 2, pp 165-75.

US Census Bureau (2001) *Demographic profiles: Census 2000* (www.census.gov/Press-Release/www/2001/demoprofile.htm 25.05.01).

Ungerson, C. (1987) *Policy is personal: Sex, gender and informal care*, London: Tavistock.

Ungerson, C. (1997) 'Social politics and the commodification of care', *Social Politics*, pp 362-81, Fall.

Ungerson, C. (2000) 'Thinking about the production and consumption of long term care in Britain: does gender still matter?', *Journal of Social Policy*, vol 29, no 4, pp 623-44.

Unikowski, I. (1996) 'Departing for a life of sunshine: background to the seminar on early retirement in Australia', in Department of Social Security, Early Retirement Seminar, Canberra: Australian Government Publishing Service.

Vincent, J. (1995) *Inequality in old age*, London: UCL Press.

Vincent, J. (1996) 'Who's afraid of an ageing population?', *Critical Social Policy*, vol 16, no 2, pp 3-26.

Vincent, J. (1999) *Politics, power and old age*, Buckingham: Open University Press.

Visco, I. (2001) *Paying for pensions: How important is economic growth? Managing the global ageing transition*, A policy summit of the Global Ageing Initiative, Zurich: OECD.

Wadensjo, E. (1991) 'Sweden: partial exit', in M. Kohli, M. Rein, A.M. Guillemard and H. van Gunsteren (eds) *Time for retirement: Comparative studies of early exit from the labour force*, Cambridge: Cambridge University Press, pp 284-323.

Waine, B. (1992) 'Workers as owners, the ideology and practice of personal pensions', in *Economy and Society*, vol 21, no 1, pp 27-44, February.

Waine, B. (1995) 'A disaster foretold? The case of the personal pension', *Social Policy and Administration*, vol 29, no 4, December.

Walby, S. (1990) *Theorising patriarchy*, Oxford: Blackwell.

Walby, S. (1997) *Gender transformations*, London: Routledge.

Walker, A. (1981) 'Towards a political economy of old age', *Ageing and Society*, vol 1, no 1, pp 73-94.

Walker, A. (1984) 'The political economy of privatisation', in J. Le Grand and R. Robinson (eds) *Privatisation and the welfare state*, London: Allen & Unwin, pp 19-44.

Walker, A. (1987) 'The poor relation; poverty among older women', in C. Glendinning and J. Millar (eds) *Women and poverty in Britain*, Brighton: Wheatsheaf, pp 199-217.

Walker, A. (ed) (1996) *The new generational contract: Intergenerational relations, old age and welfare*, London: UCL Press.

Walker, A. (1999) 'The third way for pensions (by way of Thatcherism and avoiding today's pensioners)', *Critical Social Policy*, vol 19, no 4, pp 511-27, November.

Walker, A. and Maltby, T. (1996) *Ageing Europe*, Buckingham: Open University Press.

Walker, R. with Howard, M. (2000) *The making of a welfare class: Benefit receipt in Britain*, Bristol: The Policy Press.

Walsh, J. (1999) 'Myths and counter-myths: an analysis of part-time female employees and their orientations to work and working hours', *Work, Employment & Society*, vol 13, no 2, pp 179-203.

Ward, R.A. (1993) 'The politics of age', in J. Johnson and R. Slater (eds) *Ageing and later life*, London: Sage Publications in association with the Open University.

Ward, S. (1981) *Pensions*, London: Pluto Press.

Ward, S. (1985) 'The financial crisis facing pensioners', *Critical Social Policy*, vol 5, no 2, pp 43-56.

Warde, A. (1990) 'Introduction to the sociology of consumption', *Sociology*, vol 24, no 1, pp 1-4.

Warde, A. (1994a) 'Consumers, consumption and post-Fordism', in R. Burrows and B. Loader (eds) *Towards a post-Fordist welfare state?*, London: Routledge, pp 223-38.

Warde, A. (1994b) 'Consumption, identity-formation and uncertainty', *Sociology*, vol 28, no 4, pp 877-98.

Warnes, A.M. (1993) 'Being old, old people and the burdens of burden', *Ageing and Society*, vol 13, pp 297-338.

Waters, M. (1996) 'Human rights and the universalisation of interests', *Sociology*, vol 30, no 3, pp 593-600, August.

Watts, R. (1997) 'Ten years on: Francis G. Castles and the Australian "wage earners" welfare state', *Australian and New Zealand Journal of Sociology*, vol 33, no 1, pp 1-15.

Weber, M. (1976) *The protestant ethic and the spirit of capitalism*, London: Allen & Unwin.

Wilensky, H. (1975) *The welfare state and equality*, Berkeley, CA: University of California Press.

Wilkinson, M. (1986) 'Tax expenditure and public expenditure in the UK', *Journal of Social Policy*, vol 15, no 1, pp 23-50.

Williams, F. (1989) *Social policy: A critical introduction*, Cambridge: Polity Press.

Williams, F. (1992) 'Somewhere over the rainbow: universality and diversity in social policy', *Social Policy Review 4*, pp 200-19.

Williams, F. (1996) 'Postmodernism, feminism and the question of difference', in N. Parton (ed) *Social work social theory and social change*, London: Routledge.

Williams, F. (2000) 'Principles for recognition and respect', in G. Lewis, S. Gewirtz and J. Clarke (eds) *Rethinking social policy*, London: Sage Publications in association with the Open University, pp 338-52.

Willman, P. (1986) *Technological change, collective bargaining and industrial efficiency*, Oxford: Oxford University Press.

Wilson, E. (1977) *Women and the welfare state*, London: Tavistock.

Wilson, E. (1980) *Only halfway to paradise: Women in postwar Britain 1945-1968*, London: Tavistock.

Wilson, G. (1995) '"I'm the eyes and she's the arms": changes in gender roles in advanced old age', in S. Arber and J Ginn (eds) *Connecting gender and ageing*, Buckingham, Open University Press, pp 98-113.

Wilson, G. (2000) *Understanding old age: Critical and global perspectives*, London: Sage Publications.

Wook, S. and Windolph, P. (1987) *Social closure in the labour market*, Aldershot: Gower.

Yeo, S. (1979) 'Working class associations, private capital welfare and the state in the late nineteenth and twentieth centuries', in N. Parry, M. Rustin and C. Satyamurti (eds) *Social work welfare and the state*, London: Arnold, pp 48-71.

Young, M. and Schuller, T. (1993) 'The new prospects for retirement', in J. Johnson and R. Slater (eds) *Ageing and later life*, London: Sage Publications in association with the Open University, pp 262-8.

Index

see also early exit/retirement
flexibility and informal welfare 208
limiting effect of occupational
  pensions 9, 21, 53–4, 122
pensioners as resource
  as economic expedient 187
  in post-traditionalist society 154–5,
    168, 169
  unemployment and retirement rates
    63–4, 211
  see also paid work
labour mobility 201
Labour party see New Labour
labour relations see trades unions
Laslett, P. 80, 92–5, 106, 107, 213–14
lay trustees 119–21, 130, 131
legal discourse 135, 139
Legal and General 56
lesser consumers 102–3, 108
Lewis, G. 2
Lewis, J. 196
liberal welfare regimes 175, 176–7,
  203
life assurance 18–19, 124–5
  enhanced life annuities 124, 161,
    211
life expectancy
  as basis for reforms 189–90
  'longevity risk' 159, 160
  in post-traditional society 157, 168
  women disadvantaged by 33, 36,
    158, 159
  see also mortality rates
lifestyle choice
  consumption theory 79, 80, 90, 91,
    186, 223–4
  and retirement decision 201–2
  'third age' model 92–5, 103–4, 107,
    213–14
  see also behaviour; conditional
    welfare
Lister, R. 31
'longevity risk' 159, 160
lump sum payments 24–5, 36, 95–6,
  222
Lyotard, Jean-François 147, 150

M

male breadwinner/female carer model
  29–31, 77, 192, 196–7
  in post-traditional society 153, 157,
    158
Malthus, Thomas 50, 52, 53, 186
managerialism 81, 163
manual workers: social closure 22
markets
  effects of fluctuation 56, 57
  orthodox political economy
    approach to 50–61, 130–1, 210–13
  'sellers' market' 56, 57–8
  and welfare regime models 175–6
  see also capitalism; liberal welfare
    regime
Marshall, T.H. 41, 165, 175, 185
Marx, Karl 49, 61–2, 146
Marxist theory
  and consumption 79
  of political economy see radical
    political economy
  and welfare regime comparison 203,
    204
Maxwell, Robert 133
means-tested benefits 61, 99, 214
  Age Pension in Australia 41–2
  and de-commodification of welfare
    175
  women as recipients 36, 39, 101
media
  advertising and consumption theory
    80, 86–92, 108, 213–14
  manipulation in post-traditional
    society 148–9, 150–1
  on misselling of private pensions 60
  portrays 'burden' of public welfare
    25, 26
medical discourse 111–12, 139
middle-classes: benefit from welfare
  18–19
Midwinter, E. 95, 98
Mineworkers Pension Scheme 69–70
Minimum Income Guarantee (MIG)
  36
Minns, Richard 68, 69
Mirror Group pension fund 133